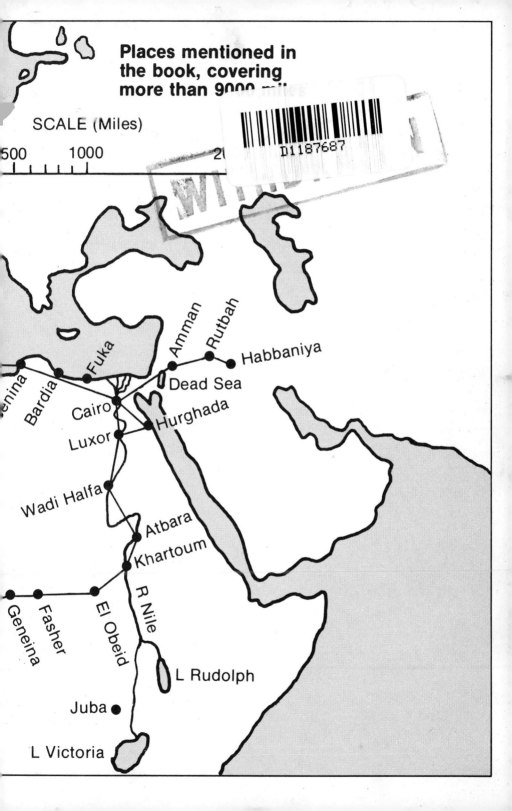

Places mentioned in the book, covering more than 9000 miles

SCALE (Miles)

500   1000

Fuka

Amman

Rutbah

Habbaniya

Dead Sea

enina

Bardia

Cairo

Hurghada

Luxor

Wadi Halfa

Atbara

Khartoum

Fasher

Geneina

El Obeid

R Nile

L Rudolph

Juba

L Victoria

Wings Over North Africa

For Mike and Jacquie

Wings Over North Africa

Air Vice-Marshal
Tony Dudgeon CBE DFC

A Wartime Odyssey, 1940 to 1943

Airlife
ENGLAND

First published 1987
by Airlife Publishing Ltd.

Printed in England by Livesey Ltd., Shrewsbury.

Airlife Publishing Ltd.

7 St. John's Hill, Shrewsbury, England.

Contents

Acknowledgements

I would like to reiterate my sincere thanks to Mr Richard Riding, Editor of *The Aeroplane Monthly,* who not only egged me on to write my earlier book but who has continued to encourage me and find space in his magazine for more of my work. Some parts of this book have already been a source of brief articles and his permission for the subjects to re-appear is much appreciated.

Introduction

In 1942 I was given a job which turned out to be a pilot's dream; *carte blanche* to fly any type of aircraft anywhere in the Middle East, at any time.

Life could hardly have been more exciting for a young man in his twenties. Experiences were many and fascinating as a trouble-shooter on 9,000 miles of routes. From dealing with gold and diamond smugglers — to flying a medical emergency to hospital by night with no flare-path to help; from sighting the ruins of the 2,000-year-old Carthaginian city of Volubilis and the Sultan's tomb at Idriss in Morocco, to taking a light aircraft to the edge of the Red Sea where I paddled for oysters and then took off to Luxor.

I still wonder which was worse; to be sleeping peacefully on a camp-bed in Morocco one Sunday morning when an officer came to say that King George VI was on the airfield, and had been waiting there half an hour for me — or finding myself piloting a crippled Vickers Wellington aircraft through a howling storm on a pitch black night after failure of all the electrics and the automatic pilot — and the navigator had collapsed with hysterics — with six-hours still to go *and* it was only my second trip in a Wellington!

I went from the steamy Gold Coast in West Africa, via the arid plains of Nigeria, Chad and the treacherous Sudanese deserts to Khartoum. Over the Nile flanked by scorching sands, past Aswan, Thebes, Luxor and the tombs of the Egyptian Kings, to Cairo and its Pyramids. From Iraq across Jordan and the Holy Land to the Western Desert. Thence along North Africa, by Libya, Tunisia, and Algeria to Morocco and Gibraltar — not forgetting brief trips over the Atlantic Ocean to the United Kingdom.

This is not just another story of wartime flying; it is a true-life adventure story on several levels which I hope will appeal to readers of all ages and interests. I wrote *Wings Over North Africa* to carry the reader through a world of beauty, fun, interest, romance, humour and some danger. I hope I have succeeded.

Chapter 1
Red Sea Rescue

There is something rather special and magical about a clear night from a few thousand feet up over the Egyptian desert. The darkness there is like velvet — soft and smooth. Above, the stars look incredibly bright, flashing and sparkling like millions of tiny diamonds. If there is no moon, or if it is low above the horizon and there are no lights and fires, you hang over an enormous void; you seem to be able to look down for ever. Somewhere below there is an earth, hard and unforgiving but to the desert aviator, beyond the reach of softly glowing lights in his cockpit, it is just a great black expanse of nothingness.

Wartime. Radio silence and moonless. I held my course, climbing steadily and checking the altimeter so as to be quite certain I should pass well above the tops of still invisible hills ahead, 4,000 feet high and lying between the Nile and the Red Sea. Nothing to do and nothing but the stars to see outside. I just sat, keeping precisely to my heading, silent and happy, listening to the sweet sound of the engine running perfectly, waiting the half-hour before the climbing moon would show me something I could recognise.

I thought over the events of the day, leading up to this flight. Was I engaged on a justifiable endeavour, or merely being plumb stupid? Should I really be flying hundreds of miles over trackless desert, with help only from the moon, a map and my personal expertise, to find a particular patch of sand? Was it reasonably balanced because one airman's life was at risk?

Normally, I polished an office chair at my very first job as a Wing Commander in a little headquarters. Our tiny staff all chipped in, taking on anything needed at any time, so it was not surprising that an engineer was doing a stint as Duty Ops Officer. Jock MacElwain poked his red hair and buck teeth round my office door, saying, 'I got problems due to the weather, and I need fresh ideas. This snag comes from Hurghada; that storage depot with a short landing-strip and no other flying facilities, miles from anywhere on the edge of the Red Sea. Remember it?'

I nodded.

'Well, there's an airman there with appendicitis. He's not dying or anything right now but their doc wants him flown out as soon as possible, and operated on before his guts blow up, because it could be fatal if they did. Yesterday, and again today, the casualty-evacuation Dominie was tasked to pick him up and fly him out. But, as you know, the wind has been rising in the daytime and creating sandstorms. Twice the casevac went there and tried to get down. Even that well-mannered, slow old biplane couldn't hack it in the heavy sandstorm, and they had to come back to Cairo. The Met are forecasting the same again tomorrow. The doc there says that it would be too dangerous to put him in an ambulance and bounce him for a 200-mile trip across the rough desert tracks. The doc also says his appendicitis could become critical at any time. So now what?'

I knew only too well that blowing sand is, from the air, an almost opaque yellow dusty fog. Looking down, it is virtually impossible to pick out the equally dusty yellow surface of a landing strip under you. And, to try and land on something you can't see, without any outside help, is unacceptably dangerous and utterly foolish. The fact that blowing sand also blotted out completely all radios and beacons was of no consequence in this case — Hurghada didn't have any of those things anyway. I thought for a few moments and then asked, 'How about fetching him out at night, when the wind usually dies down, and the sand will have stopped rising?'

Jock shook his head. 'I suggested that to the casevac crew already. No joy. Hurghada is a fine-weather daytime airstrip only. It has no air-traffic control, no equipment and no night-flying facilities whatever. So it is forbidden for anybody to authorise a flight to go there in the dark — blowing sand or no blowing sand.'

A penalty, or privilege, of seniority is that when the chips are down, as for Abraham in the Bible, the lot falls upon you. Nevertheless, a challenging rescue mission is intensely exciting and satisfying, whatever its type or scale. A flight to Hurghada on a clear night was unlikely to be a hair-raising project. I smiled at Jock and reached for the telephone.

First to the doctor at Hurghada. The lad's appendix was still grumbling but did not seem to be getting worse, yet. Also, he was not a stretcher case, for he could sit up. But, the sooner he got out the better; it could suddenly become a matter of life or death with little or no warning. Next call, to the Met office. Just as I had hoped, they confirmed there would be virtually no wind between 8 pm and 5 am the next day, and the air should then be gin clear. Third, to the Communications Flight at Heliopolis. They had a serviceable Proctor — a single-engined aircraft with side-by-side seating, and a landing light. Also, they checked that the moon was nearly full and, after the first hour or so, would be shining brightly almost all night. Fourth came a call to the Squadron Leader, an equipment officer, commanding the depot at Hurghada. Yes, he had a couple of paraffin hurricane-lanterns. No, it would be no problem to put one at the touchdown end of the landing-strip on its centre-line; he would of course choose the downwind end, if there was a wind. Yes, he could place the other lamp half way along the strip, on its left-hand side. That got the final problem settled; the first lamp would give a marker beyond which I should land, and the second would help me to keep straight during the landing run. Finally, I rang my flat and said I would be late home; certainly not before midnight, and possibly long after that.

After the office had closed down I went to Heliopolis to go through the preliminaries carefully. It was senseless to do the job sloppily and thereby build in even more problems and risks than were there already. Latest weather report . . . maps . . . knee-pad and pencil . . . make a flight-plan . . . check over the Proctor from nose to tail, outside and inside, before it was dark.

By 8 pm — an hour before moonrise — I was strapping myself in for start-up. As I taxied out, the fast-fading sunset light showed low, rounded hummocks to the east. Beyond and slightly to the right was the faint black silhouette of the first range of hills to be over-flown — the Mokattams. I took off, turned right on to my south-easterly heading, climbed into the night sky and settled down to wait in blackness for the moon.

In three-quarters of an hour the sky to the east showed the first shafts of moonglow. Fifteen minutes later, spot on schedule, a particularly large 'harvest moon' — in fact, more like a great blotchy orange football — lifted itself gently over the horizon. All too soon its warm colour was fading and changing to frozen metallic white.

The second range of hills appeared ahead, much clearer in the moonlight than I had expected. On the moonlit sides they were a deep glowing violet and on the other sides, in the shadows of the valleys, jet black. The ridges were sharp, like teeth. Fifteen minutes after that we were nearing the coastline, with a shimmering silvery pathway on my left, spread by the moon on the Red Sea. It moved along, keeping pace with me as the Proctor ploughed its comfortable way through the night sky, following the sea-shore at close to 150 mph. The silver pathway, as it moved, outlined each gentle indentation of the bays and headlands, together with unmistakable black patches out to sea which were little islands just off the coast. Map-reading with these conditions outside, and the cockpit lights turned down low inside, was turning out to be delightful and dead simple. It let me calculate our time of arrival over Hurghada to within seconds. Having by now got well past the hills, I let down gently to 1,000 feet.

At Hurghada there is a distinctive headland which confirmed final identification and, just inland with the bright moonlight, it was not difficult to see the sharp angular black shadows of the tents and packing cases, widely spread over many acres so as to minimise damage in case of a bombing attack. It was even possible by moonlight to identify the piece of desert used as a runway. Its edges were clearly picked out by two parallel black lines of camel-thorn bushes pushed back to either side. And, as requested, two yellow pin-points of light came from the hurricane-lanterns asked for, one at the end and one in the middle.

I sailed in smoothly over the first lamp. However, the touchdown did not match the standards set by my approach and it wasn't as smooth an arrival on the hard sand as I would have wished. Although the landing was a bit of a thump, it was not really bad and certainly nothing had been bent or broken.

I could, perhaps, claim two extenuating reasons for this sub-standard landing. First, we were trained not to use landing-lamps. In wartime, prowling enemy aircraft sneaked about: we ourselves prowled a lot over Germany. Any brilliant white headlamp advertised a juicy target which was being remarkably unconcerned about its self-preservation — and ready to be shot down on the instant. But here, with no flarepath and hundreds of miles from enemy-held territory, using a landing-lamp was a far smaller risk than touching down by moonlight alone. I gratefully accepted the lesser of the two evils. Second, I had never landed a Proctor at night before.

I taxied towards a car with its sidelights on. The driver proved to be the CO and we spent the first several minutes thanking each other profusely: on my side because he had put out two hurricane lamps precisely as requested; on his because I had, or so he believed, diced with death and braved the elements to rescue his ewe-lamb. Eventually, on both sides, we managed to persuade each other that it was 'nothing, nothing at all, my dear fellow'. He said that the appendix was still placid and, according to the resident doc, I could take time to enjoy some supper without risk to the patient.

I had already lived on desert rations. With no refrigeration it was going to be bully beef, or tinned bacon and sausages — either of these to be garnished with baked beans, hard tack biscuits and margarine. Perhaps, if I was lucky, there would be some mashed spuds made from dried potato powder, and the whole topped off with some vinegar and HP Sauce. To stifle the taste of disinfectant chlorine in the water it would be tea, or Camp coffee essence from a bottle, with condensed milk; very welcome nonetheless. I would naturally refuse the proffered beer, knowing that it could only come from their meagre personal desert-ration of one bottle, per man, per week.

So it was that, seated at the wooden table in the Mess tent, I almost went through the roof canvas when the CO asked, with studied unconcern, 'I suppose you wouldn't object to a dozen oysters as a starter, before your grilled rock-salmon?'

It was true! Hurghada beach had on it, lying on the white and shining sand at a depth of about one foot, rocks about the size of a football. On the rocks were crinkly-edged oysters, any number, for the culling and opening. And the Red Sea is full of the most delectable fish.

In due course, when I was feeling well fed, well content and in no hurry to leave, the doc explained to me that, even if the patient's problem went from the grumbling stage to the screaming heeby-jeebies in the air, there was no need for me to worry. Let the patient panic if he wished, but he would then be, at the very worst, only a couple of hours from an operating table in Cairo and that, according to him, was medically acceptable. I returned to my Proctor. They installed the patient on the seat beside me and the return journey was as beautiful, and unspectacular, as the flight on the way out.

I parked on the tarmac at Heliopolis and instantly an ambulance pulled up alongside. The orderlies had filled themselves with rumours of a medical crisis 500 miles away, rescue dash, no radio or night flying aids, derring-do . . . and so on *ad nauseam*. They were thoroughly irked when I, and my passenger, appeared to be perfectly normal and unconcerned as we got out of our machine. It was not justice, they reckoned, that the whole affair should be turning into a mere doddle. This did not mean that they were going to be disappointed and cheated of their chance to extract maximum blood and thunder, once they got my passenger into their clutches. Medical orderlies crowded round us and in moments, much against his will and complaining bitterly, he was forced down on to a stretcher, held there by strong arms and loaded into the ambulance which whisked him away with flashing lights and wailing siren. Luckily, I just managed to prevent the more enthusiastic of them from forcing me on to a stretcher and into the ambulance beside him, too! I went home.

Next morning a telephone call produced the information that the surgeons had been waiting for the airman at the hospital. Although there was still no emergency, they did the job there and then because they were ready for it. Within the hour he was appendixless and, at the time of my call, was reported to be doing splendidly.

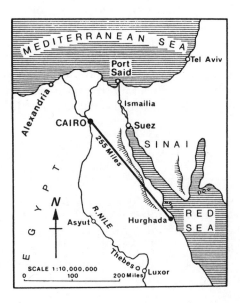

Chapter 2
Slightly Crazy

I was the youngest child of a late marriage and many people have considered me to be born more-or-less crazy, if pleasantly so. It has often been my mischievous pleasure to announce that, doubtless, I was bound to be crazy because my mother gave birth to me when she was in a lunatic asylum! It is a conversation-stopper, but true. When the stunned looks die away, I can continue: my father was a superb doctor who became a specialist in what was then called lunacy, but is now graced by the more polite name of psychiatry. He worked for the Egyptian government from the time of his marriage in 1903 until he died in 1935 whilst head of the entire mental health organisation for Egypt and Palestine. His first big job was to run an asylum at Khanka, about 20 miles north of Cairo. It was a very big hospital and was completely self-contained — it had to be. There was no road to it; they had no car; there was no public transport — only a spur railway line from the local station. The only communicating vehicle for them was a trolley which ran along the railway lines, pushed by porters. It was lifted off the rails if a train needed to pass, and then put back on again afterwards.

He was years and years ahead of his time in treatment for the mentally handicapped. The whole hospital ran as a large farming community — with the lunatics providing practically all the labour under supervision of the nursing staff. He contended that if a cobbler thought he was Napoleon, so what? Let him wear a cocked hat but it didn't stop him making good shoes for his peers. The modern term 'occupational therapy' had not been invented, but that is what it was. The same applied to the grooms in the stud farm for the horses and mules (no tractors, of course), the tillers of the fields and vegetable plots, the irrigation system from the wells, and so on: 3,000 lunatics, almost all productively employed somewhere. The only places that used none of the inmates were the power-station which housed the spinning flywheels and belt-driven dynamos for making electricity, and the machine-tool workshop. The hospital cost the Egyptian government nothing; it made a net profit from selling the surplus produce on the open market.

My father was a great sportsman. In his youth he ran 100 yards in 10 seconds — and twice came in second in the All-England 10 miles. He was a rugger international till he went to the Boer War. In Egypt, all those sports were behind him but he played polo there to a 4-goal level, and cricket with the best. He was a low-handicap golfer and at 60 he could beat the average 30-year-old at tennis. He also had the finest duck-shooting in the world on his doorstep, in the Fayoum.

In many ways my parents' life was idyllic. They were not under modern time-pressures and could take the trolley to Cairo quite often. The couple had two months' leave in England every summer and, when family and friends visited them in Egypt, it was not for the present-day package tour of a couple of weeks; it was for a whole winter.

One night there was a howling wind and rain storm, completely stopping all forms of transport. My doctor father himself brought me into the world to flashes of lightning and peals of thunder. He always reckoned that the whole affair had been something rather special for him.

My mother always told the curious that she arrived in Egypt hand-in-hand with Noah. A character of great resourcefulness, she heard that the way to fertilise a desert was to plant wattle, in the same way that you clean the ground in England by planting potatoes. So she sent to Australia for wattle seedlings and planted them in the piece of hard sand which would become her garden. The land was all barren desert but she had the great advantage of unlimited willing labour in the form of gentle lunatics, and a plentiful supply of water from the wells. Eventually an English garden was created with a tree nursery from which she supplied masses of saplings to be planted round the government buildings in Cairo. Most of her trees were lovely feathery-leafed pepper trees, jacaranda with their mauve blooms, or scarlet-flowered flame trees. In no unkindly sense, but irreverently and behind her back, she was nicknamed The Duchess of Cairo.

My father died when they were both 62. My mother had had rheumatic fever twice already and her doctors feared that she could not take the cold of an English winter, so she stayed on in

Cairo after she was widowed. Living in a small flat next to the Gezira Sporting Club, her great worry was that she might die and, her assets becoming frozen, there might be no money for a dignified funeral. So, £200 in nice clean notes was always kept in her one-brick sized wall-safe, hidden behind a little hanging carpet. Although the safe was out of sight, there can have been very few of her friends who did not know exactly where it was. Indeed, on Saturdays or Sundays, when the banks were closed, there were often panic calls to borrow some or all of 'the funeral money'. It must have financed hundreds of rip-roaring parties in its time — far removed from, and much better than, a dismal funeral.

My mother had a house-boy called Hassan who obviously fed himself very well. His Sudanese skin was shiny black and he looked like a black Winnie the Pooh. He was the great-grandson of my father's first servant, whose family considered my parents to be their personal property, and to be looked after accordingly. My mother often lost her keys — car keys, house keys, or the safe key. She would cry 'Hassan! Where is my key?' She would never say *which* key. Hassan would reply, gently, 'You put it in the bag with your curlers' or '. . . in the top drawer below your underclothes', or whichever was her latest secret hiding place. Somehow, without being told or ever having been seen looking, he always knew which key she wanted and precisely where she had hidden it. Meanwhile the £200, which to him would have been a fortune, continued to finance party after party.

It never rains but it pours. And that seems to go for good luck as well as bad. Almost everything was going my way. I had, by incredible good fortune, been prevented from getting home to England shortly after World War II broke out. I was hauled off a boat on the way home from Singapore when Mussolini closed the Mediterranean, and began three years' war in the Middle East. How many people, in that conflict, were able to spend a good part of it working from home?

I was still alive after two pretty unpleasant batches of flying against the enemy. Then, in the middle of Cairo my mother had two adjoining flats and, while serving time in a headquarters, I lived in one of them. My mother organised all my catering and there was no rationing in Cairo, hardly any shortages, no blackout, a splendid night-life, *and* I talked the local language.

On 3 May that, at the giddy age of 26, I was to be a Wing Commander; indeed, I had become one two days earlier, on May

Day, but no one had troubled to confirm it. Added to that — and best of all — on 5 May I was going to be married. Two years earlier I had fallen in love with an enchanting girl, but she had been stuck in India where her father was serving. And, during the war abroad, fiancées were not allowed to reach their swains and wives could not join their husbands. However, if perchance you married a girl locally, she was permitted to stay with you.

A little matter of 3,000 miles separation and a stack of rules would not daunt my mother. The Duchess set to work on the Embassy. In no time she had charmed a bird off the tree or, more precisely, the Ambassador's wife off her lofty perch to come down and help willingly. Permission was given to Miss Phyl McFarlane to occupy a seat from Karachi to Cairo in a civilian BOAC flying boat, so that she might take a job in the Cairo Embassy. Before she began it, however, she could take me for better or worse and we would have two weeks honeymoon in Palestine. All was wonderful and there was not much for me to weep over!

Admittedly, one apparently infinitesimal inconvenience remained: the telephone call of 3 May had told me not only of my new rank, but also of a new post to go with it, a staff job, at Heliopolis on the edge of Cairo — and 5 May, my wedding day and start of leave, was also my official date to start work. I airily presumed that the clash of dates was of small concern — doubtless my new boss would have been told by the postings staff of our wedding, and a brief courtesy telephone call to him would get matters squared away amicably so that my leave and our honeymoon would not be endangered. Although I didn't want a staff job because I was a mad keen pilot, it was not *all* bad. It did mean that we could live together in my flat and use my mother's super cook. With the unbounded optimism of youth I put the call through.

The Group Captain cut me short, saying, 'It's all most unsatisfactory; here you are telephoning me out of the blue to say would it be OK for you to appear on *21 May*! Over two *weeks* hence? No; it won't be OK . . . You're supposed to be here in two *days'* time! I've got the task of creating this completely new Group to fill a vital need which at present is nobody's baby — with you as my No 2 — and the target date was 1 May which has already gone by. I've been waiting *months* for Headquarters Middle East to nominate a Wing Commander for me, and it was only last week that HQME nominated you. Even then they said you couldn't be freed until 5 May — two days from now. And what's more, that is a Saturday, so in effect you won't be here till Monday 7 — and that's a week late. Bloody hell!! I've had enough fiddle faddle and delay from HQME already. I won't insist that you come in for this Saturday — your proper date — but the weekend is all you can have . . . Anyway, why don't you *want* to come in next Monday?'

At that moment, holding the telephone to my ear and listening to this tirade from the prospective boss whom I had never met, I saw him as a tough martinet who lacked even the usual courtesies accorded by a boss to his subordinates. It boded ill for my new job. Taking a deep breath I began 'Well, Sir, HQME only told me today — 3 May — of my posting to your new Group, and that the official date would be 5 May, the day after tomorrow. That is all I was told, and all I know. I assumed, wrongly, that you knew all about me. This telephone call was meant as a courtesy, to make my number with you and confirm that my plans are OK. It seems you haven't been told that, some months ago, I got permission from my present AOC to get married — and Saturday the 5th of May (which has now become the day of my posting to you) is my wedding day. It's all been arranged to take place in the English Cathedral, with all the trimmings. My boss here had already granted me two weeks' leave for my honeymoon . . . which takes me up to the 21st — a Monday . . . which I had assumed you knew already . . . Sir . . .' I heard my voice dying away lamely.

There was such a long pause before he spoke that I thought we had been cut off. Admittedly things happened fast in wartime and last-minute changes were rife but, even so, he must have been frustrated beyond the bounds of tolerance.

At last he spoke: 'Typical embuggeration by HQME. Not one person there seems to know what another is up to. They keep you there till the last minute before you go on leave, and then expect me to make good their balls-up. However, I simply cannot let you have *two* weeks; how about coming in on Wednesday the 9th — that would give you four days — and I'll hold the fort till then?'

After some slightly less edgy pleading on both sides, a bargain was struck: one week's honeymoon and the job would start immediately after that, on the Monday.

Planning a wedding in wartime, or any social event for that matter, was full of pitfalls. However, we were much luckier than most young couples getting married abroad at that time, for my fiancée could live with my mother in Cairo and we could be married from her flat. My mother was already 70 years old and not in the best of health, so most of the organisation fell to us, but it was wonderful to do it from my home background. Minor crises were met by loans from the 'funeral money' and luckily most of the celebrations went off as we hoped and planned — except for a couple of happenings which were totally unforeseen and resulted from the war.

The first happening was due to the fact that my fiancee's parents were in India, so that there was no possibility at all of them being there on the great day. We decided that a nice present for them would be to have a film made of the wedding. Clutching my movie-camera I found my way to the office set aside for the public-relations cameramen in the Middle East.

There must have been at least eight of them sitting around, drinking tea and endlessly smoking cigarettes. Somewhat diffidently, I enquired if by chance there was a photographer with some experience of movies who could, perhaps for a small professional's fee, do his stuff with my camera? Then, as there were so many of them there, I took my courage in both hands and added that, if it were not too much of an imposition, perhaps another of them could take some still photographs with my miniature camera? I would, of course, pay for and provide all the films they wanted. Perhaps an extra incentive would be the champagne at the reception, after the ceremony . . .?

To a man they rose and came towards me *en masse,* led by one with the physique of an all-in wrestler. It looked as if they were going to chuck me out, bodily and ignominiously, for having been so crass as to try to importune a specialist war photographer just to take pictures of a miserable civilian wedding. In some alarm I retreated as far as possible, pressing myself against the shut door at my back. I feared they might do me a mischief. The wrestler came close and appeared to be the spokesman.

'Did you mention the word *wedding?'*

Hesitantly I admitted doing so and apologised for any lack of tact on my part. An incredulous look followed by a beaming smile spread across his face as he turned and said, 'Chaps! D'you hear that? A wedding! Sir, you have before you the top photographers of Fleet Street. The *Daily Mirror,* the *Sketch, The Times, The Tatler* and all the other glossies. As for your movie — him, he's the number one cameraman from British Movietone News. We are fed up to our back teeth with troops endlessly brewing char, with guns, ships, female parachute-packers and everything else connected with the war. We'd give our eye teeth to cover an honest-to-God real live wedding again. It'll be just like home. Forget your cameras. We'll use our own which we know, and all film's free for us in any case. Where is it, and when? We're all coming — every single one of us. You won't be able to keep any of us away.'

So it is that we have one of the finest sets of wedding photographs in existence — and reckon that the astronomic and much enjoyed quantities of champagne that they consumed was fair payment!

The second happening concerned my best man. He was to be Robin Johnson, an ex-East African political agent who had joined up for the war. He was a fighter pilot in a Hurricane squadron. We had become good friends during the 1940/41 desert campaign and, although he couldn't take leave, he assured me that his CO would let him fly a Hurricane down to Cairo for the day so that he could help me take the fateful step. The wedding was at 2.30 pm and he expected to be in by about mid-morning.

On the day itself at around noon, give or take a bit, he telephoned me from Alexandria. He said he was under interrogation and it looked like going on for a long time.

'Interrogation? What in Heaven's name have you done?'

'I'm afraid I've been a complete idiot. I was bowling along from Mersa in my Hurri, thinking of not much, when I saw a Ju-88 recce aircraft ahead. He must have been sound asleep and, without thinking of the consequences, I naturally fell in behind and gave him a quick squirt up his backside. He burst into flames and went straight down into the desert. When I told Ops about it on the radio, they said to land at Dekheila and make out a quick report. Now the idiots here in Alexandria keep telling me that their interrogation is more important than your wedding. No way can I get to Cairo in time to hold your hand. I really am most awfully sorry about it.'

With the wedding only two hours away I was compelled to scoot off to Cairo and scour the streets to see which of my colleagues was wandering around, had a decent uniform to hand, and could be cajoled into being my best man about an hour later. I was lucky enough to find another good friend, Roger Porteous, by 1.15.

Roger subsequently was to gain fame and decorations for knocking out numerous German tanks in a Hurricane fitted with a thumping great shell-firing gun under each wing. It was no sinecure: every time he pressed the trigger the recoil was so great that it knocked twenty mph off the machine's flying speed. At the beginning he damned nearly killed himself when, coming in for a landing, he pressed the trigger by mistake. The Hurricane, losing twenty mph on the final approach, came within an ace of falling clean out of the sky.

When Roger said he would stand-in for Robin, I briefed him, 'Wonderful; here is your best-man's present — and I will see you at the Cathedral in three-quarters of an hour. I'll give you the ring there and fill in all the details. Do you know where it is?'

'No. Not really,' he replied.

'Then grab a taxi in good time!' I urged him.

Back at the flat once more and having completed all the final checks — presents on show, the cake in place and a sword to cut it, drinks ready, and so on, with, finally, the ring in my pocket — I gave my fiancée her last kiss as a spinster, saying, "Bye, darling! I'll see you at the church in half an hour!' and left. Some say it is unlucky to see your bride-to-be after midnight before the wedding. Maybe, but we had no option and now, after 44 years, I can say with conviction that it can not have been *too* unpropitious for us!

We had chosen to honeymoon at the King David Hotel in Jerusalem. However, we could not leave Cairo on the day of the wedding. For one thing, my new wife would have to have a passport in her changed name, and the local consulate would not issue this until office hours the next day. Another, stronger, reason was that the one daily airline flight to Palestine would have left before the wedding was over. Anyway, it would be no great chore to visit the passport office next morning and catch that day's flight, but these were not the only reasons for booking into Mena House Hotel for the first night.

Mena House, about 20 miles west of Cairo, must have been one of the most romantic hotels in the world. It was a large and comfortable Egypto-Victorian building, surrounded by fig, palm and casuarina trees. Bougainvillaea spread pink, orange and purple blossom up the walls. Among them were the blue and red trumpet-shaped flowers of morning-glory which twined and writhed up the bougainvillaea. The Egyptian aspect showed in the Moorish arches, floors of veined marble partly covered by fine Turkish carpets, wall mosaics of eastern conception and, for after dinner, carved wooden chairs beside local tray-tables made of brass inlaid with silver. Then, just outside the front door, rising high into the sky, were the enormous pyramids of Cheops and Chefren, with the smaller pyramid of Mycerinus in support. Some distance to the left, the head and back of the Temple of the Sphinx stuck out of a sheet of sand. The temple doorway, flanked by the animal's gigantic forepaws, only came into view many years later when the sand was cleared. These four great monuments of sandstone looked yellow in daylight, a wonderful reddish-orange in the last rays of the setting sun and a mysterious silvery charcoal-grey in the moonlight. The whole place positively oozed romance for a wedding night.

Not only romance; the Victorians liked their comfort, too. It was to be found in the bedrooms with vast bathrooms, large sitting-rooms, comfortable sofas, a superb cuisine and an excellent cellar, backed by immaculate service. I reckoned that, taking any rough with the smooth, we would manage at a pinch to survive the rigours of Mena House for one night.

May 5 was hot beyond belief. The bride's absent parents were spared that dubious pleasure of standing in a receiving line, feeling the perspiration trickling down inside your clothes, knowing that your face is shining like a navigation beacon on a clear night. However, the knot was successfully tied, the speeches were made and then it was all over as far as we were concerned. Someone else would sweep up the crumbs and throw out the empty bottles. With the usual cries from well-wishers, including the happy and slightly rocking Fleet Street photographers, we sank thankfully into the back seat of a luxurious taxi and waited for Mena House to appear. Once there we went to our room and, prompted by some simultaneous urge, both said: 'What I need is a swim!'

We changed into swim-suits and went down to the pool. Selecting a table and lounger chairs, we ordered a couple of very long, very soft, very cold drinks. The water looked gloriously enticing. Just before we dived in, a girl got up from the other end of the pool, came mincing up to us and gushed: 'It simply *can't* be true! *Phyl* McFarlane of *all* people! How *wonderful* to see you. I had no *idea* you were in Egypt! What are you doing *here?*'

Artlessly and languidly, Phyl lifted the third finger of her left hand showing the little gold band which had been made to my special order by melting down a half-sovereign the same age as herself. She answered casually, 'My name's not McFarlane now; I'm married, you know.'

The other girl's eyebrows shot up. 'I had *no* idea! Good Lord! What *marvellous news*. How long have you been married?'

Phyl tried not to giggle, saying, 'About four hours.'

Instead of bursting into hoots of laughter as we both did, and then joining us for a drink, she muttered some ludicrous remark about not wanting to intrude on the love-birds, and scuttled away. Phyl told me that she was a fairly silly girl and her performance had been about par for the course; we were not missing anything.

Our one week at the King David went by in a flash. I know not how, during that flash, we squeezed out enough time to see the Wailing Wall, Golgotha, the Holy Sepulchre, churches and markets, not forgetting Bethlehem with its several birthplaces of Christ (each claimed by some Christian sect or other), the Dead Sea, and all the other places that tourists to the Holy Land always have to visit. It was a marvellous honeymoon.

At dinner on the last evening, Phyl looked at me soulfully, saying: 'Darling; sometimes you write poetry. Would you, please, darling, write a poem about our honeymoon? It has all been so wonderful and special. I would like to remember it that way.'

I turned the menu over, took out a pen and after a few moments I wrote:

> The honeymoon was simply grand.
> I dished out *quids* with either hand!

Phyl gave me a dirty look. 'You are a stinker. You're a Philistine with no sentiment and, moreover, you sound as though you'll be happy to economise by getting back to work sooner than we originally expected. I am not sure that I love you after all . . . you rat!'

*   *   *

Some months later, in common with most of the British women in Cairo, Phyl was doing her Florence Nightingale act, visiting the sick and wounded in hospital. She made her rounds of the wards, stomaching the tannery smell of burned and putrefying flesh, laced with disinfectant. She pushed a trolley of books, wrote letters home for the illiterate and tongue-tied or for the desperately wounded, trying her best to cheer the patients up. Most were deeply grateful just to talk to a girl when their families and girlfriends were kept thousands of miles away from their bedsides.

She came to a bed where the occupant was heavily bandaged, but seemed alert enough. To open a conversation she asked him where he had been wounded. He answered that he had not been wounded in the fighting, but he and some chums were using a battered old building for shelter when the roof fell in. He had been fairly seriously injured by the falling beams and they had brought him in to Cairo in a casevac aircraft.

'Oh! Was it your first flight in an aeroplane?'

'No; not my first; it was my second flight. The first one was tremendously exciting! Can I tell you about it?'

'Of course.'

'I got the most appalling go of appendicitis. There was no hospital nearby and they couldn't get me to one because there were no roads and no one could fly there because of the bad weather — so I was all set to die! And I would surely have been a goner except for a crazy Wing Commander who saved my life because he was a super pilot! He actually flew all the way from Cairo, through those appalling sandstorms, with no radio, *and* in the middle of a pitch-black night! He landed on the desert totally in the dark with no lights and . . .'

Phyl listened, fascinated as he unfolded his wildly embroidered and dramatised story which, by curious coincidence, she had heard before in different terms. The airman, flattered by the rapt attention of his audience of one, pulled out all the stops. At last, he came to the end and waited for the admiring comments. Eyes sparkling with laughter and pleasure, she said: 'Funnily enough, I know that crazy Wing Commander you mentioned. I married him.'

Chapter 3
Mahogany Bomber

The 'Ferry and Transport' Headquarters that Group Captain Bunny Russell designed and created, known as No 216 Group, was tiny. It had its being in a medium sized rented apartment of about half a dozen rooms, not too far from Heliopolis airfield and about seven miles from the centre of Cairo. There were only a couple of staff officers from each of the disciplines — Operations, Equipment, Engineers and Signals — plus one accountant, a few clerks, some radio operators and one car with a driver. Bunny turned out to be a fabulous organiser and his men soon learned that his battle-cry was 'Why have more? You are paid to get things done. Don't ask me what to do. Find an answer — and *do* it! Tell me *afterwards* only if it goes wrong, or you think I *have* to know about it.'

A great deal was achieved by doing things without asking, instead of bleating that 'they' should be doing something — the faceless 'they' that so many people think are around to be leaned on. Douglas Viney, the chief signaller, for example, was no slim and spry little pixie. This didn't stop him shinning up on to the roof of the apartment block and putting up a tall aerial there so that he could be in direct and instant touch by radio with any of our units. HQME weren't in contact with them, but Douglas was.

Everybody helped each other to do anything that was necessary, went flat out all the time and prided themselves that it worked very effectively. Bunny made it work so well that the mighty Headquarters RAF Transport Command was formed in March the following year, using Bunny's 216 Group us as the model — but bigger and on a world-wide basis.

Day One, Monday morning, Bunny was briefing me on my new job: a desk job, known with derision to all ground-borne pilots as 'flying a mahogany bomber'. I was in a sour mood. Having been away from operational flying for a year, I had hoped to get back to piloting fighting aircraft on a full-time basis. Now, to be given a second office-job in a row was bad enough, but this task was a brand new one. The group being formed had no real counterpart anywhere in the world — except, in a few respects perhaps, a group in England which oversaw the ferrying of aircraft across the Atlantic from the United States. This meant that there was no one to whom we could turn for guidance, asking 'How does one . . .?' or 'What if. . .?' We would have to work it all out from the grass roots as we went along. And, moreover, the things that Bunny was telling me sounded dismal. I wanted to be *flying*! And planning conferences were heaving menacingly over my horizon, with piles and heaps of bumf — *and* a shiny seat to my trousers — all of it stretching far, far away into the distant future.

Bunny explained in the fashion of a child with a delicious pudding (keeping the best bits to the end) 'As the Mediterranean is enemy controlled, all the short-range fighting aircraft have to be crated and shipped to Takoradi on the Ivory Coast in West Africa. After assembly they are flown 4,000 miles to Cairo. They make several or a few landings on the way, according to their range — fighters often, light bombers less often. They use little airfields called staging posts, each with just a landing strip and a few men. Two hundred pilots do the job, commanded by a chap called Dan McGinn, who lives and works from a houseboat on the Nile.'

I thought 'What a mess! How does one ever try to get output from that load of rubbish?'

He continued, 'The flow of aircraft to the Middle East front will be vital for the life and death battle with the Germans, which is going to come, sure as eggs is eggs, in the Western Desert, sooner or later.

'Up till now Wing Commander Dan McGinn, and his pilots, and all the little staging airfields spread across northern Africa, haven't been anybody's baby in particular, except that sponge-like mess that calls itself Headquarters Middle East. Let us consider what happens if, say, some Flight Lieutenant or Squadron Leader, hundreds of miles into the southern desert and not belonging to a battle-tasked outfit, needs something urgently. He can try a wireless link — but they only work if the weather conditions are suitable, and then only at night. Or perhaps a passing aircraft will take a letter for him. Either way, sooner or later and usually later, it gets to HQME. His impassioned plea raises the level of some staff wallah's pending-tray by one sheet of paper. Those desk-bound minions keep up their morale by pretending they are vitally busy with fighting the war in the desert, far to the west. In fact, most of them keep busy putting sand on the office steps — so that they can wear their desert-boots. Nothing much happens for the poor fellow 2,000 miles away down south.

'From now on, everything to do with moving aircraft, or stores or people in aircraft, belongs to us. Our parish stretches from the Ivory Coast in the south, to the front line in the west, to India in the east. The people far away, out in the blue, must have *somebody* they can turn to directly; someone who can — and will — *care*! And that is going to be *us*!'

I sat feeling slightly stunned and depressed while Bunny paused a moment, thinking. Imagine! I was being sentenced to sit at a wooden desk just so that people, anywhere in an area 4,000 by 3,000 miles, could shuffle their belly-aches and wails on to my shoulders . . . It was a miserable prospect.

Bunny went on: 'We'll set up a few strategically placed control points, each manned by a small, highly efficient team, who can cope with nearly anything. They'll look after a clutch of staging posts in their area. Only when a problem comes up which they can't solve will they apply direct to us. We can win their battles with Middle East on the spot. Dan McGinn will bring the fighter aircraft up here from Takoradi in batches, led by a senior pilot with a navigator in a light-bomber. They'll fly in short hops, for the 4,000 miles to Cairo. Local problems are the job of the chaps on the spot. Only if it's beyond their scope, they apply to us — and *we* get results!'

That sounded better. Not *all* the complaints would come to me.

'Here, in Cairo,' he continued, 'we'll have an Ops Room to tell where the aircraft are and what they need if something's amiss. We've got our own wireless links and we'll create our own really efficient postal service, using the aircraft always flying up and down our routes. It can't help being a damned sight better than the official one! Let's face it, we're going to be good! We must put on pressure *before* things get drastic.'

The widespread ramifications of this task were beginning to sound a real challenge which could be fun to meet. But the best was yet to come — here was the *bonne bouche:* 'Naturally, getting the aircraft here is only the first bit. We will deliver right to the front-line squadrons, up in the desert. That means arming them and training the crews to fight their machines effectively, should they be intercepted by the enemy . . . And another thing, our crews get flown everywhere on top priority; no crews on the 'available' roster means no fighting aircraft delivered, and that could be critical.

'As I see the division of labour, my job will be here minding the shop and getting things done. I've more experience than you have, and more rank to kick HQME off their fat arses when needed. In your office, you are wasting my time; you're to be my eyes and ears, up and down the routes, ensuring that what we do here matches what they want there. Things at the sharp end have got to really *hum!* And, if they don't, contact me to do what's necessary. You simply hitch lifts down the routes in one of Dan McGinn's Hudsons, and fly yourself back in what you choose from the assembly line at the far end.'

He gave me a quizzical look. 'Do you think that sounds reasonable, and do you think you could cope?'

Oh brother! Reasonable! Being encouraged to fly any and every type of aircraft that came on stream? My mouth must have been opening and shutting like a goldfish's. If I couldn't cope I would die trying! What a desk-job for a Wing Commander! Responsibility for the effectiveness of 200 pilots, both ferrying and fighting? A dozen airfields to oversee? Deliveries over more than 4,000 miles right into the battle zone? *Carte blanche* to travel anywhere in the Middle East, on top priority, on my own say-so? And a boss who felt that efficiency where things *really* happened, out in the field, was what mattered and not skill at bumf-shuffling in an office? I was going to have the most airborne 'mahogany bomber' in the entire Service!

Chapter 4
An Ugly Bird

Every day brought masses of work and, mostly, more and more satisfaction. What had started for me as a lively curiosity had now burgeoned into my major interest and passion — piloting and comparing as many different kinds of aircraft as possible, designed and built by different people for different kinds of work. My so-called desk job was being unbelievably kind to the type-hog that I had become.

It was fascinating to see how separate designers had used their individual pet ideas to solve the same basic problems. Over the past few months chances galore for self-indulgence had come my way. I had delivered British and American fighters; Hurricanes, Kittihawks, Tomahawks. I had done local trials on a captured German Me-109 fighter and a German Me-110 twin-engined fighter — searching for tactical weaknesses we could exploit when our machines had to fight against them. On top of that I had ferried some American twin-engined light bombers — Bostons, Baltimores and Marylands — assessing them against our Blenheims (incidentally to the latter's severe disadvantage).

It was intriguing that, over and above the technical variations, even national factors showed themselves. For example, Britain is small so the British fighters climbed quicker, but the American machines, coming from a big country, usually flew further. The British machines were more manoeuvrable and nippy, but the Americans were more stable and relaxing on long distances. They had more spacious and comfortable cockpits; they frequently provided ashtrays and arm rests on the flight decks; we had a rigid 'no smoking' rule. The Germans had gone for technical efficiency, but the crew comfort was miserable.

Another out-of-the-ordinary and intriguing job came my way. In 1941 Air Headquarters Iraq* had seemed to me to be pretty

*See Chapters 20-23 of *The Luck of the Devil,* by the same author, published by Airlife.

restricted by the rule-books.| Now, in|1942,| they|were running true to form. The signal in my hand said that they had a Grumman Goose amphibian on their airfield at Habbaniya; this I knew was a baby flying-boat with retractable wheels, twin-engined and built in the United States. They asked us if we could send them a pilot qualified on that type, to test it and fly it to the Nile Delta, because they had *no one there who could do so . . .* I could barely believe that a place like Habbaniya with its Flying Training School could bring itself to send such a signal. It was a positive insult to · their highly qualified and presumably competent flying-instructors by the dozen.

I read the signal again and decided I had been right the first time; it *was* too good to be true. I trotted off to see the boss. Bunny Russell grinned widely and agreed that matters would be greatly simplified for a rule-besotted outfit like AHQ Iraq if I claimed to be the only Goose pilot in the Middle East. Perhaps I was a goose myself; who could say? We sent an answer to AHQ Iraq saying that a qualified pilot *for* their Goose (carefully not saying 'qualified *on* the Goose') would arrive as soon as transport could be organised: we always stopped short of actually telling flagrant lies.

A few telephone calls to HQ Middle East unearthed some rumours and very little substantial information. They said that the machine had belonged to an American millionaire who had been caught by the war and could neither fly it nor ship it back to the United States, so he had generously presented it to the RAF for communications work.

I had various things in my past experience which led me to assume (unwisely) that this new (for me) machine would not present significant problems. Pre-war I had flown an amphibian called a Walrus. I chose to gloss over the fact that it had been a *biplane* with only *one* engine and an abysmal speed range; probably the only similar characteristic was that both could sit on water without sinking. The two engines in the Goose were apparently the same as the one that I had flown behind in an American Harvard training landplane. It was basically a civilian aircraft, so (I blithely presumed) it would be simple and viceless for amateur pilots, unlike the dedicated professional which I pompously took myself to be. I thought (ingenuously) that, given a careful study of 'Pilot's Notes', no grave problems lay ahead.

I discussed the machine with Bunny. We decided to grab this heaven-sent opportunity with both hands. We would make it our own private executive aircraft! It had two engines, which made for safety on the long desert-hops; it carried about five passengers (so far as we knew), so we could use it to shuttle ferry crews around; it was amphibious, so we could land on the Nile, or the Niger — or go shooting crocodiles for that matter. Indeed, we convinced ourselves, it was tailor-made for our own purposes and pleasure. First things first; go and fetch it before AHQ Iraq changed their minds. Meanwhile, Bunny would peddle our ideas in HQME. Clutching the signed piece of paper, saying 'he can fly it' (and omitting the words 'he hopes') I hitched the first available aircraft going the 800 miles to Habbaniya.

The Goose was on the airfield and I can record that I had no problem in recognising it instantly for what it was. This was not surprising; it could not conceivably have been anything else. It was plumb ugly, and it looked ungainly and faintly ludicrous. It had a deep, chesty fuselage with, each side, a fiddly little wheel poking out. Stuck up on top was a wing with two engines fixed in it. Two floats hung down from the wingtips, one at each end, and at the back was a very high rudder. The whole shebang was painted a sinister matt-black. I was reminded irresistibly of the organ-grinder's comment on getting his monkey: 'My God you're an ugly bastard — but you're all mine now.'

No one appeared to know anything about it save that it had been given a number — *HK 822* — and prepared for a flight to Cairo: prepared, that is, in the light of common sense. My questions did not receive answers which were exactly helpful. No — they had no aircraft or flying history records. No — they had no Engineer's Handbooks for a Goose. No — they had no inspection or maintenance schedules. No — they had no Pilot's Notes. No — no one had yet flown it because of its reputation; it was said that the owner's Parthian shot was to warn of its diabolical tendency to swing viciously to one side on take-off and on landing, but to *which* side, nobody knew. A Squadron Leader, sweating through his khaki shorts and shirt as he answered my queries, looked at me quizzically. Surely, as the only fully qualified Goose pilot in the Middle East, I knew all about that . . . didn't I? I put on what I hoped was a knowledgeable look. However, I wished I had not been so smug: flying a strange aeroplane with the help of nothing but a lot of unsubstantiated warnings would need considerable care.

The door was in the side and the cabin proved to be spacious and higher than I expected, because of the deep flying-boat hull.

This Percival Proctor sitting on the sandy airfield might not be considered an ideal ambulance aircraft, but it was adequate for me to go and rescue an airman whose appendix had begun to grumble, hundreds of miles from any hospital.

(via The Aeroplane)

This powerful character, my mother, went to Egypt at the turn of the century. Much beloved by everybody, she was known sometimes behind her back as 'The Duchess of Cairo'. She was a keen bridge-player and an inveterate gambler – at both of which she made a lot of money.

The 'Duchess of Cairo' managed to charm the Embassy enough for them to give permission for a flight by my fiancée, Phyl McFarlane, from India to Cairo – in wartime! Here is her BOAC 'Empire' class flying boat touching down on the Nile at Rod el Farag, just in the suburbs. The magic of 'the big iron birds' had not yet fled from the local populace! (Imperial War Museum)

This is the house where I was born. It never had a name. When my mother went there it stood isolated on sandy desert, with one tap – and twenty miles from the nearest English-speaking person. And there was no road. That redoubtable lady sent as far as Australia for seedlings: every single plant, shrub and tree that you see (and a great many more that you can't) was planted and nurtured by her.

Phyl and me, taken in my mother's garden. The official photographers to the armed forces were all tip-top Fleet Street men in civilian life. At the promise of champagne and cake they came in a body to take wedding photographs.

A Grumman Goose was a type of aeroplane which I had never seen before. There were no books, no instructions and no one had flown it who could help me. It was a happy challenge to air-test it and then fly it 700 miles from Iraq to Egypt. This is a photograph of the actual machine – No HK822 – at RAF Habbaniya. (via The Aeroplane)

The fort at Rutbah was on the oil pipeline from Kirkuk to Haifa. It was the first and only landmark for 200 miles on a flight from Habbaniya to Cairo. I overflew it many times. This was a time when, in 1940, a bomb had been dropped to try and flush out some rebel Iraqis who had occupied it – they stayed put. (Imperial War Museum)

Towards the front was a strong metal bulkhead; the wheels were attached at the bottom and on the top were the engines. Good; if I did a heavy landing, the engines up there would not force themselves down on to the back of my neck. I climbed into the cockpit through a hole in the middle of the bulkhead. Sitting in the pilot's seat I began a long and detailed inspection . . . it was not encouraging. A few American dials of long-ago manufacture were scattered like confetti all over the instrument panel, not logically grouped like our British ones; mental note — do not try to fly it by instruments, ever. No radio, no radio-compass, no auto-pilot; oh dear — to be flown by eyeball and seat-of-the-pants, all the way. Throttles and engine controls *hanging from the roof!* Oh my God! — as you value your life in a panic situation, do not grab at the usual place, which is sprouting from the floor! On the bulkhead was a heavy-looking handle for winding up the wheels; next note — always be sure to carry a passenger to do the heavy manual labour. The two fuel gauges each showed 60 gallons; 'full'. After an equally careful re-check I could find no reason for putting off an air-test any further. There were no other sources of useful information to be tapped. My invitations to sundry pilot-spectators to come for a ride as co-pilot, and to give me a hand in discovering the intricacies of this interesting machine — in reality primarily to wind that damned handle — were all politely declined.

I proceeded very gently. She taxied beautifully because the tail-wheel turned with the rudder, so she steered like a boat. Before take-off, and twitching with nervousness because of the proclaimed 'vicious swing', I put her very precisely into the wind. Slowly, smoothly, carefully, I opened the throttles. She rolled forwards, straight as a die, and no trace of a swing appeared. When she had enough speed, we lifted into the air, like a bird. I gave a deep sigh of relief. The next three-quarters of an hour was spent in doing every test I could dream up to check settings and handling, with and without the wheels extended. To mix a whole stack of metaphors, she was sweet as a nut, docile as a lamb, ugly as sin — and I could find no vices.

Just as carefully as on the take-off I came in to land. It was dead smooth and easy. I did several more 'circuits and bumps'. She rolled herself off and she greased herself back on to the ground, every time. Ugly as sin she might be but she was a dolly-bird to fly; a real 'old gentleman's aeroplane'. Within an hour she had become the apple of my eye.

Several of my invited passengers 'happened' to have been sitting in the flight-office, watching the viceless comings and goings. Two or three now sidled up and artlessly enquired if, by any chance, I could now see my way to giving them a checkout flip, and letting them fly it too. Their craven tails got a contemptuous twist when I pointed out that they had each been asked for help earlier, which they had declined to give. Now was too late!

My plan was to take off next day at about 8 am, before it got too hot. I had done calculations from my speed tests, and from my knowledge of the engines in the Harvard trainer, and reckoned we might just make Cairo in one hop, with luck and if the winds were not unkind. Anyway, if I was running a bit short of fuel I could always drop in for a top-up at Ismailia, or Fayid, about 70 miles nearer and on the edge of the Suez Canal. The crew of a Blenheim, looking for a hitch-flight back to Cairo, asked if they could scrounge a lift and I magnanimously agreed. Guess who was going to wind up the wheels?

The morning was perfect. Our first turning point was Rutbah Wells, about 200 miles away. On the map, a road was shown, marked by one thin red line. Below, on the brownish sand itself, there were hundreds of wheel marks made by the lorries and Mr Nairn's air-conditioned Mercedes buses, which had plied since long before the war between Baghdad and the Lebanon. The tracks varied wildly from the so-called road because each driver chose and followed his own preferred route — as long as it went in the right general direction. There were the usual wadis, seldom placed as shown hopefully on maps made some years back. Although the wheel tracks gave me no help on distance flown, they confirmed that we were pointing more or less at Rutbah; and ninety per cent of them would converge there eventually.

It was delightful. The weather was good. The machine was almost flying itself, except when the Blenheim pilot in the right hand seat was happily flying it for me. I was the Rajah, or Pasha, or Great Panjandrum in the skipper's seat, watching them do any work necessary. The engines were running at economical settings and were quiet. The Blenheim W/Op had nothing to do, and slept, while the Blenheim navigator got steamed up because he had no real job, and worried himself silly because for two hours I appeared to do no navigation and, he reckoned, paid no proper attention to his efforts. See if I cared — we were over an old stamping ground of mine and I knew it like the back of my hand!

Rutbah turned up in due time, to the navigator's surprise and slight annoyance considering my inattention, and we turned slightly left to follow the 'pipeline' towards Amman, 250 miles further on. The 'pipeline' was a bit misnamed, because there was no pipe to be seen: it was buried underground. However, there was a straight track beside it for the lorries and the buses, a telephone line on poles, and a little packed-sand landing ground beside each pumping-station for the oil. Following those markers would be easier and more reliable than a radio-beam. Navigation, in good weather, posed no problems.

Having noted the time to Rutbah I settled down to checking fuel consumption, to calculate the time we were due to pass over Amman and to see if we could make Cairo in one go. This first set of sums is always an intriguing task, particularly if margins are close. Will we, or won't we? The early figures give a rough estimate and then, as the flight proceeds, later figures become progressively more precise and refined. Consequently, the answers become more accurate. Naturally, one always hopes that the last sums show the first ones to have been accurate too. You pat yourself on the back and doff your cap to such good navigation and airmanship.

So it was that, metaphorically, I hit the roof: the readings showed that far too many gallons were disappearing somewhere. I checked my figures again . . . and again, from the beginning, *very* carefully. Something was most definitely wrong. Was there a fuel leak, with a risk of fire, or seriously mal-adjusted carburettors? The latter could mean plugs and valves burning out, followed by engine-failure. Or had the tanks not been filled properly and the 'full' readings on the gauges were wrong? Was it the result of no maintenance documents, compounded by the fact that at Habbaniya they had no Harvards with a similar kind of engine to be copied? Whatever it was, it was no laughing matter. From the instruments and switches I could detect no rough running nor signs of poor performance. The Blenheim crew, sniffing nervously and peering through the windows, could smell no petrol and see no black smoke from the exhausts. I prayed that it would get no worse, and that we could reach Amman. One saving grace: if we went down it would be beside the pipeline, and we should be found before we died of thirst.

Reaching Cairo was out of the question. So, for that matter, were Fayid or Ismailia. It behoved me to get down at the nearest RAF airfield as soon as possible — and that was Amman, in

Jordan. The endless multi-shaded brown desert slid by underneath with maddening slowness for a very long two hours. The lorry tracks and the telephone poles stretched from horizon to horizon ahead and behind. Each pumping station gave me another pin point to check and recheck the excessive consumption, in alarm and disbelief. I saw each landing ground come towards me with relief, and saw it go behind with regret. Finally, the greenery and houses of the Jordan valley came into view and I dropped her on to Amman with a great big sigh of relief. We had used three-quarters of the fuel on far less than three-quarters of the distance; let's say, roughly a fifth more than we ought to have used.

I called for wheel-chocks and gave the engines a full and comprehensive ground test. There was absolutely nothing wrong. We took out one of the sparking plugs to see if it was oily or burned: perfect. I thought it through carefully, twice more. There could only be one answer; those civilian-type engines, for some unknown reason (maybe connected with on-water operation?) used more fuel. That being so, there was no reason not to fill up and go straight on. We would do just that, and have ample fuel to reach Cairo. I told the petrol-tanker driver how much fuel had been used, the Blenheim crew went off to find sandwiches, and I sat in the shade under the wing to answer questions if needed.

My reverie was broken by a stream of four-letter words from above my head. They came from the mechanic who was sitting on top of the wing as he handled the fuel nozzle. His sunburned face was tortured and he eyed me with blame and resentment.

'Didn't you say about 45 gallons a side, Sir? I only got in a bit over 35 and, whambo!, at full flow she overflowed and the fuel slopped over everywhere. And now I've got petrol in my crutch and it hurts like buggery!'

Petrol on the privates had once happened to me, and it is mortal agony indeed. Some time later, having sorted out his immediate problem, we checked for an air bubble, found none and then filled the other tank particularly carefully. Most odd: she had taken 37 gallons in one side and 38 in the other — just what my calculations for fuel consumption had been, before we took off! But the gauges had said . . .? I climbed into the cockpit. Both the needles had gone up by 45 gallons and were at 'full' once more!

And then the penny dropped. Clot! Half-wit! My finger trouble, and up to my elbow at that! What a stupid bloody-fool I was! Gallons are not always the same as gallons. American gallons are a fifth smaller than British ones. As I should have twigged at once, I was looking at American gauges in the Goose while I was used to British gauges on tankers and in our Harvards. No wonder I was apparently using more 'gallons' to fly the distance; they were smaller and I needed more of them. Never would I live it down if the story got out. Without a flicker of expression I thanked the mechanic, hoped his crutch felt better and apologised profusely to him for misreading the gauges, thereby causing him so much pain and grief. He went off with a look which said, deservedly, 'How do such over-ranked idiots get airborne, let alone arrive at where they want to get to, if they can't read a gauge?' I reckoned he was not far wrong, in this case. In due time the Blenheim crew came back with a sandwich for me and we set off again. I was very non-committal in answer to their questions!

The rest of the trip was unremarkable. First, over the fertile Jordan valley where the white and brown walls of the town of Jericho are 1,200 feet *below* sea-level. Next, over the sizeable town which was once the little village of Bethlehem and then out over the desert again. We brushed the long curving coastline where the sapphire-blue of the Mediterranean at El Arish was separated from the red-brown of Sinai by a white beach and a few green date-palms. At last we crossed the Suez Canal, remarkably wide, stretching northwards from Ismailia to Port Said and southwards from the Bitter Lakes to Suez, then it was over the Nile Delta with its lush green acres of maize, lucerne and cotton crops, before letting down to land at Heliopolis.

Bunny Russell was a most thoughtful man. Whenever he got a signal saying I would be back, he used to send his car and driver to fetch Phyl so that she could come to meet me. The driver was called Ludwick. He was a thin, cadaverous individual, a true Cockney who had been a London bus-driver. Phyl and he had become great friends. He used to suck his teeth before producing such gems as: 'The Group Captain spoke very sharply to me, Ma'am, when I got his car stolen. Very 'arsh, 'e was.'

As I turned into the circuit she pointed to the unmistakable Goose and said confidently, 'That must be his aeroplane — there.'

Ludwick looked up at the black-painted beast, with its high-mounted engines, the deep boat-shaped fuselage with wheels sticking out at the bottom, its very tall rudder, and the floats hanging down from the wingtips. Pensively he watched it for a full quarter of a circuit. Then he turned, sucked his teeth carefully and delivered his considered judgement, slowly and without a flicker of emotion: 'Most peculiar thing Oi've ever seen . . . 'cept my mother-in-law, of course.'

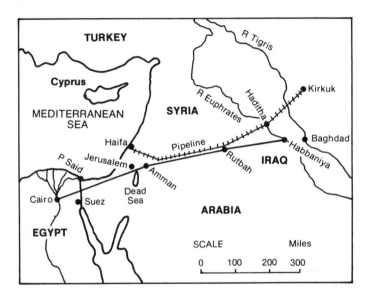

The end of the story is sad. Bunny and I fought HQME hard and bravely to keep our hands on the Goose. They, in their wisdom, had decided to use it for Air Sea Rescue duties. At first thought, it sounded a sensible idea but we emphasised, in vain, that the machine was designed for use only on lakes and rivers; it was not strong enough to withstand waves at sea. They knew better and, having had it painted yellow with a Red Cross, to my frustration my honey-bunch went to ASR. Within a day or two of arrival someone put her down in mild sea-conditions just outside Benghazi harbour, to see how it went. She broke up and sank. Saying spitefully to HQME 'I *told* you so!' couldn't bring that ugly and attractive lady back.

Chapter 5
Know Your Desert

To the west of Cairo lie about 20 miles of cultivated greenery. The green vegetation then stops suddenly and, beyond, there are miles upon miles and miles of multi-coloured rock and sand — give or take a bit, 3,000 miles of it; desert, reaching away into the distance as far as from London to New York. This open space, with its dried-up river beds, sand dunes, hard patches of sandstone, rocks, hillocks, and with its many colours from near-white to dark ochre, makes a pretty tapestry. Here and there, the water table comes near the surface so you have an oasis with palm trees and, usually, some hutted inhabitants. From above, it can be beautiful even if a lot of it lacks individuality. In the cool air aloft, you do not sense the varying temperatures. When flying, you are not stopping in one place. If you do stop in one place down there for any reason, away from the oases, the desert can be harsh company.

Thursday
Major Cloete was a squadron commander from the South African Air Force, working up his squadron of Blenheims before taking part in the Western Desert campaign. They were based at an airfield alongside the Suez Canal. His real name escapes me, but that one will do for now.

'We're going to do a proper navigation exercise. Not this backwards and forwards around the Nile Delta, but we'll do something worthwhile. Going to somewhere you don't usually see. Way out in the desert. To an oasis — Siwa. Siwa's about 400 miles south-west of us and nearly 200 miles from the coast, south of the German forces. We can pick up some fuel from the barrels stacked there, eat a packed lunch and come back by Wadi Halfa. From there we can fly over Luxor with its ancient Egyptian temples and so forth — it'll be a *really* interesting trip.'

There was a murmur of approval from the crews gathered round him.

'We'll take three aircraft and we can have an extra technician in each machine; it'll do them good to get out for a change. Take-off tomorrow, good and early. I'll lead. Precise details and crew lists will be on the board shortly.'

Friday

The three Blenheims were in loose formation, droning steadily over the apparently limitless expanse of desert. There were no definitive landmarks. One saw the occasional wheelmarks of a vehicle, apparently having come from somewhere and going nowhere in particular, but obviously having had a purpose at some time or another; probably Colonel Popski's Long-Range Desert Group which went everywhere that was unpopulated. The sand changed colour from brown through russet to yellow and back again. Here and there was a wadi, bone dry and goodness knows when it last had water flowing in it. The whole place was so arid and empty one could believe that the last water seen was in prehistoric times. The three technicians were each crouched in the central well of the fuselage, looking forwards between the pilot's and the navigator's heads. After an hour or so they had seen it all and were thoroughly bored.

It was a simple navigation error but, at the scheduled time which Cloete's navigator had calculated, Siwa did not appear ahead and below. The desert, with its spaces, and hummocks, and wadis, and patches of colour, stretched limitless in all directions. They kept going for another 15 minutes — 50 miles, roughly — and still Siwa Oasis did not appear. Surely, they could not be as far wrong as that? Cloete didn't want to admit readily to having made an error and appear a fool before his pilots. He would make a quick search.

He discussed it with his navigator. Perhaps they had gone past Siwa to one side or the other. Surely they couldn't have gone over the top without seeing it? The situation was unbelievable. It was a great big oasis, marked clearly on the maps — how could it have vanished? Time slipped by. They decided to return, about 15 miles north of their outward track just in case Siwa was over there, to the place where they had thought it was in the beginning. Then they would start an area search at that point. Cloete called up his Nos 2 and 3 who, up to this time, had observed the wartime rule of radio silence, and said he was turning back for Siwa; they were to hold formation while he got on with the job.

Almost two hours went by as the three machines flew backwards and forwards, round and round, across the featureless desert while Cloete and his navigator became more and more frustrated. Nothing, not one single identifiable landmark, could they find to give a firm start-point from which to fly to safety. Cloete did a careful calculation on his knee-pad; his fuel remaining would not now get them back to the Delta — and to reach the coastline meant going over the Germans who would find the vulnerable Blenheims to be most succulent targets. Siwa *had* to be found. Finally, the pair of them admitted that they were utterly and irrevocably lost. The other two crews, having been dragged around in formation with no knowledge of what was going on in their leader's mind, were no better off. They must all land, at once, before anyone ran out of fuel and crashed.

The piece of desert Cloete chose looked flat, free of boulders and, God willing, hard. He told his 2 and 3 to watch and, if he broke it, to try somewhere else, nearby. He didn't break it and the other two made equally successful landings, taxied up, parked alongside and switched off. The 12 men got out and took stock. They had their pack lunches and a bottle of beer apiece. There were the three rubber dinghy packs which had in them some emergency rations — malted milk tablets, hard-tack biscuits and chocolate were the only ones of use; water-purifying and de-salting chemicals were not exactly appropriate in their case; each machine had a four-gallon can of water on board . . . and that was the lot. As the flight had been planned for a comfortable altitude they had not worn flying suits or special clothing — they were wearing shorts and short-sleeved shirts, to be comfortable.

They decided to sit under one of the aircraft wings and hold a council of war while they had their lunch, and enjoy their beer while it was still cool. The council did not get very far. They were lost, about 400 miles from Cairo. There was nothing they could do, or think of doing, to improve their position. Nobody in the Delta knew of their situation yet and no one, including themselves, knew where they were; so, they reasoned, the first and foremost necessity was to register their plight back at base, and somebody could then initiate a rescue operation — and the sooner the better. For openers, therefore, the wireless operators would get back to their sets and, in case one had better results than another, take turns in transmitting.

It was now high noon, in mid-summer, and the heat was appalling, so most took their shirts off and sat stripped to the waist. The worst off were the operators, inside the fuselages whose metal skins in the blazing sun were too hot to touch. Several, including some outside the aircraft, doused themselves with water from the containers in a vain attempt to keep cool. If they just sat on the ground, they seemed to roast in the glare off the sand; some wandered around because the faint movement of air on their sweaty skins made them feel cooler. They drank a lot of water because then they sweated more, and that was better.

By evening the good news was that the sun was going down and, blissfully, the heat was leaving their tortured bodies, although most were showing early signs of serious sunburn on their torsos. The bad news was that first one operator, then another, and finally the third had each come out of his oven and reported that he had been unable to raise base-station — further, that the accumulator in his aircraft was now flat as a pancake. Being terribly dehyrated from the heat in there, each needed a long draught of water.

Saturday
The night had been almost worse than the day before. Soon after sunset the temperature fell like a stone and during the night it had gone down close to freezing. In their thin khaki-drill shirts and shorts they shivered as if they had ague. They huddled together for warmth, first inside the aircraft till the frigid metal seemed to chill the very marrow in their bones, then outside on the sand in acute discomfort till most of them took to walking about and flailing their arms to try and generate a semblance of warmth.

Dawn, and the gentle rays of the rising sun were a merciful relief. They told themselves that by now their absence — three aircraft and a squadron commander — would have started a major scare and a comprehensive search operation would have begun. Help would be at hand shortly.

By 10 am the grilling heat of the desert was upon them again. Their sunburn of the day before was excruciatingly sore; some thought it was better to wear a shirt, and some went stripped to the waist, risking the sunburn getting worse. By mid-morning the water was all gone.

In the early afternoon, one of them said that he had a deep-down feeling, amounting to a certainty, that Siwa was 'over there' and he pointed south east. His intuition had come in the night and grown steadily till now he knew for sure. Someone pointed out that they had been on the ground barely 24 hours; why not give the rescuers a bit more time? Nothing would shift him from his obsession; he proposed to walk 'over there' till he reached Siwa. He could keep to his direction from the sun by day, and from the stars by night, until he arrived. He would then return with help.

Although the man was a bit weak from heat exhaustion and dehydration, he was, perhaps, in slightly better state than the others. None of them felt tough enough to make a big fuss so, if he felt fiercely about it, why not let him try? They wished him luck and he went off on his lonely journey. They watched him languidly from the shade of the wing as his figure got smaller and smaller in the distance. Twice they saw him fall, but he got up and went on. After a while they realised that he had disappeared; maybe he had gone behind a hummock, or perhaps he had decided to lie down till the cool of the evening?

Sunday
Saturday night had not seemed quite so bad as the night before. They were becoming dehydrated and numb with exhaustion. Sensibly, most of them just sat around and waited, dozing, shifting to ease an aching muscle, rubbing their stomachs to quell the throbbing pains, conserving their physical resources till help arrived — as they ought to have been doing from the outset.

Several tried to wet themselves with their own urine which gave a momentary relief from the heat — and then it became stinking and sore on the sunburn. Some tried drinking it to quell their raging thirst, but it made them retch. They would have vomited, if they had had anything in their stomachs to throw up. They were apparently unaware that to drink urine makes one even thirstier because the body has to neutralise the salt in it, which it does by extracting water from the muscles — which already are screaming at one's system for more water anyway.

At the end of an interminable second day, night fell.

Monday
As our Group was not a battle organisation we did not run a full wartime schedule of 24 hours a day, seven days a week. We had

an officer and a couple of airmen on watch but most of us could, and did, get the weekends off; mainly, that is, at home on the end of a telephone.

Naturally, for security and enemy intelligence reasons, all signals had to be transmitted in code. The first thing Bunny and I did on arriving at our offices, any morning, was to flip through carbon copies of all the written stuff that had come in or gone out in our absence. We could thus keep a finger on the pulse of the outfit. I was just reading mine when Bunny came charging in. He was as near as I ever saw him to being in a towering rage.

'Have you seen this one! Came in on Saturday, and no one has done a damned thing!'

He thrust the paper under my nose. I hadn't yet reached it. It was a 'Request News' for three Blenheims. When they had not appeared at Wadi Halfa as planned, on Friday evening from their long navigation exercise far out into the desert, a Request News had been enciphered that night and sent off. Wadi Halfa, being a tiny landing ground, did not have cipher machines; encoding had to be done by hand, in book-cipher. This took a long time. No particular need for urgency was apparent — the aircraft could easily have landed safely at some other airfield; that often happened. The signal went to all airfields, as was normal procedure. If anyone had news, they would send it; if not, no action was required. If nothing came back to Wadi Halfa after a decent interval, it was up to them to start something helpful.

Wadi Halfa was one of our units so, although we were not an airfield which might know of the missing Blenheims, we had been sent a non-priority courtesy copy. Our copy of the signal, arriving only as a batch of unintelligible non-urgent figures, reached us during Friday night. On Saturday morning, our duty cipher-officer got his books out and had decoded it by lunchtime. The ops room staff looked at it and, as they had no aircraft to report, put it in the 'out' tray and that was that.

What urged Bunny into piling on the pressure and treating it as a matter of life and death, I could not see. The Blenheims could easily have been — and almost certainly were — down somewhere safely. They belonged to some operational formation, somewhere, and it was their job to do anything necessary. It was well on the cards that everything was all in hand and, as they were not ours and we were a non-flying unit, no one had bothered to tell us where they were. But Bunny was right and I was wrong. Wadi Halfa had tried to press the alarm button on

Saturday evening and, over the weekend, no one had done a damned thing.

By making the wires red-hot we managed to put together some salient facts. The aircraft were indeed lost. Four men in each machine. No special kit with them beyond the standard dinghies. The senior flight commander at their base said that each Blenheim carried a four-gallon can of water. Bunny heaved a deep sigh of relief, saying, 'Thank God! Eight pints per man; one pint per day to maintain body-fluid needs — provided they sit in the aircraft's shade, are not hurt and they keep quiet. That gives them till next Saturday. Then, if they don't do anything rash, they should survive another five days. In short, this is the third day and we should have ten more days — till Thursday week — to find them alive.'

By that evening, Monday, we had put together a flight of aircraft, crews, food, water, a doctor and medical kit, and Bunny had agreed a plan of campaign. We would go into action at the crack of dawn on Tuesday. With luck, we might get help from a message picked up during the night by the stepped-up radio watch on the emergency frequency. Personally, I thought it would be an unproductive affair unless we got radio-contact. Three minuscule aircraft, in a million square miles of desert, gave our searchers an almost hopeless task. Moreover, it was one of grave danger in the event of any kind of radio or navigation failure amongst them. It was three needles in 50 haystacks, to be located in short order. Should we risk our men to that extent? Bunny gave an unqualified 'Yes'.

Tuesday
The searchers were away when the first streaks of pink and yellow showed in the eastern sky. And, due to a simply unbelievable freak of chance, a searching aircraft located the Blenheims early Tuesday afternoon. The rescuers gave a cheer and metaphorically shook hands in self-congratulation. Three machines, apparently undamaged, neatly parked, could be seen to have landed safely with the wheels down. The crews could also be seen, lying in the shade under the wings. Nevertheless, it was odd and disturbing that they did not get up and wave.

The leader thought it over. Landing miles from anywhere if you have no option is one thing — but to put down on an unknown surface, in the middle of nowhere, hundreds of miles off any beaten track, may merely compound the serious problems which are on the plate already. However, down there were people who appeared to be in a bad way, so the grave risks had to be taken.

First, keeping a wary eye on the Blenheims in case he lost sight of them, the leader climbed up high and contacted base on his radio. He gave the position as accurately as he could and told them what he was going to do. Then, down he went. Noting carefully the tracks of the landed machines, he touched down on the same area, found it held well, and rolled to a standstill beside the parked Blenheims. The rescuers got out and walked across to the motionless bodies under the wings. The doctor bent down. All 11 of them were dead. He couldn't believe his senses. At that very moment it was only four days — 96 hours — since they had touched down with no damage, presumably in good health, and with a gallon of water each. Further, what had happened to the 12th man; did that have a bearing on the puzzle?

There was no way that the rescue team could dig 11 graves in a packed surface that was hard enough to carry a landing aircraft, so they laid the bodies out neatly under the wings. It was unlikely that any carnivorous animal or bird of prey would be there, many, many miles from other life. HQ Middle East could later decide how, when and whether to send out a ground party to collect or bury the bodies and recover the aircraft.

The doctor went over each corpse meticulously; the rescuers searched each Blenheim with a toothcomb, gleaning every scrap of paper, notes, maps, logs, knee-pads, jottings, last words written in desperation to wives or loved ones — collecting every single fragment of evidence which might conceivably help us to put their story together.

From those efforts we analysed the tragedy, how 12 fit young men killed themselves in under four days although each one, properly trained and led, could have had a minimum of 14 days of life remaining. Fourteen days alive during which, as things worked out, we would have rescued them. The only crumb of comfort for me was a hope that our future teaching of desert-survival would be improved — so that 12 deaths would not have been wholly in vain.

Chapter 6
The Route

In my new job I had a lot to learn, and fast. It was not long before I took my Group Captain's advice and went to see what I could see at the far end of our 'parish'.

In 1940, when the Battle of Britain was at its height and England was reverberating to the thud of German bombs, Winston Churchill is reputed to have written something like: 'The Middle East is where the turning point of this war will be. Be sure to plan and put in place the necessary organisation to have adequate forces there during 1942.'

Even if it was not Churchill who wrote it, someone in authority at that time must have thought similarly. The facts are there; it took two years to create the supply lines and then fill them to capacity. So, unless that vital order had been given in 1940, Bernard Montgomery would not have been the General in the Middle East who at last had adequate forces to beat the enemy, and to start the string of major successes which began at the Battle of Alamein — in 1942, as forecast.

And, what an organisation was necessary behind it all! When I was fighting in the Western Desert, arrivals of fresh reinforcement aircraft were taken totally for granted. I had had no idea of the enormous distances and problems involved in getting them there — stripping, crating and shipment, followed by re-assembly and flight-delivery — all the way round enemy forces in the middle; say 8,000 miles to travel all told, by sea and air from the factories where they were made.

The ferry aircrews who fetched the aircraft were run by a bluff, hard-drinking, no-nonsense Wing Commander with an enormous moustache called Dan McGinn. He had them all based on a convenient and pleasant houseboat tied to a bank of the Nile in the middle of Cairo. It provided him with his floating offices, his operations room and the aircrew's Mess — and they were all immediately under his eagle eye. Most of his crews were British but his outfit included a strong spattering of refugees who had joined us from other nations' air forces. They lived with their own special problems, such as limited command of the English language, the personal risk to them of being eliminated (maybe out of hand, or maybe very messily) if they were shot down in battle and captured, and perhaps even a political embarrassment for us in using neutrals. So, for these nomads, the ferry outfit was an admirable home from home. There was a small number of Free French, an Austrian or two, Czechoslovaks and Yugoslavs, some Scandinavians, and others. We had a fair number of Poles who were inveterate gamblers and not above any profit-making enterprise whether legal or not. Two pilots we suspected of being Americans; however, having joined us clandestinely (and probably illegally) long before their compatriots came in on our side, they never discussed their backgrounds. We asked no questions and accepted their continuing support gratefully. Dan had the ideal character to run these aircrews who were a motley but nevertheless effective collection.

Dan McGinn it was who said he could give me a lift to Takoradi. Takoradi, on the edge of the Ivory Coast in West Africa is more than 3,000 miles from Cairo in a dead-straight line and nearly 4,000 along the refuelling stops. Everything began for us there because that is where the boats came to deliver our crated aircraft for assembly. So it would be my starting point, too.

Patiently I waited on the tarmac at Heliopolis for my 3,750-mile flying hitch in one of Dan's freighter Hudsons from his communication flight. A Lockheed Hudson was new to me. Even before the Japanese attack on Pearl Harbor we were getting masses of American aircraft, built in the United States and delivered to us for war work. A Hudson, for those days, was sleek, smooth and remarkably fast — compared to the stick and string biplane Valentias, wallowing their airsick passengers along at not much over 80 mph. By modern standards it was somewhat like a tadpole, but a great advance on the old warhorses.

The navigator was Polish. He came and gave me a stiff shallow bow, saying, 'Do you play breedge?'

I admitted to knowing the rules.

'Escellent, escellent! Eet is a leetle deeficult to make up four peoples wizzout using our pilots. And, "George" ze automatic pilot is vairy good but eet is not happy to be in the cabin and play breedge for long times wiz no life pilot in ze cockpit. Now you can be in ze pilot's seat, or playing breedge, and we have four OK. Poker is better; you can play tree. Two/tree days is long times to get to Tak.'

Obviously, it was impossible to play normal bridge inside an unlined fuselage with two 1,100 horsepower unsilenced engines roaring just outside. Having arranged suitcases or a packing case to play on, the intrepid four, wearing flying helmets to deaden the appalling noise, would huddle round the 'card-table'. Play was by using gestures only. A shake of the head meant 'no bid'. The number of tricks was indicated with fingers, and the suit by a hand-movement. Show a knuckle (as though you were wearing a ring) and it meant Diamonds; a scooping movement for Spades, a little swing of the wrist indicated Clubs, touch your chest for Hearts and make a zero with your finger and thumb to show No Trumps. If you were getting vicious and wished to double, you crossed two fingers; to show, by redoubling that you declined to be pushed around, you crossed four fingers. The Poles were notorious for playing harsh, but good, bridge for high stakes. You had to keep your eyes skinned and your wits about you. House (or aircraft?) rules were that if you did not see a gesture, or made any mistake, that was just your bad luck and the appropriate penalty was exacted for your error. There was one great advantage — the noise completely excluded any discussions, arguments, recriminations or post-mortems on any hand.

About 19 hours flying time and what felt like 19 hundred bridge hands later, we touched down on the Takoradi runway. The Poles had ensured I was much poorer. Stepping into West Africa was like stepping into a Turkish bath. The hot humid air fell over you like a warm wet blanket. This did not dull the feeling of urgency and output all around. Down one side of the airfield were some hangars and innumerable packing cases, out of which had come all the bits to make up complete aircraft and which now served as offices and stores. Beyond them were the beige roofs of leaf-thatched huts and green-topped palm trees stretching away into the distance. Near the edge of the runway were dozens of aircraft, either getting their last touches, waiting for air-test, or ready for the long haul back to the Mediterranean coastline.

The airmen bustling around and doing the work were all stripped to the waist, dripping with sweat and brown as walking-shoes. I was intrigued to see how the NCOs solved the problem of wearing rank badges without sleeves; they had them on wristbands, opposite side to the wristwatch. There were a fair number of Hurricanes, the odd photographic Spitfire, Blenheim bombers and several American machines such as Kittihawk and Tomahawk fighters, together with Baltimore, Boston and Maryland twin-engined bombers. I went to the packing case which served as a despatch section, partly to give it a checkover but also to make plans for my flight back to Egypt.

At Despatch the business took only minutes. It was disturbingly easy-going and uncontrolled: 'You want an aircraft to fly to Cairo? Just say which one and we'll tee it up for you . . .' Being reasonably circumspect and on my first trip, I decided to take a Blenheim. The basic type was an old friend which had served me well in the past, though this was a later development, a Blenheim V — Army-Support/Attack-Bomber — called a 'Bisley'. The main differences to be seen were that it didn't have a sort of greenhouse in the front for the navigator to sit in — it had machine-guns — and the gun-turret at the back was a massive affair, but otherwise it looked fairly familiar. Its two engines, radio and a crew, would permit me to fly unescorted, taking my time and visiting wherever I wished. The excitement of flying the different, faster and more exotic types could wait till later on another trip. This time, the important thing was to have Bunny discuss with Dan the slap-happy despatch of valuable aircraft, after my return.

At that time quite a number of crews were hanging around, waiting to get to Cairo. The UK authorities used it as a jumping off point for Middle-East replacements and reinforcements. Many, even, had come straight from training schools. The idea was that the men would jump into a suitable aircraft and deliver themselves and the machine to Cairo. The results of this simple and fine-sounding plan were appalling. The crews would have to try to fly nearly 4,000 miles over unfamiliar and barren territory. They would have few or no recognisable landmarks, using radio of doubtful efficiency, and having maps the like of which they had never met before. Specialised training, careful briefing and intimate knowledge were essential, but absent. The easy-going despatch procedures ensured that the route was littered with crashed aircraft in various degrees of disrepair. No wonder! Dozens more precious aircraft were lost before Bunny Russell brought down a great chopper on the malpractices.

Nevertheless, at that moment, it meant that there was a navigator and a wireless-operator available to make up my scratch crew. They were an ill-matched pair. The navigator was tall, skinny and wore glasses; he reminded me of an assistant I once met in a haberdashery. The W/Op was a short, stocky man; you would wish to be on his side in a pub-brawl, if you got into a pub-brawl. No matter if they were straight out of flying-training. Under my experienced supervision, they would save me a lot of work on the way. Or so I thought. I was to learn differently, later.

The first leg, to Lagos, was a simple 360 miles along the coast. We flew fairly low to enjoy the blue-green sea and the golden beaches. Inland were a million patches of cultivation with waving palm trees just off the coastline. The only discomfort was that the Bisley carried so much weight of armour-plate and hydraulically-powered turret that it didn't really *fly* properly; it simply wallowed through the air and had to be cossetted every inch of the way. Even when one glanced at a map, the beast climbed, dived or swung off to one side or the other.

My W/Op told me after about half an hour that the battery was not being kept properly charged. There was nothing we could do in the air, but he would get it put right on the ground. The navigator was also having his problems; the rivers on his maps did not seem to fit the streams or dried up beds that he saw on the ground. This was hardly surprising as they were quite likely to change course with the rains, or vanish altogether in a dry season. But it played hell with his meticulous calculations. As the thriving town of Lagos is on the coast, he had no trouble in finding it and we put down on its airfield, just inland.

The W/Op assured me that he would get the charging problem sorted out, and the navigator said that after his initial difficulties he was getting the hang of it. Having looked at the airfield's minimal facilities and chatted up our little servicing team, we went to the Mess-hut for a snack.

Lagos was not much of a town really. Most of it was a conglomeration of thatched huts, unpaved roads which became a quagmire in the rains, and market stalls selling cheap-jack goods. Later I was to wonder why it was such a favoured night stop for the convoys, only 360 miles into their long journey? It proved to be the gold bazaar. You were not allowed to buy gold but the Poles discovered quickly that if you did so, and flew it northwards, the further you went the more you could sell it for: twice as much in Khartoum, where the police were not a problem; three times or more in the bazaars of Cairo, but where the risks and dangers were far greater. The Poles, gamblers, mostly took their gold to Cairo.

One Pole was picked up by the police in Lagos gold bazaar — a forbidden area for foreigners. They were fairly kind and, after reproving him, fined him what he had on him — about £100, which was a fair sum in those days. Two or three weeks later, on his next trip, they caught him there again. This time they were very angry and threatened to put him in their gaol — an unsalubrious building, insanitary and *very* uncomfortable. Eloquently he pleaded the importance of his task, the value to the war effort of the aircraft he was flying, the effect on his career, and much more. Generously they again accepted to fine him what he had on him, and call it quits. They were surprised to pick up over £1,000. I was to learn, but not as evidence, that on his next trip he evaded capture and made up both his previous losses together with a nice profit on top of that.

Much later again, and very frustrated by rife gold smuggling, we decided to enlist the help of the Lagos police to try and put a stop to this unbridled illegality. They told us that a convoy, mainly flown by Poles, was carrying a lot of gold — many thousands of pounds worth bought in Lagos. At least, having bought it, presumably they were carrying it. The aircraft were Blenheims and the only places where they would land and also where the gold could conceivably be disposed of were two — Khartoum, and the destination airfield which would be one of the maintenance units near the Suez Canal. At Khartoum the aircrew were escorted from the aircraft with only their night kit, and the machines were kept under heavy guard. Next day, after take-off, a wireless message was sent to them in the air, forbidding them to land as planned at Kasfareet in the Canal Zone and telling them to land at Heliopolis, Cairo.

At Heliopolis they were met by a large posse of Military Police. They were searched. Their baggage was searched. The aeroplanes were searched. Nothing! We were looking for over twenty *kilogrammes* of gold, so it was not something they could hide up their bums or in their mouths. The Poles were led away, looking like pictures of injured ignorance. Next, we began to take to pieces every bit of the aeroplane which could have been dismantled at Lagos without actually cutting metal, which would have shown up at once. Purely by chance one of the searching engineers found a small scratch where no scratch should have been. The gold was found *inside* the axles of the undercarriages. These were hollow to save weight and, apparently, sealed for ever during manufacture. The Takoradi mechanics had managed to unseal them and make the ends removable, if you knew the secret. Inside were cylindrical tins containing the gold. . . like Tate and Lyle's golden tins, but more golden than any tin known to *that* company.

Their background organisation, as it gradually came to light, was based exclusively in Lagos at one end and Kasfareet at the other. It proved to be superb: first, getting prior knowledge of which Blenheims were going to that particular depot at Kasfareet; second, unsealing their axles during assembly at Takoradi, and hiding the fact; third, filling at Lagos only the 'modified' axles with gold; fourth, warning the mechanics, at the far end, which axles held gold; fifth, devising a method of extracting the gold at Kasfareet with no mole discovering what was going on; sixth, transferring the gold to Cairo and selling it; and finally, seventh, distributing correct and appropriate cash shares to all the dozens of people involved — including the Poles. One was forced to admire the masterminds involved; we would love to have had them working in the *official* organisation on our operational problems.

After our snack we took off for Kano, another 540 miles further on. This time for me, doing my own check navigation, it was easy — apart from the Machiavellian tendency of the Bisley to wander off course every time I tried to calculate. There was a proper road which criss-crossed our track now and again. We flew over the mighty Niger river which never dried up or changed its bed. There was enough cultivation to support several medium-sized village-towns which were big enough to stay where the map said they were. The streams and the lesser villages, which moved frequently by distances from yards to miles, could all be ignored. My poor navigator, who did not yet know which landmarks to take and which to leave, found it awful. I think he credited me with a sort of unfair clairvoyance, and not just a deal of experience in the business.

In the headphones, the W/Op could be heard clicking away. When asked how he was getting on, he said he couldn't raise anybody. As we were right in the middle, 200 miles from the nearest station, and in daylight, this was hardly surprising. Only at night could you cover substantial distances to our low power ground stations; no one had told him that that was all we had. I suggested he kept quiet till we were within 50 miles of Kano, and then he would be heard. The clicking still went on, nevertheless. As it kept him happy and occupied, it was of no concern . . . or so it seemed.

Kano was quite a sizeable town, mostly of circular houses built of mud bricks and with slightly domed conical roofs, although there were a few square ones in the style of Western civilisation. It boasted a hospital, some government offices and the British Resident's house. I paid the gentleman a social call that evening.

Over a drink of beer the Resident presented me to a local Arab trader who had spread out his wares on the verandah. I was not attracted by the poorly made and embroidered bags, slippers and robes. Then the trader asked if we were interested in diamonds? My host explained at once that, properly, it was illegal to buy diamonds. They would have been smuggled out of Sierra Leone, if indeed they were diamonds and not glass. However, let us see what he had got. The trader reached deep into the folds of his robe and produced a small, soft wash-leather bag. Having untied the neck he spilled out on to the verandah ten lumps of what looked like pitted and frosted glass, each about the size of a lump of sugar. He then produced a small piece of glass and scratched it with one of the lumps. My host sniffed disdainfully, saying, 'Might be diamonds — but could easily be quartz.'

After a few words with the trader in an Arabic dialect which I did not understand, he turned to me: 'He wants £10 for the ten. Which is roughly the going rate. If you want them, there is no' grave reason why you shouldn't have them. I won't look. Lots of people buy, but remember I cannot assure you that they are real.'

I was sorely tempted but £10 was all the cash I had, bar a few odd coins. 'Can I buy one lump?'

'No; it's all ten or nothing.'

So I declined the offer. Ever since, I have wondered — ten diamonds the size of sugar lumps . . .? If even a bit of *one* had been of reasonable quality . . .? On the other hand, to spend my all on ten little bits of shapeless quartz . . .?

The Poles jumped on to this diamond bandwagon pretty quickly. It was another bit of smuggling that we had to try and stop, but with meagre success because the size of the contraband was so much smaller and lighter, so the hiding places were more plentiful. At that time it was not very serious because the diamonds were almost all of very poor quality; they were only of use for industrial purposes — for which there was no market in Egypt. Later on, and some time after I had left that organisation, matters changed dramatically.

The change came in 1943, when General Montgomery and General Bradley had opened up the North African coastline.

Diamonds commanded vast prices in Gibraltar. Very promptly it was explained to the Poles, and to the other aircrews, that such stones went straight through the Spanish border at La Linea and onwards into the German war factories which were critically short of industrial diamonds. This was no longer petty smuggling, but trading with the enemy and costing lives on our own side.

One fellow would not listen. Twice he was caught and was severely reprimanded. The second time he was also told that if it happened again he would be tried by Court Martial as a traitor. It did happen again and he was court martialled and found guilty. I heard that he was shot as a traitor, which stopped the smuggling effectively.

Next morning the wireless operator explained that neither the Lagos nor the Kano maintenance teams had been able to repair the fault. The accumulator still was getting no charge and another, fully charged, battery had been put in. I explained what that meant for us. I told him, 'Right; we have to be careful. If we force-land, it will be vital to have a fully charged battery when we get down. So, tune in your set, on the ground, while you can draw power from the still-connected ground supplies — then, don't use it at all, unless I tell you to. OK?'

He said he understood.

The navigator poor fellow, a Pilot Officer, was practically twittering with alarm and despair after his performance the day before. He was behaving as though he feared that the almighty Wing Commander, meaning me, would have him castrated with a pair of blunt scissors at the next landing if he got lost again. I encouraged him to relax; I would work in parallel with him while he could follow my pilot-navigation and learn something of desert flying, I hoped.

We set course in fair weather for Maidugri, another 350 miles. This landing strip was one of the more important ones for it lay at a convenient distance for a first night stop, roughly half way from Takoradi to the next convenient overnight at Khartoum, on the Nile. It therefore boasted better-than-average accommodation and maintenance facilities for the overnighters. It merited a close look and, with luck, they could also solve our problem with the generator.

We had only been airborne about ten minutes when in my

headphones I heard the clickety-click of the wireless transmitter being keyed. When the operator transmitted in a Blenheim, he couldn't hear the rest of the crew so it was quite a while before I attracted his attention. I was not amused. 'I thought I told you to leave that set alone, unless I wanted you to do something with it?'

'Oh, but you see, Sir, my signals instructions require me to make contact as soon as possible after take-off, for safety reasons, and then to be back in touch every 30 minutes.'

'Listen carefully, boy. I don't give a fish's tit for your written signals instructions. Our lives are at stake here, and they are much more important than any books of any kind. In the air, my instructions from the pilot's seat are what count, so far as you are concerned. I said not to use it, unless I told you to, and when I say something I mean it. You are not to touch that key in the air until I say so. If you do, I shall hear it, and I shall place you under close-arrest immediately we land, for disobeying a specific order . . . Are you quite clear on that point?'

'Yes . . . Sir.'

When we landed at Maidugri I took some time off, partly to have a good look around but also to collect my thoughts on how to handle the young and inexperienced W/Op; also to simmer down and not be bad-tempered with him.

The buildings were all typical native-type huts of mud bricks with thatched roofs, suitable to the country and its climate. The accommodation was clean and the water from the wells was tolerably pure. There was no doctor but the medical orderly (and he had not known I was coming) had a spotless and, to my unprofessional eye, well-equipped dispensary. The doctor from Takoradi visited regularly by hitching flights up the route and back.

A little shop sold local products. The python skins, for purchase at so-much a foot, were fascinating. They were dirt cheap and I bought several to take back to Cairo with me for Phyl. Carried away by my enthusiasm, my purchases later became turned into shoes, bags, a jacket and even a snakeskin suitcase. The bags and shoes were all right but the snakeskin jacket — stiff and crackly — was a disaster. It got worn only about a couple of times out of kindness to me before being consigned to a rummage-sale, with my whole-hearted blessing. The suitcase, with a strong steel frame which made it weigh a ton empty, was not too welcome either.

At last, when I had had a good look round, I decided to deliver my homily to the two very green aircrew. I had not realised how woefully unbriefed these lads were in the possibilities and perils of desert flying — so I tried to put my warnings in a helpful and gentle way. Luckily, the python skins had smoothed down my ill humour and put me in a reasonably benign mood for dealing with the W/Op.

'I want to give you an idea of what we may be up against,' I began. 'First, I am sure no one told you any of this at school. It is just local know-how that one has to work out for oneself. You must appreciate that we are crossing thousands upon thousands of square miles of barren country. Roughly every 200 to 500 miles along our route there is a tiny British-run airstrip. Manning is minimal and everyone is busy with their daily routine. There are no telephones or telexes. Radios (and there is only one at each airfield) are of limited range and they don't work particularly well in daylight. Aids to navigation and landmarks are, at best, scanty. If for *any* reason we go down — lost maybe, or engine failure — probably no one is going to lift a finger, because they won't know about it, for several hours. Suddenly, probably after work has stopped, somebody catches on to the fact that we are not where we ought to be. OK so far?'

They both nodded, interestedly.

'But, as you can imagine, from then till late evening the air and every wireless set is going to be clogged solid with high-priority signals, asking everybody everywhere if there is any news of us, and by midnight all the answers will be in saying 'No'. At that time we have some things working for *us,* and we use them. Darkest darkness gives the conditions when radio signals go furthest and sound loudest. There will not be too many people chattering on the airwaves in the middle of the night. *Then,* without further delay in case the night-watch operators begin to get tired out and sleepy, we act. Midnight is the time, and not a minute earlier, that you first touch your transmitting key. That is when every operator all over the Middle East is straining his ears to be the first clever-boy who hears the faint peep from our set. That will be the moment that we need every watt of power we can extract from our precious battery — so that *you* can give us our best chance of not dying. Does that make sense, Mr Wireless Operator? You are one of the trade . . .?'

The boy nodded again.

'You press your key and — surprise, surprise for the listening world! — there you are, popping up loud and clear on the distress frequency. If your acc is good, you've at least a sporting chance of getting a message through. Now you'll see why I was so enraged — and I am sorry I lost my temper — when I heard you squandering our one and only source of life-saving power, because of something in a fart-arseing book written by a man who perhaps has never been off the ground in a risky situation. Get it?'

The wireless-operator scuffed his shoes in the dust and nodded once more. I went on: 'If that fails it will be serious, but it's not necessarily the end of everything. We could perhaps be lucky because in many areas this side of Khartoum there are quite a lot of tribesmen, herders mostly, spread thinly over the desert. They are very curious, and very very nervous. It is quite possible that one of them will have seen us come down. He will come to look at this peculiar monster bird that has flown down out of the sky — but for sure he won't let the monster see *him!* If we sit still and make no alarming gestures, sooner or later curiosity will prevail and bit by bit he will come closer, provided we are very careful.

'Let me tell you a true story. A ferry pilot went down and he was alone for three days, getting more and more frightened. At last, some way off, a herder appeared with his goats. Overjoyed and making loud cries of welcome and relief, the pilot ran towards him, believing he was rescued. His hoped for saviour promptly ran away, disappeared, and did not dare to look again for two more days. Luckily, he *did* look again and, by then, the pilot had cottoned on to the situation. Suffering agonies from thirst he nevertheless had the nous to sit perfectly still. If he had made another sudden move, the herder most likely would have left him to die first. Why not? That would have solved all queries and been perfectly safe. After all, the herder had all the time in the world . . .

'So, to meet any emergency properly, we conserve our resources with the utmost care; we wait patiently and only move to help anybody who might want to save us when the time is ripe — for *them* — and when it will do the most good. Quite clear?'

Somewhat sheepishly the young man said 'Thank you, Sir.'

Next morning it transpired that the Maidugri team, too, had been unable to fix up the generator. Another fully charged battery had been put in and, after breakfast, we were on our way with a very subdued W/Op.

From Maidugri it was only a short hop of 130 miles to Fort Lamy. We had very few airmen there because it was only used as an emergency landing ground. Fort Lamy was in the French province of Chad, near Lake Chad, and it belonged to the French Foreign Legion. Vichy French during the war might work with Hitler and his German Reich, but the French Foreign Legion in Chad worked firmly and unofficially with the other side; our side.

The runway, not very long, was paved entirely with bricks. I'd never seen that before. Luckily it had not been raining; I was later told that landing on those wet bricks was like landing on a police-training skid-pan, liberally doused with oil. Unprepared, I would assuredly have gone clean over the edge. Having passed the time of day in French (my second language) with 'Mon Colonel' I took off on the next hop of 550 miles to Geneina. Geneina, just outside Chad and into the Sudan, was another landing ground alongside the native huts of a little village, primarily for emergencies or a fuel top-up in doubtful weather. We only stayed a few minutes for an encouraging chat with the tiny and remarkably enthusiastic servicing team. Then, it was on again for the next 150 miles to El Fasher.

I decided that my W/Op was too chastened, frustrated and depressed to be amused by the story of an earlier happening on the Maidugri/Fasher leg. Both those airfields were small, isolated and quite tricky to find without outside assistance from the radio. A ferry pilot had as his operator a deeply religious young man. Somewhere around the half-way point the intercom went dead. He scrambled forwards along the fuselage and handed the pilot a piece of paper on which was written: 'The radio has gone unserviceable — but be not afraid, God is with us.'

The pilot read it, borrowed a pencil from the navigator and wrote on the paper before passing it back: 'I hope He's got some petrol with Him.'

The young operator was deeply affronted and, after they landed safely at El Fasher, complained formally of blasphemy. Unsurprisingly, he did not get very far with it.

All the way across the 1,700 miles between Kano and Khartoum the surface as it spread itself out beneath us was beige, ochre, yellow and reddish. All around and into the distance as far as the eye could see, it was sparsely spotted with black-looking little tufts of camel-thorn and desert scrub. Occasionally there would be the outlines of a few tiny 'fields' which were merely little cleared sandy patches which would never show greenery unless, once in every several years, there had been some rain.

Apparently, according to the map, we had plenty of landmarks to guide us on our way: rivers, roads, hills. But, knowledge said, 'Beware! The map can be an unmitigated liar!' Experience, coupled with a jaundiced view of all map publishers, was invaluable. A 'river', known universally as a 'wadi', would be a dried up watercourse whose bottom probably had not seen water for many a year. *But,* as like as not, the wadi had changed its track to skirt some sand-hill which had blown in since the last rains! A 'road', clearly marked in red across the map, should have provided a splendid navigational check-point. However, this 'road' was merely the surveyor's idea of where many camel-caravans and feet of the caravaneers had gone as, since time immemorial, they crossed the endless desert from one oasis to another. If the surface was rocky they had probably left no marks at all. If it had become very soft since the map was made, the chances were that the guides had avoided that area altogether and gone elsewhere, to find an easier surface to walk on. Map-reading needed special care, and a good measure of acquired skill. Therefore it was a question of checking, rechecking, adding, and averaging all the different answers together until enough evidence had accumulated to make a change of course reasonably certain.

My frequent and apparently unreasonable disbeliefs, when the map clearly said otherwise, drove the navigator absolutely scatty. Finally, we reached El Fasher in good order — last stop before Khartoum.

El Fasher was another reasonably important landing ground. It was about half-way from Geneina, at the edge of the Sudan, to Khartoum. It therefore supported, administratively, Geneina on the one side and El Obeid (another emergency landing-ground) on the other. This saved manpower because one doctor, one engineer and one signals specialist sufficed for all three airfields. They hitched flights either way on passing aircraft as often as necessary. Morale was enormously high and their pride was unbounded for the technical miracles they worked in getting damaged and ailing aircraft back into flying order again. But, failure to mend my dud generator was a terrible blow to their self-esteem.

The next day was to be a fairly short one — only 550 miles to Khartoum; just one single three-hour flight. All across featureless desert admittedly, but we were flying west to east; Khartoum is on the Nile which flows south to north, straight across our track. So, sandstorms and plagues of locusts aside, we *ought* to be able to see below us the longest river in the world as we crossed it.

After breakfast we climbed aboard and I tested the engines for the normal pre-flight checks. All was well. I waved my hand for 'chocks away'. To my amazement a half-grown lion ambled up and pulled the chocks aside, gripping the handling-ropes in its teeth, first on one side and then the other. The airmen had acquired a young cub, trained it and kept it as a special surprise for pilots visiting Fasher for the first time. Indeed it was a surprise and the beast had scared me to a jelly in case it ran into or jumped at the propellers. A great talking-point, but damned dangerous. I would discuss it with their boss in Khartoum.

We didn't stop at the emergency landing ground by El Obeid, although I would have loved to do so. The village had an importance far beyond its size for, being at the very end of the Western Sudan railway, it was a main trading centre for the local populace. Livestock were herded there across the desert even from as far as French West Africa, 2,000 miles distant. Pre-war the little village of El Obeid supplied 90% of the world's consumption of gum-Arabic. Men climbed and cut the local acacia trees to get the resin; it arrived at the village in sacks, carried by camel-convoys. It was then sold by auction and exported, via the railway, to be used for stamps, envelopes, paper, cardboards, pastes, varnish and hundreds of other materials. Even now in the days of synthetics it is supplying 90% of the world's needs; it is used in sweets, soft drinks and jellies — and for which no suitable substitute has been found! I would dearly have liked to visit its bustling local market with the gay colours, smells and the noise of voices raised in hard bargaining.

The Nile was where the map said it should be, so we reached Khartoum with no problems. Its airfield had existed pre-war and was well established — that was why we had chosen it for our local Ferry Control headquarters. We also had a pious hope that, as the place had a telephone line all the way from Cairo, we should be able to speak to the CO direct. It turned out to be pure wishful thinking. Contact went through the Egyptian civilian telephone system and (apart from being totally insecure) speech over 1,100 miles of Egyptian wartime telephone wires was beyond even the miraculous. Naturally, the CO there found that being separated by more than 1,000 miles from his bosses had a lot to commend it: he could get on with the job and avoid detailed questions on what the hell he was playing at.

The CO of the Ferry Control at Khartoum was an old friend of mine — Wing Commander Denis 'Ricky' Rixson. We had first met in 45 Squadron during 1940, then based at Helwan some 15 miles south of Cairo, while we waited to go south to fight Mussolini's Italian air force in Eritrea.

Ricky was a great man. He oversaw all the staging-posts northwards to Cairo, south to Juba, west to Kano and east to the Red Sea; say, the efficient operation of over 20 airfields spread over a million square miles. It was no mean task for a 27-year-old Wing Commander with a staff of only five or six to help him.

Of course, he needed to be mobile to look after that lot, so he profited from Bunny Russell's edict that Control COs could delay an individual aircraft if it benefited the majority. Ricky carried his interpretation of 'delay' to outer limits. A Bisley like the one I was flying 'went missing'. Then he removed four tons of armour plate and turret. Next, he stripped it of every possible non-essential piece of war equipment — guns, bomb-racks and so forth — that his fitters could get off. Thus lightened, but still with its extra-powerful engines, it became an extremely fast personal executive aircraft with an excellent range — and, unlike mine, a delight to fly. Having one's personal airborne runabout is very satisfying. It might not have met with the approval of the big bosses, but it enabled him to run his outfit extremely effectively. It was good for morale too; as well as his normal two aircrew, he once squeezed in 11 additional and enthusiastic airmen for a trip to the fleshpots, giving them a well-deserved and welcome break from the constraints of staging-post life.

After landing at Khartoum I tried very hard to discuss with him the Fasher lion which had scared me so. Ricky sent me on my way with peals of laughter echoing in my ears. He found me a charming blockhead: did I not see that airmen sentenced to months and even years with no outside facilities such as a cinema or a bar *needed* to have some distractions? What better than the looks of horror, alarm and distress upon the faces of visiting pilots who found a chock-pulling lion helping them on their way! And, if perchance there was a minor accident, I could be assured that it would never reach the ears of higher echelons. And, in retrospect, Ricky was perfectly right not to see or know too much. The morale in his 'parish' was, accordingly, very high.

Ricky was a great man in more senses than one. He weighed 22 stones — in other words, a little matter of 300 pounds or 140 kilogrammes! This did not stop him playing a first-class game of cricket, and tennis, and squash-rackets. In later life he swore he had never exceeded 19 stones, but this claim must be treated as pie-in-the-sky, and strongly open to question. Consider the facts; after his flying-training Ricky had wanted to fly fighters (didn't we all?), and had been turned down because his bulk simply would not go into the cockpit of a Hurricane. Moreover, why else had he chosen a twin-engined bomber as his personal aeroplane, whilst most of his colleagues with similar privileges filched fighters? His claim to be a mere 19-stone stripling cannot be sustained.

Ricky was everybody's friend and sometimes he used to walk with a three-year-old boy to and from the swimming pool. Their route passed the famous statue (now moved to England) of General Gordon riding on his camel. It was erected in his memory and honour after he had been besieged, captured and killed there by the Mahdi in 1885. Ricky explained to the child that the statue was of Gordon, and that Gordon had been very famous and important. Every time on the way out the boy would stop, look up and say 'Hullo Gordon'. And on the way back it would be 'Good night, Gordon'. In due course the family were to leave Khartoum and nothing would satisfy the lad but that Ricky should take him to to say goodbye to Gordon. Standing in front of the statue and holding Ricky's hand the youngster took his slightly snivelly leave, with a promise one day to return. As they turned to go he looked up and said, thoughtfully, 'Uncle Ricky, who is the man sitting on Gordon?'

As Khartoum was so far out of anybody's way, entertainment tended to be home-made and, occasionally, raucous. Naturally, the club with its facilities for sport and its well stocked bar was a focal point. The secretary, a civilian, was often harassed by the high spirits of cooped-up young Air Force officers. He made a number of rules which, in normal circumstances, might perhaps have been unnecessary. One was that no one must jump off the roof of the club into the open-air swimming pool.

One hot evening some officers and their civilian friends had been sitting on the club's verandah, laying down ever more forcefully how the war would be ended in a matter of weeks — if *they* alone held the military and political reins of command. Naturally the conversation had been lubricated and enhanced by countless draughts of beer, whisky, gin and other refreshments. Merely clapping one's hands brought the barman running. There was no closing time. It was getting pretty late and quite dark when finally, someone said, 'Let's jump off the roof into the pool!'

'Brilliant idea!'

Without waiting a second before putting this splendid plan into action, they all ran across to the back of the pool-building, up the fire-escape and sprinted across the flat roof. At the far edge, fully clothed, they flung themselves into the night — handing all further proceedings over to Isaac Newton and his law of gravity. Ricky told me that, all the way down, he was trying to work out what day of the week it was, because they emptied the pool for cleaning on Thursdays. Luckily, it turned out to be a Friday.

When at last Ricky came to the end of his time in Khartoum he was given a memorable farewell Dining-Out night. He had intended to fly his Bisley the following morning to Cairo, and report to Headquarters in the afternoon. However at breakfast-time his staff had a quick planning conference and came to the mature and unanimous view that Ricky might not be fully fit for flying duties, yet. Ricky did not demur for he was still unconscious from (as legal pundits would put it) . . . previous indulgence in alcoholic stimulants. Having rustled up a crew which was competent to fly the executive Bisley, they loaded him on to a sick-quarters stretcher and, largely unclothed, he was borne by a team of stalwarts to the aircraft. Poured into the back of the bomber through the top hatch, he lay on the floor with a damp towel across his ample stomach. He came to about half-way to Cairo.

My most cherished memory of him comes somewhat earlier when, after an evening's high drinking in the low haunts of Cairo, a dozen of us fetched up in my flat for some more slugs of alcohol. Suddenly, Ricky was missing. He had found the fridge, and eaten the best part of a cold chicken which was to have been lunch next day for my 70-year-old widowed mother. We eventually located him sitting on her bed, pulling the wishbone with her. She was absolutely enchanted by him and said it had been a long time since such a *nice* young man had been on her bed at 2.30 am.

Ricky was, indeed, one of my *great* friends.

Onwards and northwards from Khartoum was the easy part. Eleven hundred miles more-or-less following the Nile all the way, except for cutting a few corners and leaving out the twiddly bits. Best of all for the navigator, the river gave him a trustworthy check on courses and speeds — the Nile, at least, does not shift from its bed. Also, the glint on the water, the occasional green of irrigated fields, the few static riverside towns, all are easy to pick

After the retreat from Dunkirk in 1940, the Middle East was cut off from reinforcement by short-range aircraft. They were shipped to Takoradi on the west coast of Africa, assembled and then flown nearly 4,000 miles in short hops all the way to Cairo and the Western Desert fighting. Here, local labour is helping to get Hurricanes out of their crates. (Imperial War Museum)

After assembly, the short-range single-seaters were flown to Cairo in convoys of half a dozen, led by a light bomber with navigator and crew. Here is a rather scruffy bunch of ferry-pilots, bored to distraction while waiting to take off, posing beside a Hurricane (and a dog) for the benefit of the News Photographer. (Imperial War Museum)

This Hurricane is taking off from Takoradi on air-test after assembly. It must be an air-test, or it would have long-range tanks fitted under the wings. (Imperial War Museum)

Bristol 'Blenheims', on which I did most of my bombing raids, were notoriously vulnerable to enemy fire. This one, re-named 'Bisley', was fitted out as an 'Army-support and attack-bomber'. It had front guns, a powerful rear-turret and so much armour-plate that its engines (albeit beefed up) could barely haul it into the air on a hot day. I unsuspectingly, agreed to fly one to Cairo. (via The Aeroplane)

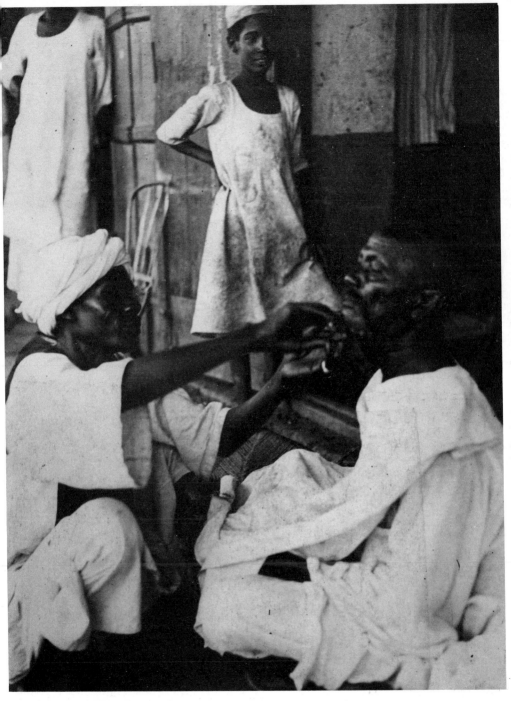

In Kano, one did not go to the barber's shop. He brought it to your own front doorstep.

The Africans' quarters along the ferry route from West Africa to the Sudan were
simple and primitive. These huts had round wooden walls, thatched with the local
grasses. They kept out the sun and the rain but, inside, when cooking was in
progress, the atmosphere was thick enough to dig bits out of with a spoon!

The big village or small town of El Obeid had two claims to fame. It was at the end
of the Western Sudan Railway, and the near-barren area round it produced (and
still produces) 90% of the world's gum-arabic. It comes from the resin of a low
Acacia thorn-bush and is used in jellies, sweets and soft-drinks. Pre-synthetics it
was also used for envelopes, stamps, varnishes, glues, making cardboard and a
hundred other materials. After men have picked the resin off the trees, it is brought
on camel back to El Obeid for sale and onward transport by rail. (Imperial War Museum)

out and can be seen from far away. Moreover, it was nice for all
three of us to have something attractive to look at for a change.

We flew happily at about 10,000 ft in the cool air, relaxed and
keeping a check on the river below which bent first to our left and
then to our right over the 200 miles to Atbara. The glare of the
sun on the sand, despite my tinted goggles, made me screw my
eyes up. We kept well within gliding distance of the river which,
below us, was like a great scar across the landscape. I knew that
away from the river, on this side, there were few (if any) living
people. The scrubby vegetation had gone. There was nothing on
which to feed even a goat. The heat would be appalling and, were
we to go down there, our life span would be fairly short — unless
somebody found us. Our capacity to walk would be negligible —
about ten miles — although someone shot down in the Western
Desert did once achieve 20. Indeed to try and walk would be
tantamount to suicide. A tiny khaki speck in an ocean of blinding
khaki sand would simply vanish. A far better chance of living
would be to stake one's all on the hope that somebody might see,
on the yellow desert, a comparatively large aeroplane for, even
though it was camouflaged sandy beige, it had a large, hard-
edged black shadow.

At Atbara, which was a collection of mud-brick houses, the
Nile swept round and away to our left. It would go in a gigantic
half-circle, 150 miles across, to our left until it came back to join
us again at Wadi Halfa. However, we could fly straight on in
comparative safety because there was, underneath us, a road and
a railway beside which we could land and wait patiently. At Wadi
Halfa, joining the Nile once more, we made a half-right turn to
Aswan where, then, there was only a low dam and a little lake.

Then came the last leg, back on to a northerly course of 400
miles to Cairo. We made a slight diversion to come lower and
look at Luxor, the temple of Karnak and the Valley of the Kings.
Gradually the cultivation at the river's side became thicker and
lusher; at first, stretching only a few hundred yards from the
river's edge; then several hundred yards.

At last, the great smudge of a township that was Cairo came
into view. To our left lay the enormous Pyramids, looking
insignificant at that distance, and the Sphinx was invisible. On
our right, the bleak sandstone cliffs of the Mokattam Hills, with
their great caves from which much of the stone for the Pyramids
had been quarried, 30 centuries before. Now, those caves
contained the treasures of Tutankhamun's tomb and other

priceless artefacts from the Cairo Museum, safe from any bomb then known. Ahead was a great green arrowhead of cultivation, spreading ever wider as it faded away towards the sea, 100 miles away. Its green was a staggering contrast to the dusty beige of the desert which runs right up to its very edge. We had flown to the start of the Nile Delta.

On the eastern edge of Cairo lay Heliopolis airfield, my destination. Thankfully I eased the beast on to the sandy surface and taxied in. Gratefully I shut down the motors. Soon I was standing on the sand and saying adieu to my long-suffering crew. I felt that the W/Op was almost disappointed that we had not force-landed somewhere and catapulted him into the position of being our maestro and saviour — after midnight, of course. The navigator was kind and courteous; he said that, although he felt he had not contributed constructively, the trip had brought home to him, to his astonishment, just how *much* his training had left him still to learn! I didn't say so, but I remembered vividly how much pain and grief it had cost me to find out the same thing. I had learned a great deal myself from the trip, too.

I signed the machine over to the engineers and storemen so that it could be ferried onwards to a Maintenance and Storage unit alongside the Suez Canal — Kasfareet maybe. There, it would be completely checked over, and the generator mended, before it went to a squadron for fighting the war. Its 8,000 mile delivery journey would be ended.

I felt great sympathy for whichever crew might be called upon to fight in it. An operational Bisley (unlike Ricky's) was to my mind a detestable flying device; you had to keep your wits about you for it had several foibles. Perhaps the worst one was that there was so much weight in armour-plate, guns and rear turret that its beefed up engines barely got it off the ground on a hot day. This meant that even a minor mismanagement of the controls could have catastrophic consequences. For example, the engine-cooling shutters had *always* to be open on the ground to avoid overheating; omitting to close them as you began your take-off run would cause you to race, still on the ground, off the far end of the airfield. This resulted in a sheet of flame, a great roar and a dirty black mushroom cloud of exploding petrol. End of one aeroplane and its crew. Not a kindly and forgiving machine and no wonder it became known amongst my pilot colleagues as the Grisly Bisley. A dictionary defines 'grisly' as 'causing horror, terror or superstitious dread.' A trifle strongly put maybe, but the sense was right. I said I would never fly another, and I never did.

Now, there was a mass of things to be done with Bunny Russell before the route could be a smooth, safe and effective pipeline for aircraft coming to the war. And, if my trip was a foretaste of what my boss wanted from me, I was going to have a superlative 'desk-job'!

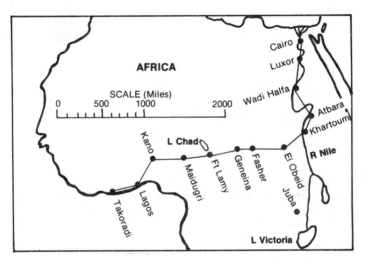

Chapter 7
The Little Bastard

'Lord above, how I envy you, Sir!'

Burned brown as a berry by the Egyptian sun, Corporal Jason was stripped to the waist and, standing on a wheeled platform several feet above the hard sand of Cairo-West airfield, was making some final checks and adjustments to the innards of a mighty 18-cylinder radial engine. The engine was one of four powering a super-long-range Liberator. It was one of half-a-dozen aircraft based in England which had been converted to carry, in the most spartan conditions, about 20 passengers instead of the bomb-load which its American designers had intended. So as to have maximum fuel, even the seats had been left out; the passengers had cushions on the floor. Jason was talking to its captain who had come out from Cairo to chat him up as he prepared the machine, and to see how the job was progressing.

Flight Lieutenant Algernon Llewellyn eyed him. 'How do you mean — envy?'

'Well Sir; my wife is in Dorset. I haven't seen her for two and a half years. We've got a little girl aged about two. I've never seen her at all. And, the way things are, God knows when I will see them or how long I shall still be here, waiting for your Libs to come in from time to time, working on them and doing my best to be sure that they get back safely. That's the way things are, in war. Two days ago, you were in England. Tomorrow night you will be back again. Tired perhaps, but at home with your family and your children. Therefore, Sir, if you don't mind me saying so, I envy your good fortune.'

Algy made some non-committal remark and went very silent as he pondered the corporal's words. Jason was a superb fitter and no task received anything but his unremitting efforts that it should be performed immaculately. He would turn out at any hour of the day or night to tend the metal monsters to the best of his ability. He was loyal beyond the call of duty and all this for crews and machines who did not 'belong' to his own unit and for whom he worked only indirectly. And, as a good officer, Algy knew perfectly well what a fine technician he was. Further, that his own life and those of his passengers and crew could well be lost but for the sterling efforts of all those like Corporal Jason at Cairo-West.

After a very long pause, Algy said, 'In return for all you do for us, I'll do something for you. It is a one-off affair and so you'll have to keep it utterly quiet. All hell will be let loose if it comes out, or if your chums start saying something like "why him and not me?". You would assuredly drop yourself in the clag but I, as the skipper who broke every rule in the book, would be even deeper down. Here's the deal. I will be back in ten days — Thursday week, in fact. If you can somehow break adrift from the camp for a couple of weeks, I will fly you home to England. And bring you back ten days later. There's a small space down by the nose-wheel compartment of the Lib, where you can park yourself, and no one except my crew need know you're there. The extra 150 lb of your weight is not going to make a hoot of difference to me lifting off the 44,000 lb of the whole outfit when we go. The crucial point is, do you think you can disappear from this place for a couple of weeks with nobody, but *nobody,* finding out, or even suspecting where you might be? Think it over and let me know tonight when I come to the aircraft for take-off.'

Algy Llewellyn was one of a small number of Flight Lieutenants who, as individuals, were as different as chalk, cheese and china. But they had one trait in common: they were superb aviators. They took turns to fly one of their Lockheed B24 Liberators from Lyneham airfield in Wiltshire non-stop to Cairo-West airfield in Egypt. On board were super-priority passengers and a tiny amount of vital freight. As the whole of Europe, and the whole of North Africa except for Egypt, was occupied by the enemy, it was quite a feat — one long hop of 18 to 22 hours, twice weekly.

To cut down the risk of being intercepted and shot down, the stretches of crucial danger were flown in the dark. They took off in the early afternoon and flew over southern Ireland, going far out into the Atlantic. Then they turned south, well clear of the long-range, radar-equipped, German Ju88 fighters based in France. Next, the flight was timed so as to cut back across the narrowest bit of Spain, high over the Pyrenees, and thence over the Mediterranean, navigating mainly by the stars. From there, south again to get past the Atlas mountains and to the safety of the empty desert, behind the German lines, before dawn. Finally, well out of reach of the Axis forces near the coast they would edge back again to reach Cairo-West around midday.

The trip was extremely tiring. It had to be done at about 20,000 ft with all the passengers wearing oxygen masks and fur-lined flying suits because cabin pressurisation did not exist. Total radio silence had to be observed for safety, thus depriving them of any kind of direct ground control or help; and, probably, of all chance of rescue if anything went seriously wrong. There were very few radio beacons, and the enemy tried to jam even those and to make them as confusing as possible. Forty-eight hours later the crew flew back. All in all, each flight was a masterly piece of navigation and captaincy. Twice a week they ferried those few people and papers whose presence at the other end of the war zone was considered to be vital.

These Flight Lieutenants had graduated to their job, not only because they were highly competent and skilful pilots, but because they also were fine captains of crews and they exercised tactfully a firm command of their passengers, who were often of dizzy rank and status. In those days many older officers felt — nay, *knew* — that because of their status they had a God-given right to bark an order at any junior, be he captain of the aircraft or no. It had not yet become aviation law that an aircraft's captain, of *any* rank, had unquestioned authority over his passengers, however senior they might be. It took a very special Flight Lieutenant to tell a General or an Air Marshal, tactfully, to piss-off and leave him alone.

Being more or less in charge of operations at the Cairo end, I got to know three of the captains very well. They were always visiting and eating and drinking with us, and were all, in their own ways, delightfully eccentric characters.

Edwin Freshfield was a solicitor in time of peace and a pilot for war. I discovered that, curiously enough, there was an earlier connection between us; his grandfather, also Edwin, had drawn up the legal documents for my mother's marriage settlement at the turn of the century. Edwin the younger may well have been, in a way, quieter than his other two pilot-colleagues but he could put away more whisky (with or without a mixer) than anyone I have ever known, whilst apparently staying totally sober. Only his nose betrayed him for it looked, to use an old-fashioned expression, 'very expensive'. He and his crew were a marvellous team.

One night, somewhere over Spain, Edwin was having a lot of irritation. The controls on those Liberators were maddeningly sensitive, even with an automatic-pilot fitted. One man, moving aft or forwards, would upset the balance so that the machine had to be re-trimmed by hand to fly level again. This night there was a General as a passenger who, because of the cold or something, seemed to need to go aft to the Elsan loo every five minutes. Edwin trimmed out the change on the General's aftward journey, and re-trimmed as he returned. Finally, he could stand it no longer. He turned to his Scottish flight-engineer: 'Look, everything is quiet up here. Take time off to go aft and persuade that elderly goon to sit down and stay down. He can't possibly need to nip back and forth like a dog who needs to lift its leg on every lamp-post! But be polite to him for God's sake.'

'Yes, Sir!'

The Scotsman was gone for about a quarter of an hour and thereafter total peace reigned. After an hour or so of complete and satisfying quiet, Edwin asked, 'You seem to have been very successful. What did you say to the General, and was he touchy?'

'Och, I didna have to say a word. I jist sat meself doon beside his place. When he came back, I pinched his oxygen tube till he passed out in aboot three meenits. Then I let the tube go and, by the time he came to, he wuss asleep.'

The second captain, 'Baggy' Sach, was somewhat portly with a pink and boyish complexion. He laughed easily, frequently, and when he did so his raucous cackle could shatter glass at 40 paces. Once, when I had no idea he was in the country, Phyl and I were at the cinema to see a comedy film. I heard a laugh at the other end of the auditorium. It was unmistakable. I stood up and shouted 'Baggy!' Everyone near me said 'Shush!', 'Shut up!', or worse. Baggy stood up and cried 'Tony!', to the displeasure of almost the entire audience which became very restive. It was quite enough for us. With no further words, we met and renewed our friendship in the foyer afterwards.

For several years after the war, Baggy made valiant attempts, every six months, to pass the written exam required before promotion from Flight Lieutenant to Squadron Leader. He failed them all, for writing at a desk did not come easily to his kind of mental apparatus. He had put in several impassioned pleas to be excused the exam because of his past record, but the rules for allowing anyone to escape the axe were positively fierce. If it was *reasonably* possible to take the exam, there was no mercy!

Five or six years after the war had ended he was in Japan where, as he truthfully said, there were no proper facilities to take the exam on the appointed days; once more, could he ask to be exempted? It so happened that I was doing penance in a London staff-job and, of all people, it was I who was the final arbiter on who might be excused. The administrative examiners, and their civil-servant advisers, had decided that he should not be excused, because he could easily skip across to Hong Kong and sit at the established exam centre there. Fortunately, they had not looked at an atlas. I was able (and delighted) to point out that Tokyo to Hong Kong is about the same as London to Cairo. Aeroplanes being what they then were, he would have had to make a cruise, by boat, both ways, and be away from his job probably for a month. I excused Baggy from the exam and — surprise, surprise — he was picked by the next promotions board to become a Squadron Leader!

Algy was more serious, and expansive. Much of the work these three did was highly sensitive but he felt he could talk freely to me, as his local boss, in the privacy of my own Cairo flat; and, anyone under stress needs the safety-valve of someone to talk to.

At that stage of the war we were desperately short of watches of sufficient reliability for airborne navigators to take their sextant-shots of the stars. It did not matter if the watch gained or lost; that could be allowed for. The crunch was that its gain or loss should not *vary* by more than four seconds in every 24 hours. We didn't have such watches and didn't make them. The Swiss had, and did — but they were surrounded by the enemy. Luckily, the Nazis wanted gold, which we could get. Occasionally, therefore, top quality Swiss watches were flown to Lisbon, in Portugal, by the German Luftwaffe in their three-engined Ju52s. Algy would also take his four-engined Liberator there. Why not? It was a neutral country. Algy's gold would be exchanged for watches, and both air forces flew their machines back the next day, with what they had come to get.

One evening in Lisbon, Algy and his crew were at a loss for something to do, so they decided to go to the Casino for a little flutter at the tables. They hadn't much money but they felt it would be an interesting experience. Choosing one of the green baize-covered tables, they sat down. Somewhat to their surprise they found themselves opposite the German crew. The RAF men began to play, and won. There was no flicker of expression on the croupiers' faces. The Germans seemed to have a lot of money and by degrees the heap of chips in front of Algy and his men was piled high. At last, the enemy crew was broke. They rose, clicked their heels, bowed and left.

Quite quietly four or five Portuguese slipped into the vacant seats and began to play. Algy's team started to lose. Slowly but steadily the pile of counters dwindled on the British side of the table and grew on the Portuguese side. Still the croupiers were totally impassive. Finally, the British crew was broke, too. They indicated that they also were pulling out. The whole place broke into roars of applause and back-slapping. All the German money, and the British money, had been pleasantly and effectively transferred to Portuguese pockets. For the rest of the night all the drinks, and the food, and dancing, were 'on the house'. It was a terrific party. The fact that Algy's team spoke no Portuguese brought not the slightest disadvantage. The small hours were getting quite large when they were all decanted into a pre-paid taxi and ferried back to their hotel. The Casino outing had been a deal more interesting than Algy had expected!

Algy said that flying the Prime Minister, Winston Churchill, was another of his memorable experiences. The old man would come up on to the flight-deck and stand just behind Algy's shoulder. 'No Smoking' was the rigid rule but Winston was not deterred by rules: rules were only for those who needed them, in his view. He would stand there, cigar in one hand and oxygen-mask in the other, taking alternate puffs from first one and then the other. There would have been an almighty blaze of crackling flames if the glowing cigar-end had come in contact with the oxygen — but he simply wouldn't listen to what he didn't want to hear.

On one of those trips, Algy got an unfavourable weather report and decided to turn back. Churchill was told the news.

'What did you say, young man? Bloody nonsense. I've got a very important meeting to attend. I'm prepared to take the risk in going on; so if I can, you can! Full steam ahead, at once!'

'I'm very sorry, Sir,' replied Algy, 'but I think the risks are unacceptable, whether you are prepared to take them or not. We're going back.'

Churchill was furious. He began by thumping Algy's shoulder and wound up by returning to his seat, muttering threats and

imprecations all the way home. Then, after landing, he came up
to Algy and said, gruffly, 'Quite right my boy. Very inconvenient
for me, but you were perfectly correct to do what you judged
best.'

Then he stumped off to his waiting car. They were both
singular characters. It takes quite a Flight Lieutenant to tell the
Prime Minister to go jump in the lake, figuratively speaking.

One day, having a pre-lunch drink with us in our flat, Algy
asked Phyl if she could help him, and his wife in England. He
began: 'Her problem is that the only brassieres one can get are the
"Utility Clothing" grade. Catherine feels they make her look like
a couple of under-filled flour bags. And, as if that was not insult
enough, they require our precious and scantily-rationed clothing
coupons. She asked me to see if I could buy her two on my next
trip. But I am not at all sure of myself in this department and I
wondered if you would help me?

'My dear Algy,' Phyl replied, 'you know I would be only too
happy to help, but bras are a very personal thing. I don't know
what shape she wants, or how big she is, or what kind of straps
she wants, with or without lace, and so on . . . and anyway it's
Sunday, so Cicurel, where I go for mine, is shut.'

Algy took a deep breath. 'Phyl, please don't think me too
personal but as far as the size is concerned you look to me to be
just about the same as she is. More; the shape I like, and which I
think she would go along with, is like yours too. To hell with the
lace and fiddly bits; they're all underneath and only I see them —
at least, I hope its only me — and so I wondered if, on your next
shopping trip, you could buy yourself a couple of nice bras which
I could collect and pay for next time I'm over here. Might that be
possible?'

Phyl gave him a long look before saying, 'Well Algy . . . if you
feel as sure as that, I do have a couple which I bought last week.
One hasn't even been worn yet. If you want to take a chance on
making her hate me for evermore, sight unseen, which I should be
sorry about, you can have those.'

She got up and Algy followed her into the bedroom. A little
later he came out again, beaming all over his face and tucking two
brassieres into his pocket: his shopping commission had been
completed. Algy always swore to me that the second bra, when he
got it, was still warm. Phyl hotly denies it.

When Algy landed at Cairo-West on that pre-arranged
Thursday, Corporal Jason was not there. He had got a leave-pass

for two weeks privilege leave. Ostensibly he had already left for a fortnight in Palestine — off the camp and out of the country. But he and the crew met up in Cairo. They all came out in the aircrew-transport and he was smuggled aboard by the crew, together with a spare flying suit and oxygen mask that they had brought from England for him. In due course the important passengers came aboard and Jason was tucked into the little space alongside the nosewheel when it was retracted.

The great machine, pregnant with tons and tons of petrol, lumbered down to the start of the long tarmac runway. Algy pointed down its length and steadily opened the four throttles while the engineer's hand followed along just behind his. When Algy took his hand away, the engineer set each engine precisely for absolute maximum power. The speed built up steadily, the wings developed enough lift, Algy eased the stick back gently, and the flight was on its way.

Twenty hours later, cold and stiff, Jason unfolded himself from his cramped quarters in the nose. He climbed down and joined the aircrew as they went to Operations to sign off. As far as Customs and Immigration were concerned, he was just one of the people from the Lib, so he went through like anyone else. For the Movements Staff, he was merely an airman on two weeks leave, as shown by his leave-pass. They asked him where he was going, and gave him a free railway-pass to Dorset. To that they added a free bus-pass to Swindon where he could catch his train. Hardly believing his good fortune, he was gone. What on earth would his wife say when he walked in the door? What on earth would he say to his wife?

Ten days later Jason did virtually the same thing in reverse. He took care not to re-appear amongst his friends at Cairo-West, or on the camp itself, until his 14 days absence 'in Palestine' had expired. On his return he showed round some picture-postcards of the Holy Land which, prudently, he had bought for that purpose. He took up his job just as assiduously as before and that was that . . . apparently.

Roughly nine months later Mrs Jason wrote in to the Air Force authorities, saying she had been delivered of a fine bouncing boy, and could she have the extra allowances for a second child? 'No way', the Air Force wrote to her. 'The child is illegitimate because your husband is in Egypt, and has been for years, so he has not had couvrage. You must paddle your own canoe. We do not finance bastards.' . . . or words to that effect. Mrs Jason was, unsurprisingly, rather upset and confused. Knowing it was a private deal that had brought her husband home, she prudently wrote to him first, saying 'What do I do now?'

Corporal Jason weighed up the pros and cons and decided to seek the advice of his Commanding Officer at Cairo-West. The CO was positively enchanted with the bare bones of the story. It was precisely the type of reward he would himself dearly love to have manipulated for an airman as deserving as this one. Naturally, he asked 'Who was the aircraft captain?' Jason told him, very politely, that he had given his word not to reveal it, and his lips were sealed. The CO understood this loyalty perfectly and said he would write to HQ Middle East, explaining the matter and that Master Jason had in fact been born legally, in holy wedlock. He could then be duly registered on the books and allowances paid.

HQME wrote back a very sharp letter. It was monstrous. It was scandalous. Corporal Jason was alleging that an experienced captain had broken the rules; if true, the extra weight he had carried would have reduced the range, endangered the safety of his aircraft and jeopardised its precious cargo. There should be a Board of Inquiry, to establish the truth of what was being said and with a view to taking disciplinary action against the captain if it was found to be true. Corporal Jason, in his own best interests, must be ordered to say who the captain was, and give the date. The whole thing was such an unlikely tale that in no way would child-allowances be paid, without proof, on the uncorroborated word of one man.

Corporal Jason said, very politely, that he had given his word. He did not break his word and no way would he go beyond the fact that it was a pilot who flew from Cairo-West to England, eight to ten months previously.

Middle East wrote even more fiercely in response to this insubordination. How dare a Corporal, a mere Corporal, flout a direct order? Orders were to be obeyed and, if they were not, it was a chargeable offence. Corporal Jason was to be interviewed by his commanding officer and informed that if he persisted in this false sense of loyalty to an unreliable captain of His Majesty's aircraft, he would find himself formally charged under the Air Force Act and the Manual of Air Force Law. He might be court martialled and if, as appeared inescapable, he were found guilty, he could lose his Corporal's stripes and it would probably put paid to any chances he might have of any promotion in the future.

The CO of Cairo-West went hopping mad. He knew, and wrote, that all that stuff about extra weight, endangering aircraft and own best interests was a load of cock. He regretfully crossed out 'cock' and wrote 'codswallop'. It was no more than petty spite to think of taking action against one of the superlative captains who made the dangerous flights twice-weekly. And, for that matter, hammering a damned good Corporal, too.

Corporal Jason, on interview, said very politely that his word was his bond. If they wanted to punish him for his private sense of priorities, and his loyalty to a man who had done him an enormous favour, so be it. But he would not give them a name or a date.

So HQME, to the fury and disappointment of almost the entire Command, insisted on a Court Martial for Jason. The sentiments of the members of the Court itself may be gauged by the fact that they gave him the smallest possible punishment that it was in their power to award, even though he pleaded guilty to the charge.

HQME got no credit for being far more astute than anybody realised at the time. Once a Court had found Jason guilty of going to England as a *fact* — and thereby had had couvrage — it became official and legally acceptable by the Air Force that Master Jason was no longer a bastard. And therefore nobody could refuse to give Corporal and Mrs Jason all their allowances, backdated to their son's birthday. Further, Corporal Jason had been 'legally punished' for breaking the rules and no one could ever make it any worse.

Corporal Jason never succumbed to the terrific pressures put on him to say who flew him home to England, for what must have been a memorable ten days.

Chapter 8
Birthday Boy

'Darling, I'm terribly sorry but we can't have my birthday party on the day. I have to do a job near Luxor staging post, and that's the day I've got to go. We'll just have to have it on another day.'

Phyl looked disappointed because it was the first time we would have celebrated my birthday since our marriage, but she shrugged her shoulders and, like a good Service wife, put it down to the terrible privations of war. Privations? Living as we did in our comfortable Cairo flat, with no rationing and lush conditions, such little sacrifices were few and far between and *not* very significant!

Unlike most of our out-of-the-way airfields used as occasional stopping places, the parent town of Luxor nearby was on the telephone. Also, it was a favourite place to go and spend some leave, sightseeing around the famous ancient monuments and tombs. So, next day, in the office, I cast around on the telephone to find out which of my chums would be there on my birthday, and if it might be possible to drum up a party for that evening. It took some pretty intensive work but I managed to run a trio to earth. One was a great friend of my wife and myself, Sally Perry who worked for the Red Cross. She was being escorted by two other friends of ours. One, a man much older than me, had known me all my life; his name was Gerry Baird. The other was Colonel John Barraclough, just in for some leave, having done over six months in the Western Desert.

Sally was a honey. She was very tall with model-girl looks and shape. She had been brought up with her identical twin. They were truly identical — nobody could tell t'other from which, unless they dressed differently. On the other hand, in character they were poles apart. Other-Twin fully enjoyed company, dancing and a good party. However, her difficulty was that she was desperately shy and nervous with strangers: for her, breaking the ice was as welcome as murder. Sally, on the other hand, was extrovert, full of *joie de vivre* and had no trouble making friends with anybody. However, she rapidly got bored and irritated when men started to get too earnest, which, with her stunning looks and enchanting personality, normally did not take long.

The pair of them had used their remarkable outward similarity to mutual advantage. Sally would happily meet a man and have a splendid time — being taken out, theatres, cocktails, cinemas, or whatever. Other-Twin would be kept fully in the picture and given the chance to get a good look at him. Sally therefore knew whether Other-Twin thought she might like him or not. So when, as was virtually inevitable, he became all serious, Sally exercised one of two choices. She could turn him off for good, or, if Other-Twin had thought him attractive, she would make a date and Other-Twin would keep it. There was her escort, beautifully prepared, soft, slushy and as nicely broken in as anyone could wish. And, Sally assured me, the man never knew the difference until Other-Twin chose to tell him — by which time he usually didn't care. And, if needs be, Sally probably by then had another escort ripe for handing over.

We arranged to have dinner together, the four of us, at the Luxor Palace Hotel. The cooking was good and the cellar passable. The hotel agreed to have some champagne on ice, and I said I would provide oysters as a starter.

'Oysters? In Luxor? Not possible!'

'Yes; possible. In Luxor. Courtesy of His Majesty King George VI, my employer.'

I reckoned a Miles Hawk was just what I needed to nip down to Hurghada and then across to Luxor, so I borrowed one for a couple of days from the Communications Flight at Heliopolis. Earlier, when I commanded a squadron in the Western Desert, I had had one for my personal use. It was a splendid runabout for zipping around at zero feet looking for wells dug by the Bedouin Arabs, which might augment our meagre water ration. You could always land alongside, and peer down to see if the inside was wet. So I borrowed a Hawk from the Heliopolis communications flight.

It was crazy to take the needless risk, really, in that little wooden two-seater single-engined monoplane with no radio. I knew, but didn't choose to consider, what the result of an engine-failure en route would be. I had quite simply decided it was going to be a delightful trip. After all, it was on my birthday, and special accordingly. Looking back, I was really taking a devil of a chance!

I took off in the early morning, with a sack tucked into the empty passenger seat in front, and set course for Hurghada, which I had not visited since the night I collected the appendicitis case. I reasoned that the Hawk lands slowly and you can put it down almost anywhere quite safely; engine failure is going to be a potential disaster at whatever height it occurs — so why not fly low and enjoy myself? To hell with it; the Hawk has a Gipsy engine and they are notoriously reliable. So I didn't fly above 50 feet for all the hundreds of miles of barren desert, and it was fun to look closely at the colours of the sands, the wadis and the craggy mountains near the coast. Of such stupidities fatal accidents are often made.

Hurghada, fortunately, turned up as required and on landing I renewed my acquaintance with the engineer CO.

'May I go paddling to collect some oysters?'

'How many?'

'Well . . . there are four of us . . . and it's my birthday . . . should we say 60 or 70 . . . a dozen and a half each?'

'No problem. Help yourself.'

It soon became clear that the Hurghada team had learned to appreciate oysters. There were none clinging to the boulders on the beach just in front of the camp. They had all been eaten. Imagine! I had to paddle all of three hundred yards along the sand to find the necessary clusters . . . Soon I was trotting back with six dozen oysters in my sack. I strapped it carefully into the front-seat and expressed my sincere thanks to the Squadron Leader. He grinned and wished me 'Many happy returns of the day — and have a nice dinner.'

The second leg of the trip was comparatively short: only 80 miles of empty desert. The weather was good and the Nile across that brown sand would stick out like a sore thumb. No navigation problems, and so it came out, just about an hour from Hurghada. I was happy as Larry.

I snatched a great opportunity. Normally, I plodded along at several thousand feet over Luxor, minding my business of getting from A to B. This was a wonderful chance to fly round and see all the old tombs and temples from a low level. How lucky that a Gipsy engine was so unobtrusive and no one would complain at my buzzing around like an overgrown wasp!

The roofless temple of Karnak stood out well. Its rows of

carved lions held their endless watch on the great hall. Ruined it might be, but from the air its plan and shape were wonderfully clear. I could visualise what an imposing edifice it must have been in its day, filled with pomp and ceremony. And how, in Heaven's name, did they get those monumental pillars erected before the days of metal girders and cranes? The Valley of the Kings was dull; just excavations to see from the air; the real sights were underground. I landed on the airfield and taxied in as directed by the airman.

The CO, a Flight Lieutenant, was there to meet me. He was both surprised and a bit miffed when I told him I wanted to go into town after doing the work I had come for. He had prepared to give me a regal welcome, with a dinner in his tiny Mess, as befitted a visiting senior officer. Why rush off to a little Arab town which I did not know? He was even more amazed when I said it was to do with oysters in a sack. Thinking I had come straight from Cairo, he decided that I must have gone off my rocker. Sun-stroke? He began to look as though he thought I needed the local doctor, and treatment in his hospital to boot. I managed to mollify him only slightly by showing him the oysters, and telling him how and why I had got them, and giving him half a dozen for his supper.

The words of Air Marshal Tedder sprang sharply from my memory: 'The more senior you are, the more polite you must be to your juniors.' Once, as a squadron commander, I had airily suggested to him that, as Commander-in-Chief, he could do anything he chose without giving a damn about what his juniors thought. My lesson was gently put but very firmly — that I had better absorb the manners of man-management and of rank, fast. He explained that what one says and does becomes far more telling as one moves up the tree of promotion. For example, a ticking off by a Flight Lieutenant to a junior officer is not epoch making — but the same words coming to a Flying Officer from an Air Marshal would be nothing less than shattering. So, the higher I went, the more delicately I should walk.

I apologised sincerely to the Luxor CO and pleaded birthday privilege, promising that I would come back next morning and take the opportunity to have a good look round his unit with him, and have lunch in his Mess. Perhaps he could also make the time to show me round some of the ancient monuments before I left for Cairo? I think that it helped, but nevertheless it was unforgivably cavalier of me to have upset all his arrangements without warning.

The hotel staff knew nothing about oysters. They had not got, and had never heard of an oyster-knife. I went back to the airfield and grovelled to the CO, returning in triumph with a large screwdriver. I do not know if I am the only person in the world who has used a screwdriver to open 66 oysters — particularly the tough, curly-edged kind. I never wish to do it again . . . I would prefer to go without oysters. At dinner I was obliged to reveal that the red streaks visible on many of the oysters were spots of my blood — not signs of bad oysters; no one need worry, its taste would be lost in the lemon and tabasco. Sally blanched a bit but ate them just the same. The other two were totally unconcerned. The oysters were superb and greatly appreciated; the champagne was delectable — it was a splendid birthday party.

Sated and happy, we looked outside the front door of the hotel. The air was balmy and we could smell the frangipanis. There appeared to be twice as many twinkling stars as usual. What better than a stroll, up the road and back before turning in? We linked arms and ambled up the Luxor street. Most of the windows were shuttered but some let us see people contentedly playing cards, or gossipping. Sometimes a gusty laugh would float out. Our conversation was not about the war; we talked of happy things — parents, homes, blood relations, gardens and Britain. It was quiet, peaceful and the air felt smooth and velvety.

About half-way between two crossroads a ground-floor window was open. Inside, a single electric light bulb hung from the ceiling, bare and lighting the room harshly. We could see that it was a bedroom. Inside, a girl was moving around, perhaps preparing for bed. She stood in front of her mirror. The young lady appeared to be totally indifferent that the window was uncurtained and unshuttered. Uncuriously, the four of us, arms still linked, stopped and glanced at her for a moment. She reached up and, in a single movement, slipped her cotton dress over her head. Beneath it she was stark naked. It was a bit embarrassing, with Sally there; what could one say? John broke the silence. For six long months he had suffered a monastic life in the Western desert, totally deprived of any feminine contact. Quietly and reflectively he said, 'If my memory serves me right, that's a woman.'

As might be expected, men coming in after months in the desert used to look forward to finding some way of refreshing their memories. The longer the time spent in isolation, the greater the wish for feminine company. That does not necessarily mean bed, though that was very frequently the outcome. Of course these needs were known, appreciated and catered for by sundry madams in the cities. There were two in particular who ran high-class establishments, on the lines of Mother Merrick's in London before the war.

One was near the coast, in Alexandria. It was known universally as 'Mary's House'. Its standards and professions were precisely similar to those in Madame Karoff's flat, 3rd Floor, Sharia Emad el Din, Cairo.

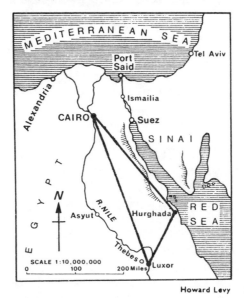

Howard Levy

Madame Karoff, known more vulgarly behind her back as Madam Crackoff, was a voluminous lady who ran a most comfortable and comforting establishment. It boasted an excellent supply of drink — which cost the earth — and it was served all night, long after even the sleaziest of joints elsewhere had closed. Reception was in the luxurious drawing-room, presided over by Madame herself because she was very choosy as to whom she (or her girls) might welcome. It was almost like a rather select Officers' Club.

You could be black-balled by Madame only too easily. Strict adherence to the proprieties and conventions was essential. An individual was ushered into the drawing-room, seated, and a drink was offered. The first one appeared to be free, but you paid for it in the end, one way or another! Conversation would continue (in any one or all of Madame's seven fluent languages) until a satisfactory interview had been completed. At that time, if it had become clear that your requirement was for drink and light-hearted badinage with your friends and the girls, so be it: the house catered for all tastes. The girls were only too happy to sit and have drinks paid for — at ferocious prices upon which they got a good commission — without having to work for them, as one might say.

The girls were equally carefully chosen for quality and variety: blonde, brunette or redhead; black, white or coffee. All were linguists, conversationalists, and none seemed to be under any pressure to work. Naturally, if the conversation with a client changed direction at any time, that could be accommodated too, at a nod and a crinkling of notes with Madame. I was credibly informed that the ignominy of having to crinkle one's notes beforehand could be dispensed with for well-liked and regular customers who were trusted to pay their bills like gentlemen. It was all very like Ma Merrick's London establishment — except that, as Ma drew her girls exclusively from the aristocracy, men did not have a variety of colours to choose from.

One night in Alexandria a lone Junkers Ju88 bomber came overhead on a sneak raid, looking for a Royal Navy target in the harbour. However, before he could complete his mission, he was picked up by searchlights around the port and coned by several of them. This, for any pilot, is most disconcerting. Even at height the glare is blinding and one cannot see the instruments properly. None of the crew can see anything outside because of the reflections on the glass and perspex. Twisting and turning seems only to make it worse. All the time you are devastatingly aware that you are a brilliantly-lit target for an enemy fighter, coming in from any direction and able to take his time over killing you carefully. The Junkers did the only thing he could in the circumstances. He jettisoned his bombs, stuffed his nose down for maximum speed and fled out to sea.

One bomb fell squarely on 'Mary's House'. The results were shocking: 11 officers were killed. HQME was naturally, and appropriately, concerned about recording the circumstances of their deaths and, particularly, about what they could say to the next-of-kin. However, they rose magnificently to the occasion. Those who were killed with their trousers on were reported as 'Killed on Active Service'. Those with their trousers off were deemed to have been 'Killed In Action'.

Chapter 9
Inexcusable Error

It was early afternoon when Pilot Officer Stanton landed his Hudson at Mersa Matruh. He was doing the return half of a routine round-trip to Benghazi and back. 700 miles home, via Tobruk and Mersa. He still had 250 miles left, about an hour and a half, before reaching Cairo. Stanton was a very sound young captain. He was a Sergeant and, having showed the qualities needed for a wartime commission — strength of character, leadership, airmanship and professional skill — he had the honour and privilege of becoming an officer instead of an NCO. It had happened quite recently and he was very proud of getting his added responsibilities.

Stanton and everyone else on board had been looking forward to arrival in the fleshpots with, above all, the chance of a good bath. But, the strong wind and the rising sand were bad; they were too bad, in Stanton's opinion. The radio was useless because of the dust-crackle. Ten billion grains of sand sent static electricity down the aerial, and all radios of that period would only produce a raucous rasping noise like a thousand sheets of sandpaper being rubbed together, to drown out all else. He flew low, and his main help had been the tarmac road running east-west a few miles inside the coast. This, from its slightly darker colour, he had been able to distinguish and to follow. His approach to Mersa airfield had been horrible. The desert was brown. The sky was brown. The air was brown. Judgement of height for touch-down had been nearly impossible, as everything was the same colour as the surface he had to land on. And the weather seemed to be getting worse. His eyes were sore. His teeth were gritty. 'Enough,' he said to himself, 'is enough; we are stopping here for the night.' He sent his navigator across to the operations tent to tell them so, while he went through the shut-down procedures in the cockpit.

Stanton was somewhat startled, a few moments later, to find

no less a personage than an Air Vice-Marshal standing beside him, bent forward because the cockpit was slightly too low for him to stand upright. Putting his face close to Stanton's leather flying-helmet he shouted against the noise, 'Don't stop the engines yet. What's this I hear about you not going on?'

'That's right, Sir,' answered Stanton. 'The weather's bad, and seems to be deteriorating. I thought it would be a good idea, Sir, to stop off here and hope for better weather tomorrow.'

'You can't do that!' shouted the Air Vice-Marshal. 'We've got important passengers to on-load who have to get back to Cairo urgently. We don't have spare accommodation here at Mersa Matruh to put up a batch of passengers just because you say so.'

'But, Sir, the weather's pretty poor and we are running downwind. It might get even worse further on as more sand gets picked up.'

Stanton turned his worried face up to the older man; he was astonished and upset, being put under pressure like this.

The AVM, on his side, was not used to being argued with by Pilot Officers; as an ex-WW1 Army officer, brought up with its rigid code of obedience to orders, he went on: 'We have had no Met warnings in from Cairo saying that the weather is in any way dangerous. You know very well that, over the green fields, visibility in the Delta is often better than it is out here. You're a transport pilot and your job is to deliver your load. Don't you know there is a war on?'

Stanton looked down and shook his head slowly as he thought it over. Here was a very senior officer who presumably had been flying for yonks years, and had a stack of experience. He, with the wisdom of an AVM, had said that in his judgement the weather should be better at the far end. And, let's face it, the landing at Mersa had been achieved, difficult though it had been to distinguish the sandy surface. Moreover, it was his duty to get through. If, now, he refused to go, would it affect his precious commission? Would it be considered as disobedience? He raised his tired head and said: 'OK, Sir. If you say so, we'll go. Could you tell my navigator that my earlier decision is cancelled, and ask him to get the new passengers on quickly, before the engines overheat. Thank you for your advice, Sir.'

As soon as the passengers had been loaded and the door shut, Stanton taxied out, took off and disappeared into the murk.

From my 216 Group office window, I could hardly see across the street to the yellow and white-washed buildings on the other

side. The weather was beyond bad; it was disgusting. The wind
was flickering around 40 or 50 mph. Straight down, the
pavements and the road had streaks of blowing sand streaming
across them, lying low and flowing like drifting snow — except
that it was beige in colour, heavy and sharp enough to sting your
skin if you went outside. It seeped under doors and through the
minuscule cracks round closed windows. Even indoors it filled
the air and got under your eyelids; if you rubbed them it was
worse. It stuck to your lips; licking them made your teeth grind as
you chewed. It was hot and the sand stuck to your sweaty skin
making a sort of patina of mud. It landed on your food and made
it all gritty; tomorrow, you would have diarrhoea. It was a fairly
typical *khamseen,* which is Egyptian for the repulsive dust-storm
which blows in from the west. I thanked my lucky stars that I was
not out in the desert with insufficient water-ration to wash
properly.

At about 5.30, when I was starting to clear my desk, I heard the
aircraft. Peering overhead I could see nothing but brown; it was
like looking up inside a brown paper bag with no seams. 'Poor
devil,' I thought, 'bloody fool you were to get up there in the first
place, but I hope to God you can get down now you've done it.'

Twenty minutes after I had heard the aircraft going over my
office, the call came through: 'Is that SASO 216 Group?
Heliopolis Ops here. One of your Hudsons has gone into the low
hills beyond the airfield and exploded. He was trying to get down
in these foul conditions. We think he was going round again. We
heard his motors roar, and then the bang. He had made two shots
at it before that one. We knew earlier that he was coming from
Mersa, and we tried to divert him back there, but we couldn't
contact him in the air because of the static. No one can get near
the crash yet with its burning fuel. We'll give you any news as we
get it. One thing is virtually certain; there will be no survivors.
Are you going home, or will you hang on at the office?'

'I'll wait here,' I replied. 'There are bound to be questions,
because of the passengers. I'll field them while you get on with the
nasty bit. Be a good chap and keep me posted, so that I am as up-
to-date as possible on what happened, and about survivors — if
there are any, though it doesn't sound likely from what you say.
OK?'

My decision to stay in the office in case of questions had been a
lucky one. A second call came through an hour or so later: 'Is that
you, SASO? There is something very odd here. There were

supposed to be 12 passengers aboard, according to the passenger list we have received. We can't marry all the bits together and count bodies yet, but one of them is a woman, and there is no woman on the list.'

'A woman! You're talking cock; no women are allowed up in the desert, and there aren't any there. Someone in your outfit is making a balls of it for you!

Heliopolis Ops came back: 'Well, there was at least one on this aircraft. The doc has come from the crash and he says there's no possibility of error. There are unmistakable female pieces. What do we do?'

'There's nothing you can do, except try to find out how many people were on the aircraft and, if humanly possible, to sort out names — from identity discs and so forth, if you can find any. Meanwhile, I'll try and get through to Mersa by landline and discover what they know. I'll tell you at once if I find anything out. Meanwhile you'll find me here, answering questions until I tell you something else.'

I put the telephone down, staring as though the contraption had invented the whole thing. The questions, both in number and fierceness, grew like a torrent as the night progressed.

I first guessed that some member of the crew — probably the pilot — had bent all the rules and taken some girlfriend up there for a ride, and to show her how clever he was. Then he found himself forced to take all the risks of coming back, so as not to get caught with her there and wind up by being court martialled. As a youngster I had done daring things to show off to girls and there were some pretty awful stupidities tucked into my uncomfortably long memory. So my guess was not unlikely.

I rang the skipper's unit and they confirmed that the pilot was both young and junior. However, they insisted that he was sound, recently commissioned, and that my guesswork was totally out of keeping with his character. 'Hah!' I thought cynically, 'I admire them for loyally sticking up for him, and saying it's not like him. However, they've forgotten the strength of basic urges and sex. Just wait and see! I'll bet some woman has — no, had — got her claws into him. And then it'll be our fault, here, for not exercising tighter control over our operations. God, what a mess!!'

Little did I know what a much worse mess it really was.

During the night and the next day the awful truth filtered through. As an exception, the Commander-in-Chief's wife had been allowed to go up to the Desert for some social work in the forward casualty-clearing units. It had been kept deeply under the covers. This had been partly to avoid any chance of a snatch-raid by the enemy for propaganda purposes. However, the main reason had been to avoid jealousies amongst wives and, more tricky, the politically powerful volunteer-organisations which had been pressing for years for their female workers to be allowed 'into the Desert to look after the troops'. The lady in question had fetched up in the headquarters at Mersa Matruh, and asked for a hitch-flight back to Cairo. 'Indeed,' they said, 'there happens to be a passenger aircraft passing through this very day. We will put you aboard and you will be at Heliopolis by late teatime.' She was, but not in the way they meant.

For weeks we fought Headquarters like wild cats, at first to protect the reputation of our unit and its recently commissioned dead captain. The staff there thought us pretty unreasonable for not letting the blame fall on a junior pilot, who was dead anyway. Why, they suggested, could the matter not be closed simply? Surely, we could accept as incontrovertible fact that: 'It is generally recognised that any skipper of an aircraft has authority. It is certain that the AVM never gave him an unequivocable order to go on. Therefore, the Pilot Officer could have said to the Air Vice-Marshal, politely of course, "No, Sir. I'm not going to do what you want." The pilot didn't refuse to fly on; therefore it is clearly *his* inexcusable error for deciding to proceed.'

It soon became clear that there was a double twist to the opinions. If the Pilot Officer was right, someone else had to be wrong. It was inferred by some very senior officers that, for the good of the Service as a whole, protection of a living AVM and his future work would justify denigration of a dead Pilot Officer. Bunny Russell disagreed and fought his seniors with unshakeable determination. He looked to the future; it might happen again. Few transport captains, and particularly not recently-commissioned Pilot Officers, had the guts and tact of an Algy Llewellyn — so we dug our toes in. We became as popular as pork pies in a synagogue.

There were no winners and no losers to that contest in the end. One could say that the whole distasteful squabble was largely shuffled under the carpet. But, there was one result: Bunny's foresight and moral courage in fighting the big guns in HQME made it certain that now, in Air Force Regulations, there is an unequivocal statement which did not exist before. It says that anyone who tries in any way to influence the professional judgement of an aircraft captain is guilty of an offence; he may, and quite likely will, be tried and punished. The rank of the persuader and the rank of the skipper have no bearing on the matter whatsoever. We could not turn the clock back, but it has since proved to be a very useful rule to have in the books.

Chapter 10
Morocco Bound

Bunny came into my office and parked one cheek of his backside on the edge of my desk, holding himself there with one leg and swinging the other gently. The boss did not usually come to my office for discussions; I went to his. He looked rather unhappy about something and I wondered what was biting him. He said: 'You know, there ought to be an Air Force motto, pinned up above every desk, saying "Haven't you heard? It's all been changed!" '

There was nothing new there. I had had that over my office door two ranks back. I waited for him to go on. He paused. 'Now that Monty has driven through into Tunisia, and is about to join up with the Americans, they're going to boost up our Group to take on extra work — roughly speaking, by cutting down on the Takoradi supply-route and opening up a new one, through from Casablanca. Not having to take stuff all the way down to the Gold Coast and bring it back up again will produce tremendous savings. And a lot of the aircraft, like the Wellingtons, will be able to fly to Morocco, instead of overloading Gibraltar. Added to which, aircraft are always spotted at Gib by German spies using binoculars from Algeciras and La Linea. More, reinforcements for the Middle East and India can just fly down the North African coast from there. Shorter, faster, and safer.'

My eyes must have lit up like green traffic lights. This was great news and an exciting prospect for creating a larger and more varied organisation. Why was Bunny not enthusiastic? I said nothing and tried to look courteously interested.

Bunny continued: 'They — the faceless "they" — have decided that to handle the elements of US Air Transport Command, which are much bigger and have people more highly ranked than us, we need an Air Commodore as the boss and not a Group Captain. So they have unearthed a Flight Lieutenant in the UK, a

Volunteer Reservist, in for the war; I understand he is half-American and in England he ran some tin-pot airline in peacetime. This makes him, they say, better qualified than I am to handle our senior Allies. They are giving him an acting Air Commodore rank, and putting him in here to run my Group. To rub salt into my wound, they asked me if I would work junior to him as his Group Captain SASO.'

Now I saw why Bunny was feeling bitter and twisted.

'I flatly refused to work for a Flight Lieutenant, wearing Air Commodore's stripes or not,' Bunny said indignantly. 'I don't yet know what is on the cards for you. I've proposed that they make you up to Group Captain, as his SASO, if you'll take the job, but we will have to wait till the new boss arrives from England and see what he wants done . . . His name is Whitney Straight.'

He got up and went back to his office without another word, leaving me in a mental turmoil. On one hand I deeply admired and was fond of Bunny Russell, so I wanted to be loyal to him. He had long experience behind him, had taught me masses of things, and had given me free rein. Though kindly he could be firm, even stubborn, if the need arose. His capacity to fight and do the best for his outfit was belied by his gentle, almost passive, looks. To put a wartime Flight Lieutenant over his head seemed churlish to me.

On the other hand, he had recommended that I should be a Group Captain! To get that rank at 27 was incredible. I knew that one or two people in the war had done it at that age, mainly fighter pilots getting their stripes by inheritance, but not many. Why in hell did my good fortune have to come at Bunny's expense?

Air Commodore Whitney Straight came in a few days later. Bunny Russell took him all round our little headquarters, showing him its ins and outs, explaining everything and introducing him to everyone. The hand-over was brief. Bunny left and never returned; we were sorry to see him go.

Whitney was charming, outgoing and obviously a powerful character, even if most of us (loyal to Bunny) were wondering uncharitably how this junior officer, wearing his broad stripe, was going to cope when experience counted.

In my office he came straight to the point: 'I have talked about you with Group Captain Russell. He thinks you ought to stay on as SASO. I agreed that your competence and experience would be invaluable to me.'

My heart soared.

'However,' he continued, 'HQME say that, with the reduction of work following the move of forces to the other end of the Mediterranean, they have eight Group Captains surplus, so they are not going to create another one. I must take one of them.'

My heart sank.

'They have graciously said I can choose which one. Sorry! I fought as hard as I could but, as a new boy here, I got hammered down. The fact that I can't get you another stripe doesn't mean that I don't want to retain your experience in the Group, somewhere. There will be a Wing Commander Ops job here, under the new SASO when we get him, which would be valuable to me if you want it. But, if you feel that having been SASO yourself you don't like the idea, I shall quite understand. To keep you, I'll give you any Wing Commander's post in the Group. You may choose which one. Think about it.'

He nodded cheerfully, and was gone.

'Oh well,' I thought, 'it was great while it lasted. At least I got recommended and someone thought I could handle it. And he's been very nice to me about it. Poor Phyl; she felt so proud of me and she'll be disappointed as hell.'

My choice was made quickly. I lined up in front of Whitney next day. 'Sir; we know that there must be a reception airfield in Morocco, to serve the North African theatre. There will also have to be two or three new staging airfields to be set up, like those we have on the Takoradi route, but between Casablanca and Cairo. Someone then has got to run the whole outfit on a day to day basis, and control the flow of aircraft along the route — matching flow with capacity. For this you will need a Ferry Control, like the one in Khartoum. That is run by a Wing Commander Ricky Rixson. Can I set that lot up, based in Morocco, and run it?'

There was no hesitation. Whitney just said: 'Yes, but there is a bit more to it than that. It is in an American theatre, so you are going to have to engender a lot of goodwill from them to keep it going.'

I could hardly believe my luck, but better was to come. I added, 'One other thing please, Sir. You know that out on the routes, Commanders have permission to delay any individual aircraft if by so doing they can improve the flow of the rest? That is going to be vital for me as I shall be out on a limb. I could always hitch a ride coming this way, but there will be no flow going back. We schedule one token RAF aircraft into the US theatre, weekly, but that only goes as far as Algiers. There is of course a Dakota, staging through Gibraltar, which carries the Diplomatic Bag; that cannot divert or wait anywhere for a passenger who wants to get something done. In brief, I've got to be able to whizz about and, right now, goodness knows what in. I couldn't spend time waiting for individual authorities. I want a Ferry Card to say I can fly any aircraft, any time, if I wish. Is that OK?'

'Sure! You write it, I'll sign it.'

I did the unbelievable, before he changed his mind. My card said: 'Wing Commander Dudgeon has permission to fly on his own authority any single-engined or multi-engined landplane, amphibian, seaplane or flying boat, and without prior check-out on type if he so wishes.' It was signed, 'Whitney W. Straight, Air Officer Commanding, Headquarters 216 Group.' This was all too good to be true!

Phyl was not overjoyed at my proposed move, nearly 2,000 miles westwards, without her. Early pregnancy didn't help either.

The next week or two were hard, but fascinating work. Whitney and I took a Boston — an American built twin-engined light bomber — and went to Algiers. He did the piloting and I navigated. We spent one night at Tripoli airfield, half-way, on the coast between the Bay of Sirte and the Gulf of Bomba. The airfield had been built by the Italians as a part of Mussolini's schemes for colonisation. It suffered, as all that area did, from a basic shortage of water, and only the shrubs and flowers that could eke out a thirsty existence were to be seen — zinnias and marigolds, with casuarina trees and some wattle. All were covered with a layer of ochre-coloured dust and looked miserable. There were long orchards of carefully planted citrus trees, nearly all dying for lack of cultivation since the start of the war. There was a cracked and empty swimming pool. It was a sad testimony to a simple and fundamentally honest man — Mussolini — who tried so hard to make his country and his people great, as his ancestors the Romans had been, 2,000 years earlier.

In the Mess we supped on desert rations with an old friend of Whitney's — Prince Bernhard of the Netherlands. He was going in the opposite direction to us, towards Cairo, flying in his American built B-25 Mitchell bomber, together with his enormously experienced pilot from KLM Airlines, Moll. Moll was to be killed three years later in a Dakota by a stupid ground-staff mistake. Somebody slipped a wooden control-lock in place, thereby jamming his flying controls solid, just before he took off.

The marvellous opera-singer Grace Moore died with him in the inevitable crash and explosion which resulted.

It was a double tragedy for me because, just a few months earlier, I had invented a special device for those aircraft. It cost virtually nothing and took only two hours to fit — and it would have made such a catastrophe impossible. The faceless 'they' in Headquarters Transport Command had rejected my idea as being unnecessary. 'Ensure' they said, 'that people are good enough to do their drills properly, and you will eliminate mistakes; good training is the proper answer'. Hah! In aviation there is, unfortunately, another potent tag; 'One cannot make an omelette without breaking eggs'. A better objective is to ensure that any broken eggs are unimportant ones. Poor Moll and poor Moore; both were virtuosos in their fields.

Next morning, bright and early, we flew westwards to go round the battle zones and then north. We climbed up over the 6,000-ft Saharan Atlas mountains, and the High Plateaux, to drop down again to Algiers. There we visited the Headquarters staff and got their agreement to our proposals.

The plan of campaign would be to set up our Ferry Control at Ras el Ma, in the neighbourhood of the city of Fez in French Morocco, where there had been a farm. Part of it had been quickly bulldozed into a gravel-strip runway by the US Construction Corps. Its name, Ras el Ma, meaning Head of the Waters, came from a stream that flowed close by. It was being run by a US formation which received squadrons and their aircraft, giving the aircrews some experience of flying in Africa before they went into battle. A mass of tents had been erected, of all shapes and sizes, and they said we could have as many more as we needed for offices, for sleeping accommodation, or whatever.

We would move in, as an RAF unit, lodging with and fed by our American hosts. Our ground personnel and ground equipment would be sent from England, but my ferry aircrews would be brought in as experienced Middle East men. I put up a scream like a factory whistle to be allowed to say what ground tradesmen I needed — fitters, riggers, electricians, radio mechanics, refuellers and so on. They assured us that the recently formed Transport Command in England knew all about these things, and would we kindly keep quiet. Whitney and I were not so sanguine, but we flew back to Cairo to manage our end of the project. Within hours some wag had dubbed me 'The Wizard of Fez'.

Ten days later I was co-pilot and navigator in a Hudson on its way from Cairo. Its captain was a well-respected Flying Officer Mackay. With us was my skeleton staff: an Ops Officer, Douglas Viney (the signals officer from Group HQ on temporary loan to set up a radio link till we could get telephones and teleprinters going), an Equipment chap called 'Tommy' Tucker to help with getting the stuff in from England, an Air Traffic Controller, an Engineer, and one or two others. Each had brought with him as much technical equipment as we could cram into the aircraft. We had permission to keep the aircraft at Ras el Ma for one week only, to nip about between Algiers and Casablanca, getting things started up. After that I was paddling my own canoe.

The weather was good and we followed the route taken to Algiers in the Boston two weeks earlier. From there, still in gin-clear weather, we flew along the cultivated Algerian countryside to the point where the 10,000-ft mountain range of the Middle Atlas swept through French-Morocco towards us. It came from our left, bent round in front and then ran away on our right to the coast on the edge of Spanish-Morocco, like a gigantic rocky horseshoe. I was gratified to note that my navigation was coming out splendidly because, dead ahead, there was a definite notch in the range; this would be the Taza Pass at around 5,000 feet.

As we approached the pass we could see, beyond it and cupped in the great hoop of mountains as in a great bath, a flat topped sea of cloud which stretched away as far as the eye could see. A light wind towards us drifted it over the nick of the pass, looking like a trickle of milk from the lip of a jug. To our left and to our right the mountains stuck up craggily through the sheet of cloud and far, far to the left-front were the eternal snows of the High Atlas. The visibility on top was superb and it was a glorious day.

I told the skipper, 'We've got about 65 miles to go beyond the pass. We don't try fiddling amongst the mountains underneath that muck. We can keep at this height, over the top of the clouds and then, as I've calculated pretty exactly our time for overhead Ras el Ma, we can see if there is any way of getting down. If not, we can fly back to Oran and wait for the cloud to clear.'

He agreed and we sailed along, enjoying the warm sunshine.

Long before the days of close control by radio and radar, a wise old pilot had said to me: 'Obviously, no one in his right mind comes down through a cloud if he believes that it has ground sticking up into it. However, if you do come down through clouds, even though you *know* they are empty, sooner or later you

We stopped at Khartoum on the route from West Africa to Egypt. A splendid statue had been erected to the memory of General Gordon who was assassinated there in 1885. It used to be floodlight on high days and holy days. It is now in England.

El Obeid did not only sell gum-arabic. It was a thriving market town. These sheep, brought in for sale, had been herded two thousand miles across the deserts from French West Africa! (Imperial War Museum)

A long-range Consolidated Liberator setting out across the ocean. Down by the retracted nose-wheel, on the right-hand side, was a small space in which Corporal Jason stowed away for 20 hours. It was a cold and cramped flight, but (for him) eminently worthwhile. (via The Aeroplane)

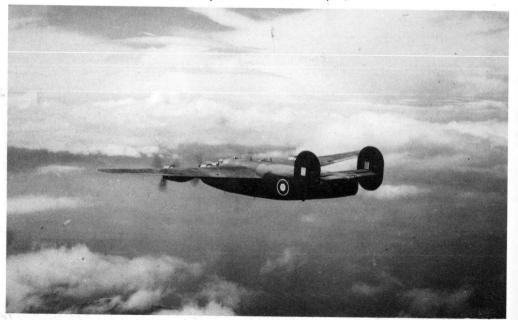

A town, village or individual in Britain could 'buy a Fighter' for the war effort, for £5,000 and the donor's name was painted on its side. That was how I came to have my own private Hurricane called Little Oakley because, as CO of a Ferry Control, I was allowed to delay any aircraft if it would improve speed of delivery for the remainder. Visiting my outlying staging airfields I carried small spares, mail and many other things needed to keep my organisation turning smoothly.

(Imperial War Museum)

Gib Ahoy! My team was in Morocco – in the American sector and a thousand miles from the battle zone. Sometimes I flew my Hurricane to Gibraltar for unobtainable British goods and spares, to be brought back in the empty ammunition tanks. After a hundred miles over water in a single-engined aircraft, 'The Rock' was a very welcome sight! (Imperial War Museum)

My view as I swung round The Rock in a left-hand circuit for landing. The airfield, hidden behind the rock, is on a little neck of land joining Gib to the mainland which can be seen in the background. A right-hand circuit, keeping the airfield in view, was not feasible because it would have meant flying over Spanish (neutral) territory. (Imperial War Museum)

The airfield at Gibraltar during 1943 – Spain on the right, The Rock on the left, aeroplanes parked everywhere, except on the runway in the middle. To increase the landing-run the strip has been built out into the harbour. Nonetheless, the waters lapping each end were very disconcerting. The dozens of aircraft that went off, one end or the other, were each a sorry tribute to a sharp attack of 'pilot's twitch'.

(Imperial War Museum)

will happen upon one with a hard centre — and you will be spread in smelly little bits all over the hillside. Indeed, flying into stuffed clouds has happened since cloud-flying began. Heed this, my Golden Rule: "If you are weathered out above cloud, NEVER descend unless you have a hole to come down through. Find a hole somewhere, or bail out if necessary." '

I had always followed his advice, religiously — and noted also that many aircraft continued to fly into mountains, every year.

Precisely on time I told Flying Officer Mackay that we should now be overhead Ras el Ma. He then proceeded to give me one of the biggest frights of my life.

'Super! Let's go down.'

'No fear!' I exclaimed. 'Just two miles north of the airfield there's a bloody great pimple of a hill sticking up a couple of thousand feet — and Fez, only five miles east, is more than a thousand feet above the countryside.'

'Hell's bells! Your navigation has been spot-on all the way. I trust it completely, and two miles elbow room is plenty. I'm going down now.'

I screamed at him, 'For Christ's sake, NO! You may trust me, but I don't. The wind I calculated earlier on the other side of those mountains could be different now and, having had no checks at all since we came over the Taza Pass, 65 miles back, a 2-mile error would easily be possible.'

'Don't fuss, Sir,' he said soothingly, 'you'll find it'll be OK. Here we go.'

And to my unmitigated horror he began to circle downwards.

I watched the altimeter with my eyes bugging out of my head. At 2,000 feet, the height of the top of the pimple, I looked ahead, waiting for the flash of dark ground which would precede by a fraction of a second the crash and fuel-explosion which would be the end of everything. Still Mackay went on down, circling steadily. My hands were clammy and my spine prickled. I was hoist with my own petard: '. . . anyone who tries in any way to influence the professional judgement of an aircraft captain may, and quite likely will, be tried and punished. The rank of the persuader and the rank of the skipper have no bearing on the matter whatsoever . . .' Should this apply if you are certain he is about to kill you? I held my peace, hardly daring to breathe, and sweated.

At 400 feet above the ground we first saw green fields below, through a gap in the clouds. Thank God, I thought, it is flat and not a hillside. Mackay went on circling. At 200 feet we broke out of the clouds into a drizzly, rain-soaked atmosphere. To the north I could see the lower shoulders of the 'pimple' sticking up into the murk. A brown, graded-gravel strip of earth, with puddles on it, was directly below us: Ras el Ma. I breathed again.

Dark olive-green tents were all along one edge of the strip. There was one small stone building and one even smaller wooden hut. Behind a screen, open to the skies above, I could see an unmistakable row of round holes cut in broad wooden planks. My eyebrows went up; open-air latrines, and a 24-seater! An old adage went across my mind: 'Any bloody fool can be uncomfortable in the field. It takes a clever chap to be comfortable.' What sort of hosts were content of a morning to sit all chums together, in the open, maybe in the rain, on a 24-holer? It made me wonder.

Mackay turned to me, grinning broadly, 'See, Sir! I told you it would be OK!'

He did another circuit and landed. When I got out my legs were still shaky. I turned to him and said: 'Very many thanks for flying me and my team over here from Cairo. It is much appreciated. I think you ought to know my opinion of your descent here. If you do that kind of thing in the future, with no radio aids to help you, as sure as God makes little apples you will die — however much confidence you may have in your navigator's accuracy. I think you are one of the biggest bloody-fool pilots I have ever met. You're with me for a week; if you display airmanship like that again I'll ground you for good — to save someone else's life. Quite clear?

'Now, I'll go and make my number with the local boss, to see if these Yanks have got a beer for us. Meanwhile, you get going with my chaps unloading the kit.'

Chapter 11
Ras el Ma

Lieutenant Colonel Schorn had his office in the small stone building. The walls were unplastered and the floor was packed earth, but it had an apparently weathertight window — and a door. In fact, it was luxurious, for a wartime set up. Various clerks were in the one other room, and everyone else in the camp had to make do with tents. Schorn came round his large, incongruous, leather-topped desk and shook my hand.

'Great to meet you er — Colonel — er — Cap — er . . . Gee, what's your grade?'

I admitted to being a Wing Commander, or Commander if that suited him better, but I added that, as my rank was equivalent to his own, if he preferred to go straight to first names that was OK by me.

He dropped the matter and said, 'Have a coffee, Commander?'

I studied him while he rather ostentatiously called a Sergeant in from next door and then waited till the man had come right round to the front of the desk before ordering two cups of coffee. Thin-faced, with a blue chin, big nose, horn-rimmed spectacles, he was probably five years older than me, and about five feet nine tall, of slight build. His nasal voice had a strong Mid-Western accent, I thought, but wasn't sure. Schorn's high-pitched, quick, giggling laugh lacked the inner assurance necessary for a good leader, in my judgement. A bit rank conscious perhaps? I would make it my business to get on with him, but somehow I didn't relish the prospect, much.

When the coffee arrived he said, 'You boys sure are fliers. We had a letter to expect you today, about 11.00. Having no radio aids here, with this weather, my operations staff weren't expecting you till tomorrow. Whambo! Eleven o'clock on the dot, your ship pops out of the overcast at zilch feet. My boys'd sure like to know the knack of it?'

'I'm sure they wouldn't.'

He was not a pilot and my reply left him a little bemused but I left it at that. I was not in the mood to tell him the facts, nor to make light of it, yet. Incidentally, the taste of chlorine in the coffee was dreadful!

He began to tell me about himself first, and then about his air-base afterwards. He had been a reservist before the Japanese attack on Pearl Harbor, and he was promptly called up. Having done a fair amount of training in the United States, he was given the rank of Half-Colonel and sent in a trooper across the Atlantic, with a sizeable bunch of NCOs and soldiers, to an unknown destination which turned out to be French-Morocco and, more precisely, Ras el Ma.

His 'base' (airfield, in my jargon) was used as a collecting point for dive-bomber squadrons which came over from the States by boat. As soon as their 'ships' (aircraft) had been re-assembled at Casablanca they came to this 'field' — landing ground — for a week or so, flying all around to get a feel for the African environment. And so on, one squadron after another. The base itself had been built by the Construction Corps, strictly according to the US manuals for tented camps on active service and, he said, it was a model of its kind. He would show me round shortly but, first, would I tell him what we were intending to do and, naturally, what we expected from him?

I outlined our plan briefly. We were going to receive aircraft — sorry, ships — from two sources. Some would be flown in direct from England if they had long enough range; others, short-range, would be assembled and flown in from Casablanca. All would be checked out here, crews briefed and then sent on to their destinations which were the forward squadrons; a number would go all the way to Egypt and India. We would handle all their technical aspects.

We hoped to have from him parking space for a lot of ships of all sizes, as well as supplies of fuel, oil, and food. Not forgetting things like sweets, cigarettes, soft and alcoholic drinks. Promptly he broke in, 'We can't give you liquor.'

I shrugged my shoulders (thinking 'that's bad news!') and went on to add that we would be needing tents for offices, ops room, air traffic control, radio — including a direction-finding station, — and tents to sleep in. We would prefer our own Messes and other domestic offices (I was thinking with some distaste of the 24-holer) if that were possible. As I said all this, it seemed an impossibly greedy approach, for an opening gambit. Still, if he knew his stuff, he would recognise that it was all fairly normal for a base camp.

Without thinking any of it through he said, 'Sure thing; no problems with any of that. Let's go out and I'll show you round. Then I'll send for my Supply-Sergeant and he'll give you what you want.'

We went out to his enormous American-made dark olive-coloured limousine with Staff-Sergeant driver.

The Colonel's camp was neatly laid out. All the tents, made of the same dark-green canvas, were closely side by side in neat geometric rows. In the middle were the domestic facilities so as to be near to all the sleeping tents. There was one large central kitchen tent, to cook for everybody and long dining tents in a star pattern, containing wooden trestle tables and benches with metal legs, led out all round.

The entire domestic area was very compact, with sleeping tents round the services in the middle. The pattern was obviously as laid down by a home based designer, who had not yet been under air-attack. Just one anti-personnel bomb near the middle would have caused utter havoc and the casualties would have been horrible.

We saw a row of 20 or 30 showers, behind a canvas screen and open to the skies. Water came from a well, specially dug 'and correctly chlorinated every day', he said proudly. Hence the coffee, I thought. The 24-seater deep-trench latrine served everybody. A small screen hid the end two thrones, for the more senior officers. In the drizzling rain the planks were wet and it looked, and smelt, singularly uninviting: constipation would be a popular disease. I wondered how I could get round this dreary prospect, later, if not by tomorrow morning. Running through my head was 'It takes a clever chap to be comfortable.'

The site for the complex, as a whole, had been well chosen. The main road from Fez to Meknes ran down one side, giving good vehicle access. The domestic camp was not too near the road. A 100-yard strip for all the technical services had been left between the living area and the east-west gravel runway. He said magnanimously, as we drew up in front of his office, 'You can have all the western half of the field. I'll send for the Supply-Sergeant and lend you a jeep.'

As the Supply-Sergeant was driving me away he asked curiously: 'Say — tell me what's your grade? Those three stripes on your arm — are you a sergeant?'

Very gently I said, 'Well, actually, no. I'm a Wing Commander, or in your services a Half-Colonel.'

'Well . . . Goddam!!'

The Staff-Sergeant had an easy sense of fun and we quickly got on friendly terms. He was much more of a realist than his CO, Schorn, whom he called 'Baldy' despite his superior's excellent head of crinkly hair. He cheerfully agreed to give me anything he could spare, but that was not a lot. Our own tents for the technical services — no problem, he could supply those and get them replaced. No separate sleeping tents for us — they had space amongst their own lines for my people to share. Own Mess tents, no; theirs were amply big enough to take us in. Own latrines and showers? No. Wheels? One jeep and one five-ton truck. And that, more or less, was it. One thing was perfectly clear: sharing living quarters would be no difficulty — but we could not *operate* without a lot more equipment than we had been offered — for example trucks, jeeps and refuellers.

I went back to see Colonel Schorn, in case he could use his rank to ease the supply problem higher up, but I got nowhere. 'If my Supply-Sergeant can't fix it, nobody can.'

I decided to send my equipment officer, Flight Lieutenant 'Tommy' Tucker, in the Hudson to Algiers. He could attack the supply organisation from the top of the tree, and might be successful. He was a good chiseller — which was why I had brought him — and if nothing else his shambling gait with caricature moustache and whiskers would leave them laughing and in a good humour for the future.

Next day the low cloud had gone. Visibility in the clear-washed air was marvellous. All round to the south and west were the ranges of the Atlas mountains, snow-topped in the far distance. Green fields stretched away to the foothills where pine and cedar forests took over. Fez stood on a rise some five miles to the east and at its edge one could see, through binoculars, the little hangars of a tiny landing-ground used by the French Air Force before the war. We learned that there was a camp manned by the French Foreign Legion in the town, and a hospital with an efficient French doctor and matron. No one on camp knew much about them 'because they only spoke French'. Fortunately, my French was fluent.

I met both the doctor and the CO of the Legion later. The latter was a Russian. He was Colonel Pravosoudovicz. I believe the spelling to be fairly accurate, but fortunately he told me, at once, that everybody called him 'Pravo'.

Tommy went off to Algiers and my little team got on with laying out our end of the airfield and putting up the technical tents. The Signals Officer Douglas Viney, a large man, to put it politely, hunched over his wireless set like a very large gnome. He tapped away at his morse-key, determined to be in touch with our Group, 2,000 miles away in Cairo, before the end of the day. I assured him that on his little out-of-date set it wouldn't be possible. That insult made him even more determined. I was delighted when, at the end of the day, he smugly came and invited me to send a message to our boss — direct, courtesy Viney.

Tommy came back in the evening. He hadn't got much, but we could have enough stuff to make our own Mess, to sleep and to eat — and start limited operations — in our own patch. More, we could disperse ourselves so that a stray bomber couldn't wipe us out completely, even though such a threat was pretty unlikely at the far end of the Mediterranean. I hoped that the people being sent from England would include cooks.

Placed between us and our hosts there was the little wooden hut I had seen from the air. The windows were broken, the doors were off their hinges and the roof had holes in it. There were three tiny rooms, the smallest being $6\frac{1}{2}$ x $4\frac{1}{2}$ feet — the exact size of an ordinary double bed — while the two larger ones were $6\frac{1}{2}$ feet square. It was full of junk — and possibilities, so I asked Schorn if we could have it. He was delighted: he apologised for not having had time in the past to take it down and burn it.

Tommy took the jeep to Fez and came back with an incredibly ancient and doddery French-speaking carpenter. We went all round the building carefully, discussing what needed to be done and he thought he could probably repair it, but for one grave problem. We asked what it was. *'Messieurs, je n'ai pas un clou.'* We clutched ourselves, rocking with laughter and agreeing with him, in English, to his total confusion that he probably 'hadn't got a clue'; nevertheless we found him the nails he wanted.

Within a few days I was sleeping on my camp-bed in the smallest room. We had tried valiantly to make the other rooms into offices, but a six-foot square does not hold a desk, an officer on a chair, and one other person for him to talk to; at least, not with becoming dignity. My offer of dormitory space for four officers' camp-beds was accepted with alacrity. In the field, a roof, *any* roof, is unbounded luxury. It was our first step towards becoming comfortable.

A couple of hundred yards beyond the end of the runway a

charming little stream wound its way across the fields to join the main river at the bottom of the valley. This was the 'Waters', the 'Ma' of Ras el Ma. At just about its nearest point it spurted over a small rocky ledge and the baby waterfall had, over the ages, created a beautiful pool beneath it, before the stream continued its meanderings down the valley.

This patch of water deserved a rather better name than pool, even though it didn't quite merit 'lake'. It was about 50 yards across and 8 to 10 feet deep. Rushes and osiers grew on its edges and, on the top of the ledge were some bushes and willow trees. The water was crystal clear, reflecting the blue sky and white clouds above. It was absolutely ideal for bathing, compared with using the fairly primitive ablution facilities in the camp. After our day's hard physical labour, putting up the camp, we had a swim in the limpid water. This was followed by a wash with soap — near the outflow from the lake of course, so as not to sully the water . . . it was pure bliss.

It was not long before Baldy sent a message, asking me to drop by at my convenience. The inevitable chlorinated coffee was produced. Would I be so kind as to stop my men bathing in the pool off the end of the base? He had put it 'off limits'. Why? Shortly after their arrival he had been asked to permit bathing but, following the stream for a couple of miles up towards its source they had found some cows, in a field, through which the stream passed. The stream was therefore polluted and he had forbidden swimming to avoid the risk of disease. Would I kindly do the same because his medical facilities were limited. Also, another of his problems would be inter-unit jealousies. I thought his veto a bit far-fetched, but naturally I agreed, he was, after all, the official Base Commander.

Although only a few days had passed, I had got to know some of his officers quite well. I discreetly sounded out their views on 'no swimming' and theirs coincided with my own. I therefore conjured up a little plan, or plot. Five days later I went to Baldy and gave him an analyst's report from the French hospital in Fez. They had tested my two samples of water, A and B. One was very much purer, healthier and more palatable than the other. I suggested to Colonel Schorn that he might consider rescinding his 'no swimming' rule, for everybody. The water from the pool (with my chaps swimming in it) was substantially cleaner than the water from his well with which we made our coffee. Indeed, I was prepared to let my fellows swim and accept entire responsibility for any diseases which might result from doing so. I looked at him quizzically across his desk. He grinned, and agreed. He too was getting more comfortable.

Towards the end of the week my NCOs and airmen arrived from England by boat at Casablanca. It was a near disaster. Somebody supposedly would have made out a list of men needed, by rank and trade. Well — they had been able to provide some, but those needed most had been the scarcest. We wanted mechanics, fitters, riggers, refuellers; people to mend the important bits and get the aircraft on their way. Mostly, they weren't there. We had droves of radar mechanics and operators (we had no radar) instrument repairers (we had no clean workshops) and office-workers. The list of 'wrong providing' seemed endless. At least, we had some cooks, even if we had not yet acquired stoves. One simple example: we had the people to work a refuelling-tanker, as on a main-base airfield, but we had no tanker; our fuel came from 60-gallon drums and had to be pumped up into the aircraft by hand. Obviously, you do the best you can. Radar operators, clerks and cooks were going to refuel aircraft and (carefully watched) wield screwdrivers on simple tasks. It wasn't difficult; they would soon learn. In fact, of course, the clerks and their colleagues simply loved leaving a typewriter to work on a real live aircraft. We knew that it was against RAF rules and regulations to misuse tradesmen. So what? We would meet that one when somebody complained. There was a war on.

In the evenings we, the half-dozen officers, congregated in my bedroom. It gave us the opportunity to talk over the day's work, to plan the morrow, to drink quantities of Algerian red wine (rough as a bear's bum and closely allied to red ink, but fairly alcoholic) and to play poker. As may be imagined, if you consider six people on a double bed, there was not a great deal of room to spare. Four men could sit on the 2-feet wide camp-bed — just — and two on suitcases either end of the remaining space, with one small suitcase between for a bar or card table. Of course, after several litres of wine, no one minded much. However, it jarred with me that Tommy, the finder and purchaser of wine, used to stack the dead-men just outside the door as the bottles were emptied. I said to him after a day or two: 'Tommy, you've got to get me some kind of a box to hide all those empty bottles. It looks bad, outside my door in the mornings.'

'Oh, surely not, Sir. No one thinks you drink *all* those bottles of wine *every* night!'

'I don't care,' I persisted. 'They've got to be in a box!'

'Of course, Sir. Whatever you say. It shall be done.'

That evening I was a bit late getting back to my room and there, lying against the wall parallel to my bed and leaving about a foot between, was a simple poor-man's wooden coffin. Tommmy gestured towards it proudly, giving his enormous moustache a tweak, 'That, Sir, is the drink-box.'

'I won't sleep with a coffin!'

'Oh, but Sir!' Tommy countered. Be reasonable! It was the cheapest box I could find; much cheaper than a cupboard or a case. It is exactly the right height to take bottles standing up; empties at one end and full ones the other. And it makes an ideal seat to sit on for playing poker. Unless we go overboard on the booze, there's even some space in the middle for your clothes. Finally, what more appropriate place could there be to hide the dead-men? Surely? . . . Sir?'

I am forced to admit that, having got over the initial shock, the coffin proved, as Tommy said, to be ideal. Every now and then someone would cry 'All change!' and those sitting on the coffin would move obediently. Backsides lifted. Lid up. Bottle out. Dead-man in. Lid down. Sit down again . . . and, without a moment's hiccup in the discourse.

We did not only talk shop and play poker. Our sessions over a pleasurable drink used to become a forum in which family gossip from home was exchanged. It was a relaxing break from the routine of flying and the humdrum of off-duty time, with no cinemas, no civilian radio, no television, no library — indeed, nothing but what we could make for ourselves. We almost became one family.

My senior administrator was a Squadron Leader Hogg — 'Hoggy'. He had been quite a big noise in Courtauld's before the war, and was going back there just as soon as hostilities ceased. He was blessed with a much-loved five-year-old son, Ian, at some school in England. We knew a lot about the boy because of the enchanting weekly letters from Mrs Hoggy. The day that the mail arrived, when Hoggy came in for his drink, almost the first remark would be: 'Come on Hoggy! What scallywaggery has Young Hoggy been up to this week?'

Whether or not she knew that Hoggy always passed on her family gems to us, her weekly letters were a wonderful breath of home. One day, little Ian was a member of a relay team at his school sports. He was the last to run and he was handed the baton with a stupendous lead over the other teams. He was far younger than the others and his little legs pitter-pattered unsteadily across the grass while the bigger children overhauled him like thunder. Young Hoggy just scraped home first by the thickness of his sweatshirt and was bursting with pride as Mrs Hoggy hugged and kissed him. At the finish of the sports, the prizes were presented by the Bishop — Bishop of Where, Mrs Hoggy did not divulge. He gave the lad his prize — a Savings Certificate! Young Hoggy looked at the oblong of paper in the prelate's hand and shook his head. He announced precisely, 'I don't want that thing; I want a Meccano set.'

The matron and all the teachers did their best to transmit to little Ian that you accepted any prize with good grace, even if you didn't like it, and particularly if it was offered by a Bishop. Young Hoggy dug his toes in firmly and reinforced his refusal with extremely noisy tears heard for miles around. Amongst the sobs could be heard the opinion, repeated crescendo, '. . . and what's more, my Daddy would *want* me to have a Meccano set!'

No amount of cajoling or threats would get him to take the certificate. At last the assembled school staff took the piece of paper, apologising extravagantly and assuring the Bishop that Ian would eventually be very grateful, when he had calmed down.

Some time later a parcel arrived for Young Ian, from the Bishop personally. In it was a Meccano set. How or where, the very reverend gentleman had found a Meccano set in wartime, no one knew; they were completely unobtainable by any normal mortal. In the parcel was a handwritten note. It said, 'God helps those who help themselves'.

Back in Africa, the RAF assembly unit at Casablanca began turning out fighters for the Algerian front. The unit was under enormous pressures and its achievements were astounding: aeroplanes were pouring out and the load was on us, too, to get them moved away. Mostly, they were Spitfires, with a few Hurricanes thrown in.

The British fighters were readily acknowledged to be vastly superior over short ranges, quicker and more agile than the Kittihawks and Tomahawks built in the United States. Inevitably, the American pilots wanted Spitfires.

The twin-fuselage, twin-engined Lockheed Lightnings were pretty good, but they had one unfortunate characteristic. If the machine was damaged in combat and the pilot had to climb out to use his parachute, the tailplane between the fuselages frequently sliced the man into two pieces as it came by — unless he was abnormally lucky. Those pilots, understandably, also wanted Spitfires.

The Airacobra had a marvellous conception, but a bestial birth. Its engine, with all that weight, was in its middle so that it could turn and twist very quickly. The propeller at the front was driven by a long shaft which went between the pilot's legs. If the machine stopped suddenly (such as in an accident), the engine behind, and the propeller in front, and the shaft through his legs, were apt to do very unpleasant things to the pilot. Those pilots wanted anything but Airacobras — preferably Spitfires. We gave all the Airacobras to the Russians for the Eastern Front, and that is probably why they do not fully trust us yet.

In fact, everyone was screaming for Spitfires. It was enormously gratifying to we Brits that all our allies wanted to fly British.

In those days in England, if you or a village collected £5,000 and gave it to the Government, you were allowed to claim you had bought a Hurricane, Spitfire or whatever. A four-engined bomber, such as a Stirling, cost £25,000. The aircraft was called after the donor — a person, a village, town or district — and their name was painted on it.

There is a village, somewhere in England which, I am sure, was deeply proud of its war effort. Perhaps they visualised 'their' fighter flashing through the skies, shooting down Germans right, left and centre. Perhaps they saw it as the favourite machine of some splendid and highly decorated fighter ace. Not so. The Hurricane bearing the proud name of 'Little Oakley' was delayed indefinitely from reaching the front, by me. To compensate for this ignominy I promoted her at once, by removing the 'Little'.

'Oakley' became my exclusive and private Pegasus — the winged steed of Greek mythology which could rise instantly to the heavens with its rider. I believe Oakley's war-effort was worth all of several Germans shot down. At any rate, as far as I was concerned that Hurricane deserved to carry my callsign. The signals staff issued me with a callsign for my radio-transmissions. Something dull, like 'Tripod'.

'Not so', I cried. 'I want something more exciting like Brigand, or Bandit, or Pirate!'

'That,' said the signallers, 'you may not have. Callsigns are chosen and issued by London. There is a big security plan designed to keep the enemy confused. No other callsigns may be used.'

'Bollocks', I thought to myself.

Remembering that someone back in Cairo had suggested I would be The Wizard of Fez, it was no problem to select my own callsign, and to hell with the signals staff. That is why Oakley and I responded only and for ever to the cognomen 'Wizard One'.

We were getting Beauforts in from England, that had flown most of the night. Crews were almost straight from school, were plumb ignorant and, as they had no automatic pilot and no co-pilot, they arrived very, very tired. Also, finding themselves at extreme range with hardly any fuel left, they did not become complacent. The first sight of a new country, and a new airfield with no hangars and no tarmac runways, added to their confusion. One morning, before we were alive to all these problems ourselves, we saw a Beaufort nearing the airfield. He then turned away. He next turned again, circling and flying around some ten miles to the west, always within view. We could not get an answer from him on the radio. Finally, after about half an hour he ran out of fuel, and crashed. Luckily, the crew were only slightly hurt and we could get the pilot's astonishing story. He was sure the airfield, which he understood was disguised as a farm, would be over there beneath him, if only he could pick it out from its obviously stupendous wartime camouflage.

From that moment onwards Oakley was parked on the edge of the airstrip, opposite my hut and my tent-office — a distance of about 20 yards. It was prepared for flight each morning, and kept always full of fuel, and my parachute and helmet lived in it. This meant that, if necessary, I could leap into it, start it and be airborne in roughly 90 seconds. The strategy paid off within a week.

This time it was a Wellington, which had much more fuel than a Beaufort. It sailed serenely overhead (we saw it go, in utter disbelief) and no yelling on the radio produced any effect. Next, Air Traffic Control saw it circling Fez; its crew was obviously looking at the little grass French airfield which, in no possible way, was big enough for a Wellington to land on without crashing. I was alerted, and sprinted for Oakley.

She fired at the first touch of the starter. I glanced back and nothing was coming in to land behind me. Ahead, if I shot off diagonally across the strip, I was clear also. I judged that the end justified the means. Breaking all flying rules and courtesies, I pushed the throttle wide open to race down the runway. A couple of Americans on foot, whom I had seen and avoided by a few yards, ran away, turned and shook their fists at me. Wheels tucked up I went lickety split for Fez.

When I got there, he had wheels and flaps down and was on his final approach to land. I curved in and cut across his bows, waggling my wings like a mad thing. I saw him swerve in alarm and then his propellers speeded up as he pulled away, retracting his wheels and flaps as he did so. I breathed a deep sigh of relief and, when he had got to a reasonable height again, came into position, slightly ahead and to his left (the pilot's side) waggling my wings to say 'follow me'. He paid not the slightest attention, did a new circuit and began to do the same again. I could almost hear him saying 'These bloody idiot fighter-boys. They don't know what discipline is. They can't fly properly themselves, and they're a menace to everybody else.'

I cut him off a second time and then came as close to him as I dared — some 15 feet off his left wingtip and slightly in front. The pilot put his finger to his temple and twisted it to say 'Madman!' I slid the hood back and beckoned to him with my arm, waggling my wings and turning gently away, beckoning all the time. Luckily, he was flying slowly so the slipstream didn't dislocate my shoulder, as is only too easy with an arm outside at speed. At last the penny dropped. He fell in behind, to formate on me as we went home. Over the airfield I lowered wheels and flaps and he came in to land behind me.

Strolling over to see him when he had parked, he turned out to be a Pilot Officer. After about eight to ten hours through the night, on his first trip abroad, getting lost, and an encounter with a lunatic in a Hurricane, he must have been very stressed, tired — and frightened. I admitted to having been the Hurricane pilot, and said I was glad to have been able to stop him crashing at Fez, which was far too small for landing a Wellington. He just gave me a dirty look, saying, 'You know, what you did was bloody dangerous . . . SIR!' and turned on his heel. He was quite right. It really had been bloody dangerous, for me too.

Baldy, prompted by his flying staff, also read me the riot-act for dangerous flying on his base. Oh well, I thought, we saved a valuable aircraft from crashing, and you can't win 'em all!

Chapter 12
Oakley

A month or so after we arrived, two things happened, one developing from the other. Setting the pace, the assembly plant in Casablanca was breaking all records. This meant that we were working like demons, getting aircraft down the ferry pipeline for all we were worth, doing overtime as though we had nothing else in hand. Even our hosts said that our pilots were 'flying their asses off'. The first circumstance of the two was that we were twisting and turning, every which-way, to try to improve our effectiveness. The second element was a chance remark by one of our transatlantic colleagues, which went something like 'Jee-zus; I could sure do with a scartch!'

It might have been Tommy who married the two — it was very much his style — or the plan may have brewed itself up on the coffin during a boozy poker game. It began with a rhetorical statement: 'Gosh, how I'd like the equipment and the wheels that these Yanks have!' It was followed by someone saying 'I'd bet we could get them, if we had whisky.' I looked at Tommy. Tommy looked at me. He said one word, 'Gibraltar'.

I nodded. Being a British outfit, the Gib mob got whisky with their rations, and duty free at that. All we had to do was devise a means of diverting some of their liquid flow. First move — to pay a courtesy call on The Rock.

Next morning I strapped myself into Oakley and started up. Politely, gently and carefully I taxied to the far end of the strip and asked permission to take off. The staccato crackle from the stub exhausts was always exciting and in a few moments she had lifted and, wheels up flaps up, I was turning on course. My general direction was west, to avoid flying over Spanish-Morocco to the north and thereby causing a diplomatic incident. I was specially interested in keeping a low profile, in making no stir, provoking no questions. However, I saw no good reason to avoid the slight dog-leg which would take me over the ruins of the old

Carthaginian city of Volubilis and its sister-city Moulay Idriss. Why not? An old guidebook picked up in Fez had whetted my appetite and given me a little knowledge. They were almost on my way.

I came first to Moulay Idriss. The Sultan Idriss, or Moulay Idriss, was a descendant of the Prophet Mohammed's son-in-law. The Moulay had founded the city which bears his name 1,200 years ago in the 7th century AD, when living in Oualili, known to the Romans as Volubilis. It is built on the sides of a small, steep volcanic mound and is still inhabited. I flew round it at a decorous height, admiring its tiny rectangular roofs looking like a grey and green mosaic. The narrow roads were wide enough for animals and pedestrians — no carts or cars. Near the base of the hill was a very fine and striking mosque-like building. The courtyard was shining white, almost certainly marble. However, its layout was a slight puzzle for I had never before seen a mosque with a square roof and what appeared to be a square minaret; all others had been domed and round. The roof was a brilliant green. I could not see whether the colour came from green tiles, or the verdigris of weathered copper. I did not go near it, in deference to the feelings of believers.

Volubilis was about five miles further west and air-inspection of a ruined city is superb. You can see it all laid out beneath you like a full sized plan of the town — roads, alleyways, doors, courtyards are all exposed to an interested airborne sightseer. You can see beautiful mosaic tiled floors, if you are low enough. Considering that it had been built by the Carthaginians more than 2,000 years earlier in the 2nd century BC, and that it was occupied by the Romans for 300 years before the appearance of Islam, the town seemed to have a singular cohesion in the sense of letting me appreciate what it had once been. As expected there were no roofs, but rooms had been spacious. The meeting halls and market places, flanked by wide roads, must have been splendid in their time. On its eastern side, pointing towards Rome and Carthage, 1,500 miles away, there were the remains of what had once been a very imposing city gate. Its pillars were high and the space between suggested a magnificent access road. The trace of the road from the gate to the centre of the town was clearly visible. The entire place seemed to be totally deserted except for a couple of Moroccans with some goats. After a couple of very low circuits to pick out details, I pointed Oakley at Rabat-Sale.

Rabat Sale with its French built airfield was a few miles from the spot where the boundary between French- and Spanish-Morocco met the Atlantic Ocean. It was 15 minutes to fly, over the fields and the little brown villages, before we got there. Its buildings made a complete contrast to the local dwellings — squat, square and sharply white in the sunshine. The foaming breakers on the yellow sandy beach, edged by palm trees, looked very inviting. I swung Oakley round the corner of the two countries, turning right, northwards to follow the Spanish-Moroccan coastline, three miles out to sea and therefore over international waters. I also pulled up to 3,000ft; it was prudent, in a single-engined aircraft, to stay within gliding distance of land for as long as one could — in case the engine failed. If you ditched a Hurricane, or a Spitfire, the radiators under the wings caught the water and pulled the whole shooting-match straight down into the deeps. You had to be a damned lucky submariner to get out of the machine at all. Ejector-seats did not yet exist.

The weather was so clear that it made the brown and green Rif mountains behind Tangier look as though they were cut from cardboard and used as a backdrop.

Forty-five minutes from Rabat we were approaching that enormous lump of rock, jutting up in unlikely fashion from the sea. There is a little neck of land between it and Spain, and across that neck a tarmac runway had been laid. Many machines had run off the far end, from approaching too fast; therefore the runway had been built up and stretched some hundreds of yards into the bay of Algeciras, to provide more than usual space in which to pull up safely. Nevertheless, what one had to cope with struck me as faintly ludicrous and made me smile inside my mask. If you came in too slowly on the approach, you fell into the Mediterranean. If you came in too fast, you ran into the Atlantic. If you made a nonsense of your approach and wanted another go — there wasn't room to turn back — you had to go right round the rock and begin again. If your engine quit on the way round, you ditched. There was no beach to land on. Yes; Gibraltar was quite an oddity, until you were used to it.

Coming in to land was a horrible feeling which I had never experienced before. Oakley got lower and slower on the approach, the waves just under her, ever closer and reaching up to grab us in. There was an almost irrestible urge to put on just a *little* more speed, to be *quite* certain she wouldn't fall out of the sky and into the sea . . . But to do so, you knew in your heart, boded disaster — as you would run into the sea at the far end.

Straight ahead, Algeciras on the other side of the bay looked ridiculously close.

Having parked and asked for refuelling, I walked slowly along the high street of Gib, admiring the shops and climbing gently up the hill to the Officers Mess. I went to the bar for a glass of sherry — Jerez, the real stuff — before lunch. I enquired politely if the officer in charge of the bar might be around or, if not, would he be in for lunch? He was in and came across for a chat. I bought him a drink before explaining that we, in French-Morocco, were living on an American base. We were fed healthily and in ample quantity, but we were deprived of drink except such as we could buy in Fez. Moroccan red wine was good for writing red figures on overdrawn bank statements, or night-flying in log books — but not much else. Could we, if it was not inconvenient to them, purchase some stocks of hard liquor and, in particular my favourite tipple — whisky, perhaps?

The bar-officer was charming but firm. Their whisky was rationed at so many tots per man per month, and there was very little to spare. If, however, I would like to purchase *one* bottle only, he could doubtless fix it for me — provided I kept the transaction strictly to myself. I nodded gravely; of course, it would never be allowed to leak and, as I was in Morocco, how could it?

His concession was not much, but it was a foot in the door. We went in to lunch. Over our food I drew the conversation round to their standard of messing. Was it good? Was it dull? Could they make it more interesting with items from across the Spanish frontier? Doubtless he would appreciate my keenness to get ideas as to how they improved their meals, as we might be able to do the same for ourselves? He suggested that if I wished to discuss food, he could get the messing officer to join us. I assured him wholeheartedly that it would be kind, if he could be bothered?

I explained to the messing officer that the sheer volume of the American food we got was astronomic. However, it all came from tins. We got Spam by the ton, followed by apple-pie-and-ice-cream till you could weep. There were jams and marmalade to go with our bacon and sausages. My listeners shuddered. These were accompanied by biscuits, spread with a margarine specially formulated not to melt in hot weather; so much so in fact, its melting point was above the temperature inside your stomach. The messing officer shuddered again. We had a lively discussion and he tried to be helpful with suggestions. Very few of his ideas were of use to us for, mostly, they depended on a supply of British rations which we did not have. He did, however, mention that he could have done a great deal more if he had eggs. I made no enquiries as to why he could not get adequate eggs from Spain. I preferred not to know.

I let the conversation ride idly for another five to ten minutes. At last it seemed a propitious moment for me to be struck suddenly by a chance idea. Might we not find some way to help each other? For example, I could get eggs in Fez market. Small ones, admittedly, from the scrawny Berber chickens not much bigger than Bantam fowls, but excellent nonetheless. I could fly them over in my Hurribird, which was sans guns and sans ammunition. Naturally I would not be so mercenary and sordid as to seek payment in cash; however, it might be possible for the messing officer, using his messing subscriptions, to make a deal with the bar officer . . . and I might be reimbursed in whisky? How was that as a stroke of genius? I tried to look as innocent as I could.

The two looked at each other with raised eyebrows, nodded their mutual agreement, and then turned back instantly to me, saying in chorus: 'How many eggs for how much whisky?'

'Well . . . I'm not too sure . . . not much, really,' I replied. 'Let's see first how many eggs I can get . . . and how much eggs cost me.'

We made a date for lunch, four days hence. A small sum of money changed hands for the whisky and I almost danced down Gibraltar high street, clutching my bottle happily to my breast, under my uniform. Oakley and I came back the way we had gone, except that we went straight home from Rabat.

After landing, I sought Tommy out. 'Tommy, listen to me; the faceless 'they' would probably judge my intentions to be technically illegal. I do not care, but I intend to keep our actions as close to the boundary of the law as I can get them. This is our first bottle, and I paid for it with my own money. We are going to make it work for our unit, as hard as it possibly can. Don't you ever forget it. If I find you (or anyone else) creaming off something for themselves, personally, the skies are going to fall upon your head. I promise that. Got it quite clear?'

Tommy nodded.

'Now, get this. They have whisky; they want eggs. Between the two lie the ammunition-pans of a Hurribuggy. You will take this bottle to Fez tomorrow and see how many eggs you can turn it into. Then bring them back to me, packed suitably to preserve them during an hour's flight. I shall need them three days hence. I have no idea at all what you may achieve, but do your best.'

Tommy went off, carrying my bottle carefully. He subsequently found that he had to surmount some difficulties. Scotch whisky was rarer than diamonds in Morocco at that stage of the war; no market stall-holder wanted, or could conceivably pay for, one whole bottle; nor, for that matter, could he supply enough eggs to make a deal at the going rate. Tommy, therefore, sold the bottle in the money changers' area of the *souk,* where there was cash. He then went to the food area, where there were eggs, and bought them as and where he could, till the money ran out.

He came back from Fez market in his jeep with almost a thousand eggs. I came back from Gibraltar in Oakley with a dozen bottles of whisky. Tommy then departed for Casablanca with eleven bottles to see what he could do with the US Supply services. One bottle was carefully stowed in the coffin for future bartering, when the need arose.

At the start, Tommy was far too lavish. He had no idea how passionately the American servicemen wanted their 'scartch'. He gave the entire 11 bottles to one man! Admittedly, he came back with two jeeps, five ten-ton trucks, an aircrew bus, a full set of kitchen equipment (stoves, pots, pans, crockery, glass, cutlery) and two powerful radio sets. But he had as yet no conception of his majestic potential for barter. I asked him if he had signed a receipt for them? A most pained expression crossed his face. He explained, as to an idiot infant, that some moronic French-Moroccan crane driver in the Casablanca docks had carelessly allowed some miscellaneous equipment to fall upon the quayside whilst unloading. It had been damaged beyond economic repair. No one wanted to buy the bits. So it had to be disposed of in the local rubbish dump.

A new day had dawned for us. One bottle for a thousand eggs to go out — 12 bottles back — 11 bottles for bartering — one bottle for 1,000 eggs to go out . . . we had hit on the secret of perpetual motion. It was not long before we were, without question, the best-equipped unit technically and the best-fed unit in the entire North African theatre. Goodbye to the drums and pumps for refuelling; we had a couple of 2,000-gallon articulated refuelling tankers, costing two bottles each. We had headquarters-style chairs and tables in each of the messes — three bottles the job-lot. The mechanics had superb toolkits and Operations had good plotting boards. We began cutting Baldy and his base in on the deal — he was learning by leaps and bounds how to be comfortable in the field.

The best thing, however, was the food. United States troopers arrived in the port of Casablanca with up to 2,000 servicemen per ship. To allow for unforeseen problems they had enough food aboard to take them all back, all the way to Virginia, on the other side of the Atlantic, without landing. And they dined like kings. Once the troops had disembarked, they had no use for the food and saw no point, really, in taking it back again. Tommy would appear with his great caricature RAF moustache sticking out sideways, capitalising ingenuously on how hard it was for we poor, starving, rationed Brits in the field; how short of goodies we were and could we for — say, a bottle of scotch — take one or two things back in that ten-ton truck he just happened to be driving? Into it would go deep-frozen best capon chickens, Virginia smoked hams, fresh-run salmon, sides of pork, soused herrings, undried vegetables, fresh bread . . . you name it. It was just a question of not taking more fresh food than the entire base — Baldy's fellows included — could eat before it went bad. American forces were being supplied by three ships to every two for the British, so there was plently of scope for initiative. The only things we would have liked and couldn't get, were refrigerators. Beyond that, the sky was the limit.

I never asked direct questions on the other side of the water, but I gathered that our eggs were supplying the Army and the Navy Messes as well. We all had a nice little thing going, with everyone gaining and being happier than they were before. Oakley was flipping back and forth and soon could almost find her way to Gibraltar without my help.

The whole shebang came to a sudden halt in a most unfortunate and unforeseen manner. A very senior officer — I heard it was an Admiral — went to his bar and, as a change from pink gins, asked for a whisky and soda. The barman blanched. He stammered some lame excuse that the expected rations had not yet come in, but it was too late. Admirals do not wait upon the chance arrival of bottles. A double pink gin with an outline of how he got his couple of eggs, fried for breakfast daily, was not enough to pacify him.

When I next landed at Gibraltar I was told of the disaster before even setting foot on the tarmac — let alone climbing the hill to put my head into a noose. They refuelled Oakley at speed and I went home. It was jolly decent of them, really, to save my skin. I never went near Gib again, and we returned to feeding like the common herd.

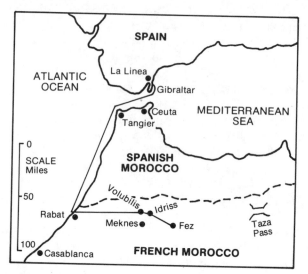

The saddest thing happened when, long after my departure, Ras el Ma closed down and the British left. They tried to give back the hundreds of thousands of pounds worth of American equipment. No member of the United States forces would accept it . . . it was not on the books . . . it never had been, so far as anyone could tell . . . it didn't exist. If someone could show it had existed, someone also would be hanged, drawn and quartered for jiggery-pokery. It was all left where it stood, to rust or be cannibalised by the Moroccans. What local man could make good use of a 2,000-gallon articulated refuelling-tanker?

Chapter 13
Don't Look Now!

One evening, long, long after the days of Ras el Ma, Phyl and I accepted a social invitation from the Sergeants' Mess. During the evening, Phyl in conversation with a Sergeant's wife said: 'D'you know that my husband always feels he would be a better CO if he had come up through the ranks, instead of coming in directly through Cranwell. He thinks he would understand *your* husband's problems better.'

The lady looked almost shocked and answered, at once, 'Oh dear me no, no, no! Not a bit of it. My husband loves working for your husband. Officers who have come through the ranks think they know all the wrinkles and spend their time trying to catch people out. *Your* husband knows perfectly well where and when to look, but especially he knows when *not* to look!'

Often, newly qualified aircrews do not accept how much still has to be learned in the dangerous school of practical experience. Youngsters come out of training full of beans and different youths need different handling. It needs a certain perspicacity of judgement to give them their heads as far as possible, while holding them back just sufficiently to preserve their lives without cracking their spirit. One can easily let things go too far in this business of when, and when not, to see. In war, men can easily get killed before they have appreciated their ignorance. Opinions on the techniques of being a senior officer can, and frequently do, differ.

The squadrons in transit, for which Colonel Schorn provided housekeeping, were full of virile young men, raring to get at the war and convinced they knew everything about ops that there was to know, after their intensive training in the United States. They flew dive-bomber North American Mustangs — a tough and manoeuvrable aircraft, solidly built and very fast at low level. Naturally these young pilots flung them about the sky with gay abandon and, unfortunately as Baldy was not a pilot, he had grave problems in maintaining flying discipline. His pilots would flash across the airfield when they returned from an exercise, pulling up into a glorious cartwheeling turn before coming in to land. It was very pretty to watch, but incredibly dangerous when performed by a green pilot at a busy working base.

I put up with it for quite a while, as long as it was done in clear weather with Air Traffic Control permission first, on the pretext of a 'dummy attack on an enemy airfield'. However, when his boys started whizzing across the bows of my tired young chaps arriving from England in the early morning, and short of fuel to boot, it was time to get ATC to draw the line. I paid a visit to Colonel Schorn, in his office.

Baldy ordered two coffees. I explained my purpose as politely but as firmly as I could. I feared seriously that one of these exuberant dive-bomber lads would either hit one of my aircraft and kill the entire crew, as well as himself, or he could easily frighten a stressed, uncertain, and weary new-boy so that he crashed. I did not wish to be difficult, but I must insist on proper airfield discipline, for us both. This 'buzzing the field' or 'beating the place up' — to use both our flying languages for clarity — had got to stop before disaster struck.

Schorn sat for a few moments, trying to arrange his thoughts and put some sentences together, on a subject with which he was familiar only at second hand. Then we both heard it coming; the crescendo roar of an Allison 12-cylinder 1,150 horsepower engine with stub-exhausts, approaching at full throttle and very low down. The noise grew in intensity and higher in pitch till it was tearing our ears out. As one man we both decided that the aircraft was surely going to hit the building and flung ourselves on the floor in the split second before it screamed overhead. The coffee cups clattered; his ashtray jumped up and down; a couple of pencils rolled on to the floor; the building shook so that the windows and door rattled and it felt as if the ramshackle place was coming down about our ears.

As the noise of the Mustang died while he pulled away in his towering chandelle, I picked myself up and dusted off my uniform. Baldy was doing the same. I was so angry I could hardly speak. I could only say, as I looked him straight in the eye, *'That's what I mean!'*

Ever so deliberately he raised his hands to the level of his shoulders, palms upwards and fingers spread outwards as he shrugged his shoulders and raised his eyebrows in the classic gesture of impotence. A sad expression came over his face as he slowly shook his head and, seeking any crumb of support from me, whispered: 'Boys *will* be boys!'

The time for me not to look was long past, and moral support from my side was not forthcoming. My message must have got home for, after that, things were much quieter on the Mustang front.

Baldy was not alone in his problems. The American army arrived in North Africa to face the German Afrika Corps, one of the finest fighting formations that has ever existed. After an early battle in Tunisia, when the Germans had knocked seven kinds of stuffing from them, it was one of their own Generals — General Omar Nelson Bradley — who coined the classic phrase: 'Goddam it! They're like bananas — most are green, some are yellow, and they smell.'

But they learned fast, much faster than we did.

One day, an Army Air Corps Major was sitting down at lunch with me, in the Mess at Casablanca. His hair was perfectly cut and brushed, he had a small trimmed moustache, his uniform was beautifully pressed and immaculate from head to toe, his shoes were polished till they gleamed, and he had medals. He was the CO of an American fighter squadron which was carving for itself a most impressive record at the front. Into the Mess came a bunch of recently disembarked pilots — lieutenants. Some were not properly shaved. Some had flying helmets hung round their necks by the headphone cables. Most were wearing sheepskin flying jackets. They had revolvers in belt-holsters. They wore flying boots into one of which was tucked a map and into the other a knife. They were being 'tough' as they swaggered across the dining room towards one of the tables, even though the nearest enemy was 1,000 miles away to the east.

The Major carefully put down his fork, wiped his lips on the paper napkin, rose, crossed the room and spoke to them quietly: 'Excuse me a moment please. Tell me, gentlemen, do I take it that you are pilots who have just returned from the front, and left your ships outside the door?'

In some embarrassment they stood up and faced this stony senior officer of their own service. Someone said something to the effect of 'Not exactly, Sir. We are on our way there.'

The Major answered crisply, without raising his voice by one decibel, 'Then wait till you have been there before you come into a Mess dressed like that. And when you've been there, you'll have learned not to do it. I have come from the front, today. Get out of this room instantly, and don't come back till you are decently dressed, as officers. Move! All the lot of you!'

He returned to his seat, apologised to me for their grossness and we continued our conversation as though there had been no break in it.

We Brits had gone through exactly the same sort of thing at the beginning of the war. Somebody wrote a song of which the words were 'We'll hang out our washing on the Siegfried Line . . .' We had not yet learned the toughness of our opponents, and all to soon the mangled remnants of our forces in Europe were evacuated from Dunkirk.

My embryo navigator on the Takoradi route a year previously had been sensible and I had been lucky. He had not resisted his lessons.

I had another lucky experience at Ras el Ma. Wireless operators 'talk' to each other with a series of dots and dashes — dit-dah, dah-dah-dit, dah-dit-dit, and so on. A run of the mill W/Op's hand squirts blips over the ether at about five to six every second. This conveys, say, 20 words a minute. The dots and dashes have no tone or change of key; there is one sound only and it is going, or it isn't. There is an interesting thing about it, incomprehensible to non-experts: each W/Op puts into this monotonic buzzing his own personal characteristics — each one has his own 'fist'. To another morse operator his 'fist' is as recognisable as his voice on the telephone.

For example, when a certain German unit was moved from Norway to Denmark, our snoop-watch listeners in England knew it at once. They could identify the 'fist' of that unit's German W/Op, tapping away on his morse-key at his new location. In that particular case the 'fist' was a disadvantage for our enemy. On the other hand, recognising a 'fist' can sometimes be helpful.

The weather on this particular day was, to put it bluntly, piss-poor. ATC had called me down to their tent — which did duty as an airfield control tower — because a pilot found himself in grave difficulties. He was up there, in cloud and the ceiling was very low; he had come from England; he must be dead tired; he had not enough fuel to go anywhere else. He was, obviously, very inexperienced.

Our only landing aid was a manually operated direction-finder, because talk-you-down radar had not been invented. It was located beyond the end of the runway. This meant that when the airborne W/Op made a transmission, the D/F operator on the ground could reply, in morse code, giving him the direction it had come from. After that, the hapless pilot was on his own, for we could give him no better help.

This unfortunate fellow had made three shots at coming down, and failed each time to be at the right height, at the right distance, in line with the runway, and pointing towards it — all four things at the same time. He had had to abandon each attempt and make another effort. Things were looking very fraught indeed *and* he was short of fuel.

The ATC officer told me that he had spoken to the D/F Op who was doing his best. The difficulty appeared to lie in the time spent between each new bearing sent from the ground; it took too long. The pilot kept finding he had got too far out of position by the time his next piece of information reached him; then, he could not get his aircraft back on line quickly enough to cancel out the error he had made. I asked to talk to the D/F Op, on the telephone.

The poor man was harassed almost to the point of incoherence. For three-quarters of an hour he had been taking bearings and passing them back, at full pressure and doing his utmost. He was only too well aware what depended upon his efforts. It was clear that he too was not very experienced. I spoke quietly and tried to calm him down for, if he cracked up, the man up there with his crew would most probably die. A mistake by this man on the ground would lead them into a fatal crash.

Having got him calmed down, between the calls from the aircraft and his replies, I asked him if he had any ideas on how we could help them better. He hesitated, and then it came pouring out: 'Oh, Sir, that W/Op up there was trained with me. I know his fist perfectly and he has recognised mine. We were real friends all through our course. Then we were split up — him aircrew and me ground trade. It is taking us so long to follow all the procedures that we've been told we must never change; the bearings go to him so slowly; if we could do it ourselves, talk with each other, I'm sure we could get bearings sent fast enough for the pilot to make a proper approach and . . .'

He tailed off, but I could almost see the look of anguish in his face. I took the chance he offered: 'Right. Throw the book and its rules away. "Talk" to him. Give him a stream of bearings as best you can. You go ahead and get your friend down, on to the ground, safely. Answer any questions yourself unless you want to ask me something, on this telephone, which I'll hold to my ear so I am right beside you. It's all yours.'

For us in ATC the next ten minutes were pure hell. Somewhere up there was a deathly tired boy-pilot, talking to his boy-W/Op, whose fist was in the headphones of his boy-chum in the D/F truck beneath him. At all costs we must not interrupt them as they threw the specialist procedures aside. At the same time we had no way of guessing whether all was coming out right or if, by 'not looking', I had signed their death-warrants. My stomach was knotted as I feared for the awful phrase coming from the truck: 'He's stopped sending, Sir, and I can't raise him . . .' Ten minutes was forever.

Suddenly the controller beside me said, sharply, 'I hear him. He's coming from the right direction.'

That was followed by 'His engines sound normal. My God! There he is! He's out of cloud. He's made it! He only needs a small S-turn before his touchdown.'

The telephone at my ear said with a slight break in the voice: 'My friend tells me he's signing off, Sir. The pilot says its OK now.'

I answered, and I meant every word, 'Well done; marvellous news — and my most sincerest thanks for saving them. It was a great piece of luck that you recognised his fist.'

Chapter 14
Forced Landing

In gin-clear weather a Wellington bomber flew sedately overhead in a straight line from the west (which was perfectly correct) towards the east (which was not). We weren't unduly disturbed because these green crews were capable of anything, but they usually sorted themselves out soon enough when they reached Fez and the rising ground beyond. Also, 'Wimpeys' normally had a respectable margin of fuel to take care of a few errors of that sort . . . but not this crew's errors.

Fifty miles further on they had to climb to over 5,000 feet to clear the Taza Pass, with the Middle Atlas rising to nearly 8,000 feet on either side. Having negotiated that hurdle, and cast around for quite a while on the wrong side of the mountains, beyond the pass, the crew decided they were both irrevocably lost and short of fuel. They were right on both counts.

The greenhorns did not, as one might have expected, trickle down to the flat plains at the foot of the mountains and find somewhere there to land; they picked a fairly small sloping field on the side of a narrow wooded valley, 5,000 feet above sea-level. They then performed their one sensible action; they landed uphill. The field was a bit too short for the hill to stop them completely but, apart from swinging violently at the far end to avoid running into the trees, collapsing one undercarriage leg sideways, busting one propeller, shock-loading one engine and damaging a wingtip, they themselves all emerged unscathed. They then walked down a track along the valley in the balmy sunshine till they were found and, in due course, brought in to me. They were astounded that I did not congratulate them on their lucky escape.

Having disposed of the idiot crew, the next question was what could we do about the aircraft? I walked over to Oakley, climbed in, took off and set course for Taza and the field beyond. I would go and have a look.

How or why that solitary grassy field came to be there I could not fathom. Up at its top end the Wellington leaned drunkenly on one wingtip. There were forests all round, no access roads and no apparent signs of habitation or cultivation. There were a few tracks, possibly suitable for a jeep, or a small truck, with four-wheel drive and low-ratio gears. An aircraft-transporter was totally out of the question. One thing was crystal clear; she would never come out on the ground. Indeed, with the collapsed wheel, and her drunken attitude, she looked as if she would never fly out either. She seemed destined to rot on the hillside, being gradually pilfered by Moroccans till nothing remained but the engines, the spars and other pieces too heavy for them to carry away.

I have always been mechanically minded by nature and training. A nice machine gives me solid pleasure. On the other hand waste of machinery, made with skill and pride, gives me something akin to physical pain. Could she be flown out, if lightened, I wondered? After all, she *had* been landed with comparatively little damage. How long was that field? How many yards were there between its edge and the far side of the valley? Could a stripped Wimpey running downhill, in the thinner air at 5,000 feet, accelerate enough to get the necessary speed to be coaxed off the ground, and to stay off? Then, could it dive to pick up adequate speed for the turn needed to avoid hitting the opposite hillside?

The best thing was to do a simulated take-off. I could keep speeds low and, as Oakley was a fighter, I should be able to climb smartly out of trouble if necessary. First, I flew slowly, parallel to the side of the valley and turned, flaps extended, to pass low over the Wellington and pointing across the field. The downslope was steeper than it had appeared to be; good. I flew low over the trees at the far end and nosed down the hill. I kept the same throttle setting to see how much more speed the slope would give me before making a gentle turn away. It wasn't much; in fact I scared myself. The far side of the valley approached much too quickly; I had to shove the throttle wide open to climb out of danger. I did another run, with slightly less loss of height and pointing more nearly along the valley. This let me fly further before I was compelled to turn. Even though I still had to pull round in what would have been a sharpish turn for a bomber, it did give me a safer and possible escape route. But, for certain, a study on the ground was essential before committing myself.

Several things were done over the next few days. The engineers and I went up there in a jeep. They reckoned that, if they made a shear-legs, or makeshift crane, from tree trunks they could lift the aircraft up. So far as they could tell without actually getting it up, they believed they could repair the collapsed undercarriage-leg, and make it strong enough to take off and land on. But there was no question of making it retract: it would be re-built down, and stay down. The damage to the rest of the aircraft appeared to be slight, and patchable. A new propeller could be fitted and, as the undercarriage collapse had occurred at very low speed, significant damage to the engine was unlikely. So, on the face of it, the aircraft probably could be made flyable. Next, might it get up and fly from there?

I paced out the possible take-off runs. The longest — about 600 yards and with the steepest slope — faced most uncomfortably across the valley and slap at the hillside opposite. Also, there was some soft earth under the grass at the far end; she might sink in a bit and slow down. On the other hand, the run which had the hardest earth and which pointed in the most favourable direction (along the escape route between the hillsides) was the shortest — barely 400 yards long — and had practically no favourable slope. I compromised between the two, 500 yards, with a respectable down slope. Then (assuming that she didn't just plunge off the end into the valley with a lot of flames and black smoke) there should be an acceptable turn away to safety. I marked trees to be felled at the far end, to give me a 50-yard gap to fly through.

It took the engineers a week to do their work. It was slow going as all their tools and every bit of equipment had to go up in the jeep, which ferried down everything it could be persuaded to carry. That included all the radio, radar, guns, bombsights, navigator's and W/Op's desks and instruments — even the Elsan loo. But a lot of the big stuff had to be left.

Every fuel tank was checked and completely drained, except for the two tanks in the engine nacelles. They were normally used only for start-up and before changing to main tanks, but they held just enough for me to fly home, plus a few minutes over — and nothing extra for mistakes. She was going to be as light as humanly possible, but everything would have to go right the first, and only, time.

Meanwhile, at base, as I could never ask nor authorise anyone else to do the job, I set about learning how Wellingtons were flown. I enlisted the help of a Flying Officer who had arrived from England on the delivery flow. He was a little man, dark, brown-eyed and with a scruffy moustache. He had an irritating habit of puffing out his cheeks while thinking. I thought he was rather pleased, at first, to be treated by a senior officer as the fount of all knowledge. He soon changed his opinion, thinking from my questions that I was closely related to the village idiot.

Why, he obviously thought, did this chap have to go through the take off and landing drills dozens of times? (Puff puff.) Why did I choose to ask pointless questions on such unlikely things as stalling when at high altitudes? When flying slowly, did one or the other wing drop, and would the controls bring it up? (Puff puff.) And then, any wrinkles about getting off the ground quickly; did one fiddle with the flaps? And at what moment? (Puff puff.) What the hell did I think I was going to do?

To most of these esoteric questions, of vital interest to me, I got no answers because he did not know them. He looked as though he longed to tap his forehead and shake his head in sorrow. I dared not give him the real reasons behind my curiosity in case he felt, in all decency, that he had to produce *some* kind of reply — I knew that an 'invented' answer might kill me. I wanted, and think I got, the sum total of his factual knowledge. For his part he wanted, and didn't get, any reasons why the authorities selected such a moron to be a Wing Commander.

Finally, after the 'plumbers' were ready and had given me the thumbs-up, the next day by good luck was perfect. A thin layer of high clouds overhead would keep off the sun, so that the air stayed cool to give maximum lift from the wings and shove from the propellers; there was very little wind to come swirling through the valley and make things even trickier than they were already.

My planned flight would take a little under three-quarters of an hour. That would leave only about ten minutes' worth of fuel in hand when I got home, mainly because of the very full ground testing for the engines — particularly the one whose prop had been bent. However, if anything was going to fall apart, far better that it happened when stationary on that field, rather than just as I got to the end of the take-off run with only a valley full of trees underneath me. Then, after the run-up, would come the take-off with both engines slurping fuel for every ounce of power I could extract. Frankly, the whole thing started to look like a hairy bit of lunacy, from beginning to end.

I entreated the controller at Ras el Ma to watch keenly for a westbound Wimpey with its wheels hanging down, and making no radio calls; he was to give it a green light and keep other

My Wellington bomber, wheels and flaps safely locked down, comes in to land after having been flown out of a tiny field, high up the Atlas Mountains.

(via The Aeroplane)

If you are stranded in England, and want to get to Africa, take an aircraft – any aircraft will do. Even one you have never flown before such as this type of Wellington, fitted with radar for submarine-hunting and nicknamed the 'Stickleback Wimpey'. You can always find out how it flies, doing an air-test round the coasts of Britain before you leave . . . or so one hopes! (Imperial War Museum)

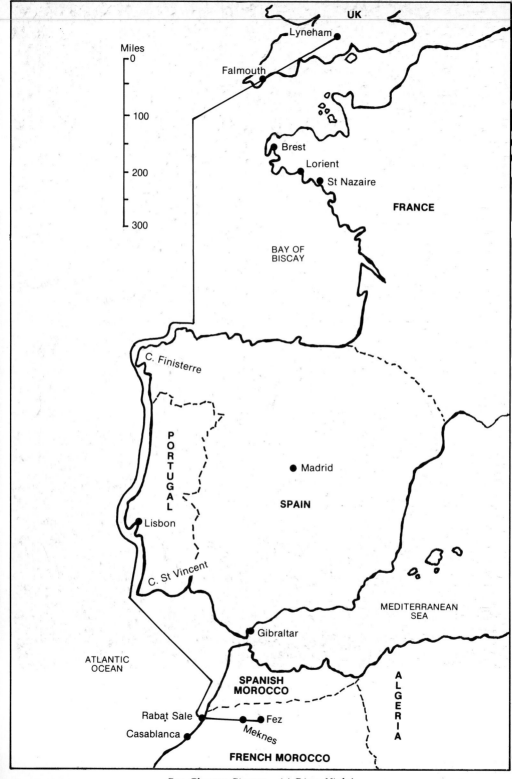

See Chapter Sixteen – 'A Dirty Night'.

A Wellington ploughs its lonely way through the night. It might well have been me, except that on my flight there was no moon and it was as dark and unfriendly as the insides of a hibernating bear. (via The Aeroplane)

A Bristol Beaufighter was a powerful and very quiet machine. It was best known to the wartime public, via the media, by its German nickname 'The Whispering Death'. There were several other non-fighter variations, such as a Coastal one for attacking shipping. I found them a joy to fly, except that the power of those two great engines could induce some unintentional and startling manoeuvres for the uninitiated. (via The Aeroplane)

Standing in the shade under the wing of his York, H.M. the King is watched by General Eisenhower and Admiral Cunningham as he greets and shakes hands with Air Marshal Tedder. On left is Mr. McMillan, British Resident Minister.

(Imperial War Museum)

aircraft out of its way, for it was in any case coming straight in for the touchdown, and no doubts about it. Then I was off on my 100-mile jeep run into the mountains.

The Wimp had already been pushed back so that the tail was in the bushes and almost touching the trees behind it, and had its nose pointing straight at the gap in the trees at the far end. I had been given every foot of take-off run that could be found. Would it be enough ? Only the next few minutes would tell.

Having carefully done all the pre-flight checks exactly as instructed by my puffing Flying Officer, I ran both engines up to maximum power. They seemed to have weathered their stay on a mountainside with no adverse effects. The instruments and the magnetos all gave results well within the limits passed on to me. My only alarm was seeing and feeling how much the airframe shook and wriggled; it felt as if it were made of hard rubber instead of steel and aluminium, and was about to fall into little pieces at any minute. This, Puffer had assured me, was normal. I waved away the chocks, feeling an absolute idiot. A nervous idiot at that.

Slowly and steadily I opened the two throttles together, holding her against full brakes. As the wheels began to slip on the grass I let the brakes off and shoved the throttles hard against their forward stops. If I had been able to push them through the dashboard and out the other side, I'd have done it. The control spectacles were held right forward, so as to get the tail-wheel up quickly to what (I hoped) would be the position for maximum acceleration.

We seemed to be gathering speed OK I supposed, but of course I had no previous experience on a Wellington by which I could judge it. Even so, we felt to be trundling down the hill far too slowly for my comfort. I didn't look at the airspeed indicator; it could only frighten me still more and do me no good. She was going to make it — or she wasn't, and there was damn-all I could do about it now, as we had passed the point of no-return in the first ten seconds.

Bumbling down that slope, I concentrated on the worst thing ahead of me at that instant — the ridiculously small gap between the trees at the far end. The felling measurements I had given made a space of ten yards from each wingtip. But, as I got faster and closer, it was looking smaller and smaller. Surely they must have skimped the job? Why, oh why hadn't they cut it wider while they were at it? Thirty yards before the field's end I put down 15 degrees of flap and eased back on the spectacles. She came off the ground, but only just, and she felt horribly sloppy. Miraculously she went cleanly through the too-small hole in the trees. Those detestable nervous prickles were running up and down my spine.

She was only just above stalling speed. I realised I had been holding my breath. I eased the nose down all I dared and went very gingerly into my turn. We came scarily close to the trees on the opposite hillside but, by that time, speed was building up and it was becoming possible to hold my height. All was well.

As I straightened up, pointing down the valley, I rocked my wings as a 'thank you' to the engineers behind me. I set the throttles to give a steady climb at the speed for flying with wheels extended and only climbed high enough to skim over the Taza Pass. That done, it was nose down thankfully and throttles back for the 50-mile drift downwards towards home.

The lads in airfield control must have had the binoculars out, for a green Verey flare arched into the sky when I was still a good ten miles away.

Next day I was on the telephone to the CO of the maintenance and repair unit. He was just a disembodied voice whose owner I had not met. He said, doubtfully, 'Well . . . we can't leave it on your airfield. You'll have to arrange to fly it in here, wheels down all the way. Our trouble is that, although we are assembling Spits and Hurries, we haven't got the equipment and jigs for a full-scale checkout on a Wimp. And, after a crash landing, we can't let it go to a squadron without that. Of course, we can cannibalise quite a bit from what your chaps haven't removed already, but on the whole it will just be scrapped.'

At Ras el Ma we debated for a while whether we could find a good use for a surplus Wellington bomber as our private executive and transport aircraft. Unhappily, proper repair of the collapsed undercarriage leg was beyond our capacity. Regretfully we flew her in, wheels down, to the maintenance unit to be junked.

My plumbers had done stalwart and innovative work, high on a mountainside, so that recovery of an extra bomber for the war effort might be possible. Understandably, they made some fairly acid remarks about this disappointing ending to their efforts, and to my first solo on the type.

Chapter 15
A Lanc

It was becoming positively irritating, the way those reinforcement aircraft from Britain were losing themselves. It seemed that hardly a day went by without some expensive and valuable aircraft fetching up, less or more bent, against some hillside, on a field or in a swamp. What made it frustrating to us was that our strip, with its hundred or so dark-green tents, was beside a major road, from Meknes to Fez. Meknes was a town of fair size with white-washed buildings which stood out well from the air — and the weather was mostly good. Fez was more beige in colour seen from the air, but it too was no tiny hamlet. Between those two was the main road. There was nothing like Ras el Ma for 300 miles in any direction. Surely, if all else failed, they could creep along the road, peering down on its right side till they saw tents, trucks and parked aeroplanes?

How on earth were they getting lost, even if they were tired, jumpy tyros on their first trip abroad? I decided to nip over to England for a few days to improve the pre-departure briefing that they were being given by the chaps at the British end. This was easier said than done. There was no reverse-ferry flow to England, upon which I could hitch a lift; all the passenger aircraft were bulging at the seams with high-priced-helps having far greater claims for priority than I could muster from my little backwater.

For some days I honestly thought that my only hope would be to hitch 2,000 miles in the wrong direction — all the way to Cairo. There I could get the boss to lean on the movements staff for one of the rare passenger seats to England. Luck, however, was on my side. Manna came to me from the skies, in the form of a four-engined Lancaster bomber.

In 1943, Air Marshal 'Bomber' Harris was sending his aircraft from England, across France, over the Alps to attack factories and other targets in Italy. Having completed the raid on Italy the bombers went on, to land in North Africa. After a rest for a day or so, they refuelled, loaded more bombs and did the same thing in the opposite direction, ending up back at their British base.

Naturally, they were never routed the shortest way — across neutral Switzerland — for that would have been diplomatically unacceptable and the Swiss would have been at liberty to shoot them down. When some crews discovered that the Swiss were far less dangerous marksmen than their German counterparts in France, quite a number 'happened' to get off their briefed track and on to the line of lesser danger. Even today, if you find an old Swiss who has a clear memory of the war, he will tell you that it was dead easy to distinguish between the noises made by German and by British aircraft. He might add, with a twinkle in his eye, '. . . of course we always fired at every aeroplane violating our airspace — but we made sure we aimed at least one mile behind the British machines.'

My good fortune was that one of the Lancasters had something go wrong with its innards and, by the time that was sorted out a few days later, the skipper had acquired a nasty go of the 'flu, the trots, or some similar affliction. Anyway, the return-raid programme had been missed and Bomber Command wanted their machine back. I got my sticky little claws on to it for a reverse-ferry. It was lucky that the crew also wanted to get home, and were prepared to bet their lives on me doing it for them.

The plan was to take off when the very last glow in the western sky was turning from orange and red to the deep blue of night, just before the velvety black of full darkness. We would then run round Cape St Vincent with its memories of Admiral Nelson, up northwards, keeping further and further away from the Portuguese and Spanish coasts. Thus we would be far, far out when we crossed the Bay of Biscay, well clear of the German long-range, radar-equipped, Ju88 night fighters. Finally, some eight hours later, as dawn came up, we would run in along Cornwall, Devon and Somerset to drop in for the required Customs clearance at Lyneham in Wiltshire.

Taken all round, it promised to be a very pleasant and gentlemanly trip for first acquaintance with a new aircraft. The crew were all very experienced and would prevent me making any ridiculous errors. I spent most of the afternoon in the cockpit with the flight-engineer, going through all taps, knobs, levers, switches and dials. He was a mine of information and gave me great confidence.

The only thing I remained nervous about was the level of the pilot's seat above the ground. I was sitting far higher above the ground than in any other aircraft I had flown before. The prospect of flying that great machine down to a landing, judging (entirely by eye) the height of the wheels above the ground, when they were far below and behind me . . . it was an alarming . thought. If we came too low the tyres would strike the ground, making the beast bound into the air like a kangaroo — if it wasn't broken. Or, come in too high and she falls out of your hands, kerTHUMP! — and you may break it that way. The flight-engineer assured me that it was enormously strong, and not to worry. I wondered.

The wind was coming from the Atlantic Ocean 100 miles to our west. So, lined up for take-off, we were facing the last traces of the golden sunset. With no bomb load she should not be too sluggish for the new boy, even though we carried full fuel tanks for safety's sake. Naturally, our Ras el Ma gravel strip was too elementary for an electric flare-path; its edges were marked by neatly designed little oil-lamps of American origin. They were hollow metal balls, about the size of a man's fist, weighted at the bottom so they wouldn't fall over, like those little plastic dolls that no child can make lie down. The ball was filled with paraffin and the wick flamed on its top. The tiny pin-pricks of yellow light stretched far away into the distance.

Slowly and steadily the four throttles went forward with the flight-engineer's hand following them. As the tail came up he set the precise power required. I glanced at the air-speed indicator to see the speed rising. Soon I could feel the aircraft beginning to bounce gently on the undulating surface, almost as though it was dancing. At first little bounces, settling back quickly on to the ground, then longer hops as the wings gained more and more lift until I could safely and comfortably hold her clear, settling into a steady, gentle climb.

I kept quite a lot of surplus speed in hand while the feel of my unaccustomed steed became familiar. I was astonished that this big aircraft was so light and delicate on the controls. Admittedly, with all that weight she did not respond smartly like a fighter or a medium-bomber, but she was positive, crisp and a joy to fly.

Another pleasure was to have an experienced and fully competent navigator. Having had one or two nasty experiences with green navigators, I always tried to keep a running mental check on the navigation — just in case. Even in cloud, or over the trackless sea, a rough estimate was possible in one's head. This man was an ace; he helped me no end. Although he was working out his courses and tracks precisely on the charts, he was also feeding me enough — but not too much — information so that I too could keep in the picture. His little forecasts were most reassuring, showing that he truly was on top of his job. He would say, 'In 11 minutes if you look half-right, and the weather is clear, you will see some lights. That will be the town of Sagres and the flashing white light to its left will be the lighthouse of Cape St Vincent.'

Then, sure enough, in 11 minutes there it was. It is a great relief, when flying with a strange crew, not to wonder just how much of the whole task is on your own shoulders, and how much they have really got in hand. I hoped they felt equally happy about me.

Half an hour before midnight, as the flight-engineer was producing a mug of delicious sweet coffee, the W/Op came forwards with a piece of paper which he slipped under a 'bulldog' spring clip fixed to the instrument panel. Laconically, he said 'Recalled', and went back to his desk. I took it down and read it. It instructed us to go back to Ras el Ma. I asked, 'Where did it come from — and why?'

The W/Op was a man of few words. He said, 'England — God knows, and he won't split.'

Somehow, this made no sense. What valid reasons could England have for sending such an instruction? There was no telephone or radio link between them and Ras el Ma, so it could not have started at my end. I decided to go on while I thought it out — we had ample fuel. I asked the W/Op to get the reason for recall.

After ten minutes the operator came back with one word — 'Weather'.

I discussed this with the navigator. First, how much fuel would we have on arrival at the far end? Enough, he said, to get to John o'Groats, or to the Shetlands if pushed. Second, could he visualise a weather situation, at that time of year, where we should be unable to find one single airfield suitable for my first landing, anywhere in the entire British Isles? No, he could not. Third, how did he feel about going back to North Africa, either for me to make my first landing in a Lancaster, at night, on a little gravel strip between two rows of flickering paraffin lamps, or to float around till dawn and do it then? He thought that either idea was lousy. We told the W/Op to send a one word message — 'Proceeding'.

It was roughly 15 minutes before the answer came back with the instruction 'Mandatory recall to departure airfield. Acknowledge and confirm.' This was a direct order, and there were no two ways of looking at it. However, mandatory or not, my job as skipper was to judge the various advantages and evils before making my own decision. I thought it out carefully, by myself. It must be something to do with the weather in the south of England — our first destination. It couldn't be for the whole British Isles and they might not, necessarily, know that we had ample fuel to go anywhere that attracted us with the entire country to choose from.

For myself, in no circumstances was I going to make my first landing in this big unknown beastie in the dark, except as a last life-saving resort — and certainly not down on a gravel strip without proper lighting. However, just flying around for eight hours, doing nothing but wait for dawn, was hardly any more attractive; becoming tired, bored and therefore inefficient, was a thoroughly poor idea.

Weighing it up, going back was a poor idea for sure; going on sounded better — but it was a judgement and not a certainty. I knew that the crew were watching keenly and waiting to see what this unknown pilot would say. I told the W/Op: 'Send an answer to the mandatory-recall message, saying simply "Negative". Then close down, go off the air, have an equipment failure, do whatever you choose, but don't answer anything else. Listen out, but keep total radio silence, please. Explanations won't do any good to them, and who knows that the Germans won't pick up your transmissions and send out the nasties to find us.'

The crew were delighted.

The W/Op thoroughly enjoyed the result. They promptly called him back and, getting no answer, switched to 'broadcasting' a stream of orders to return. Then they made a general broadcast, to anyone who happened to be listening, as a request to pass on our orders, if they happened to hear us anywhere 'on the air'. We just listened — and nobody heard a thing from us.

By degrees, and by hearing instructions to other aircraft through the night, we worked it all out. We were scheduled to go to Lyneham. At the time we were due, they were expecting a dirty great storm — rain, thunder, lightning, clouds, turbulence, hail . . . you name it, the lot. Later to our surprise, knowing the unreliability of weather forecasts, when we got there it was absolutely correct. As we sailed past we could see clearly, right there, the makings of a tremendous line-squall. The cloud tops were very high but, by selecting the least horrible bit of cloud, we got across to the other side.

The navigator introduced me to a bit of equipment, completely unknown to me then, called 'Gee'. This is an electronic box which produces sundry lines on a screen like a miniature television set. When you know what those lines mean, they tell you where you are. And that, moreover, to within a few yards.

We had decided to go to Waddington, the bomber's own base. The navigator assured me that the controllers had told him the weather there was excellent with no low cloud. Using Gee, he could bring me below cloud in perfect safety. This to me was thoroughly frightening. I remembered Mackay and our Hudson over Ras el Ma with crystal clarity. Still, if they believed I could do it without killing them, and on a first solo, presumably it was possible.

The crew were only too pleased to be going straight home with no landing on the way. Soon the navigator said, 'Start letting down, now.'

I was painfully aware that stuffed clouds collected about 30 to 40 aircraft a year, invariably with totally fatal results. Here I was, being told to go down, and that it would be safe. I was sweating with anxiety. It was horrible. I wanted beyond everything to find a hole in the clouds and go down through that, using my eyeballs. And I said so.

'No, no! I promise you it will be perfectly all right and we will come out just short of Lincoln.'

I hated it, every second of it. But he was right. To this day I can see, in my mind's eye, the view through the windscreen as we popped out of the cloud base at about 2,000 feet. There, sticking up as clearly as a victory signal, were the twin towers of Lincoln Cathedral.

Had I known what Gee can be made to do, I should have been even less happy when it was bringing me down neatly in front of the cathedral on that morning. Some years later it was demonstrated to me that Gee was *not* the panacea for all navigation problems as the navigator then led me to believe. Mistakes could be made.

Gee had a sort of miniature TV screen with lines on it. The lines had figures allotted to them and, if you chose a wrong figure, the Gee would lead you infallibly to the wrong place. We were engaged on exercises with that electronic black-box, practising night bombing with practice bombs from jet bombers. We pilots took it in turns, piloting on one trip and changing to bomb-aiming on the next. One of my colleagues got his numbers mixed up by one figure; 76 instead of 75, or something like that. His black-box aiming point then, instead of being on an observed bombing range, out in The Wash, off Ely, became The Prussian Queen public house near the coast.

Shortly after closing time the customers were preparing to leave in good order. One of the girls decided to pay a call on 'The Ladies' before she went. Relieved, she was standing up, adjusting her clothing, when a nine-pound smoke-bomb went down the pan and exploded. She did not wait to adjust her dress further, but emerged without delay, yelling bloody murder and calling upon the constabulary to arrest the landlord for having such a defective loo on his premises.

After landing at Waddington, being a well-trained transport-pilot, I ingenuously asked about clearing Customs and Immigration. They looked at me in horror, dismay and anguish as they cried: 'Customs! This is an *operational* station! We don't have any Customs around here. We'll help you get off our station, towards where you want to go, quickly and before you trigger off any bad habits!'

Probably, that was the real reason for the mandatory recall signal; an explanatory sentence probably would have said 'Go back to Morocco (using over four tons of fuel in the whole process, not counting the risks) because you will not be able to clear Customs in the morning, at Lyneham. And the rules say you should do so.'

I went on my way, as requested by Waddington, so I never learned the truth.

Chapter 16
A Dirty Night

There is indeed truth in the much-quoted saying, 'God looks after drunks, children and fools'. My Maker has cared for me under all three headings from time to time, and in several other categories as well. If that were not enough for Him, He has had to cope when, hidden under the mantle of discipline, my behaviour has been distorted by other fools.

I had a very dusty reception in England. My dialogue with the briefers and their senior bosses, for which I had just flown 1,500 miles, was completely frustrating. It was made clear in no uncertain terms that my job was not concerned with despatching from the UK. The despatchers professed to know much more about preparing youngsters for their arrival by air in Morocco than we did. My pleas, that we who saw them arrive often had to pick up the pieces, cut no ice. All my suggestions, including having them check up by map-reading and road-following, had been brushed aside as old hat in the modern day and age of 1943. Our shortages and inabilities fell on deaf ears. I was, more or less, invited to go back to Morocco and pull my finger out, thus improving my radio and air traffic control facilities so that we could suck them in better.

All those bland refusals made me feel frustrated beyond credence. I was hopping mad, thinking 'How in hell can I?' We were a non-operational unit, 1,000 miles behind the front line and the priorities of fighting RAF units, in the American zone and 2,000 miles from my own HQ to boot. What we had achieved, in the way of *materiel* begged, borrowed and stolen from the Americans, represented a minor miracle. Why blandly ask us to do still more without taking account of the impossibilities? And while green crews were at deadly risk? My reaction was precipitate and immature.

It was in a bad mood that I asked for an aircraft, any aircraft, to ferry out to Ras el Ma. They offered me a Wellington XIII, equipped for coastal duties. In my irritation, and general know-all attitude at that moment of my career, I did not mention that my total knowledge of the type was from some chit-chat with a flying officer (puff-puff), followed by 45 minutes in the air — and that was in a machine for night-bombing. Moreover, I had never even retracted the wheels. Not exactly ideal preparation for a long ferry trip, even if my general RAF flying experience was considerable.

Drunks, children and fools? When I went back to Ras el Ma from England at the age of 27 I was not a child, I was not drunk and my seniors did not get me into trouble directly. I was a plumb, dumb, copper-bottomed idiot for letting frustration and chauvinism impair my professional judgement. I accepted to fly the Wellington back to Morocco. Of such foolishness serious accidents are made. But that was just the beginning; from there on my errors were legion.

In the headquarters, where I had been so frustrated and achieved so little, we put the proposed flight together. The machine was equipped with some very fancy radar for finding submarines and along the top of the fuselage were some little aerials sticking up, so the type had become nicknamed the 'Stickleback-Wimpey'. In common with all aircraft on coastal work, spending many hours over the sea, it had a good long range, which was comforting. I would be supplied with two crew members to fly with me; one a navigator and the other a wireless operator. They were of unknown experience and background, apart from the fact that they had both been in squadrons, but I was not disposed to demur. I thought that, with all my experience, it didn't matter. Such overconfidence can be, and often is, fatal. The grim reaper's scythe was about to give me a *very* close shave!

The three of us were to meet at the airfield, where the machine had been prepared for issue to a fighting unit somewhere . . . in this case, North Africa. We would, after the take-off, make a flight of several hours, not only as a check that everything was working but also to find out how well it worked. For example, it would be folly not to determine the fuel consumption of its engines before we set off on the long leg over the ocean. Our rendezvous was set for 10 am next morning, at the aircraft.

I found my two colleagues to be very unprepossessing types. They were scruffily turned out and, when asked for details of their past experience — personal flying log-books, maybe? — there were no satisfactory answers. The only official paper they produced was their 'movement chit'. It had on it one word: 'Wastage'. That meant that they were to be used as replacements somewhere, anywhere, caused by casualties or sickness. This alone should have alerted me to the probability that, so far, no one at the sharp end of the Air Force had wanted them much; and why not? It would have been prudent to fire some very penetrating questions at them.

A third chap turned up. He was a Squadron Leader Macnama, engineer officer, and he worked for my chum Ricky Rixson in Khartoum. Ricky had given him leave and, by some monumental wangling, he had thumbed his way home to England. I was tactful enough not to ask how. He was now stuck for a ride back to Khartoum and somebody had said I was going part of the way. He knew me by sight, and also that I had a good reputation for arriving where I wished to go, so could he hitch a flight with me for the first 1,500 miles? He gratefully accepted the lift I offered. If he had had even a cracked crystal ball he would have shunned me like the plague.

After a good couple of hours with Pilot's Notes, going over the aircraft and its cockpit, making myself fully familiar with everything, we set off on our navigation/test flight. It was most pleasurable and, if I had not been so busy with the checks, it would have been a pretty drive. The sun shone. The woods were dark green and the fields were a lighter hue, spotted here and there with different coloured roofs and striped with black roads. The clouds were fluffy, bubbly and pure white like dabs of cotton wool. They were the small patchy ones, produced by a medium breeze on a sunny, happy day; not like those massive thunderheads which look so impressive and wonderfully cushion-like but which, to the initiated, bear an enormous warning on their sides saying: 'Pilots — KEEP OUT!'

Only one thing marred the acceptance-flight. The automatic pilot, 'George', misbehaved. After about two hours he suddenly pulled the machine up into a steep climbing turn. I cut him off with the safety-switch while I checked all his knobs and dial-readings. All in order. Cut him on again. Two to three minutes later, the same thing happened again. No way could I get George to behave for more than a couple of minutes. This was worse than irritating, for George could become essential.

I could normally go many hours in the seat without a break; however, the first six of the nine flying-hours to Ras el Ma were in the dark and it was always possible that, in six hours, something — a call of nature, for instance — would force me to leave the seat. The only pilot aboard was me, and the loo was near the tail. In daylight it would be reasonable to ask a crew member, non-pilot, to look through the windscreen and hold the controls while I trotted down to the rear end. For night flying, with a need to interpret and co-ordinate the meanings of several unfamiliar instruments together, it would not be feasible. Without question, George must work, and as soon as we arrived at Lyneham we asked the technicians to mend him. Apart from that, there were no complaints. We'd air-test the resuscitated George next morning, or whenever they managed to get him going properly.

The next morning was foul. There was a sheet of cloud at a few hundred feet, the wind was gusting and was forecast to increase; it was raining intermittently and getting heavier; the runway was sopping wet. As there was no form of talk-down at Lyneham, I was not going off in that muck for an air-test. Luckily, George's indisposition had been only a minor matter. The engineers had found the trouble, cured it and pronounced him perfectly healthy and responding well. So, an air-test was unnecessary, I assumed. At my level of experience I ought to have said to myself, 'Don't think — prove it.'

Our departure for Ras el Ma was scheduled for 11 pm that night. This timing was so that we should be doing the dangerous stretch in the pitch dark and far out over the Bay of Biscay — dangerous, that is, because of prowling German night-fighters. By mid-afternoon we were still in the briefing room, bored to distraction and thoroughly fed up with reading outdated and well-thumbed magazines, showing women of doubtful charms but who had grossly over-sized bare bosoms and who were trying hard to look like lascivious nymphomaniacs.

We watched the various weather reports as they came in, hoping for a change in the forecast so that we could leave before our last moment — midnight — and not have to wait another 24 hours until the next night. Suddenly, we heard the drone of a multi-engined aircraft overhead. I looked out, thinking 'what bloody idiot is fool enough to be airborne in this filth?' We heard the machine circling and we darted to the windows to have a grandstand view of the show. No one would, or should, have been trying to land in these conditions and, if they did, it could be spectacular.

Some minutes later, rumbly rumbly from its four motors, a

dirty great Liberator sailed past the control tower, flattened out over the sopping runway and, smooth as a silk bedspread, touched down in a great sheet of spray. It disappeared from sight, but it must have come to a normal standstill for, shortly afterwards, it came taxying back and parked in front of us. It was awe-inspiring. We peered closely to see what sort of hairy chested, blue-chinned superman chose to fly a big aircraft in this clag. Our faces must have shown different emotions. My crew's expressions passed from wonder, through optimism to expectation; if that man could fly in this weather, might it not be possible for the experienced Wing Commander to do the same? Mine registered a mixture of astonishment and self-criticism; if he could fly, should I?

There was a pause while the engines were shut down in turn. Then, out popped an enchanting half-pint brunette with the bluest of blue eyes, her hat at a jaunty angle and carrying a pilot-type parachute. She was followed by a hunch-shouldered man holding a clipboard and wearing glasses as thick as bottle bottoms. That was the entire crew, and the man's observer-type parachute showed he was the flight-engineer. My eyes were popping out of my head and my mouth must have been hanging open. They both scuttled into ATC to get out of the rain.

Her uniform told us she was an Air Transport Auxiliary ferry-pilot and, obviously, she had brought in an aircraft that the station was waiting for. Years later I learned that the young lady was Joan Hughes. Unknown to me during the war, she was renowned for flying anything, anywhere, anytime — and for denting endless masculine egos in doing so. Once Joan calmly arrived to collect a Martin Marauder from an American base. A Marauder bomber was a really hair-raising, man-sized machine with two great thundering engines — and any sane pilot could convince himself that its ridiculous little wings would never lift it into the air. She had never flown one before. The horrified and reluctant American CO, having failed to dissuade her, rang up her destination beseeching them to have the fire-engine and an ambulance standing beside the runway, because he knew she was sure gonna crash it on arrival. She didn't. It is also on record that the chauvinistic C in C of Fighter Command rang up her ATA boss, saying: 'I will not have that delicate young girl delivering our big, new high-performance Typhoons direct to the fighter squadrons in my command — it is ruination to my pilots' morale!'

Now, a telephone call to ATC advised me that a taxi-aircraft from the ATA was coming to pick her up, with her flight-engineer, on its routine rounds. That was the final straw; air-taxi on routine rounds indeed! I don't think I ever felt so humiliated. Me, dyed-in-the-wool tough professional aviator, CO of a ferry control, with ten years and many types under my belt, sitting and waiting for the weather to clear. She, a petite 'in-for-the-war' ATA pilot, 'Attagirl' to the rest of the world, flipping around ferrying heavy aircraft in the muck as though it was a lovely day. Life was bitter and unfair, I thought. I felt knee high to an ant. No; a snake would have towered over me . . . and a grovelling snake. at that.

By ten o'clock that night it was blowing 50 mph straight down the runway. Rain was teeming down and the clouds were below 250 feet. I knew that we ought to cancel, unpack for another night and kick our heels all through the following day. However, Lyneham felt dreary, and the bar would now be shut. The sunshine of Morocco was tempting. I said to my two minions and one passenger: 'It's foul down here, but we could climb up on top of the clouds and let George do all the work, till we get there. How do you feel about it? What do *you* want to do?'

The instant response from all three was an enthusiastic 'Let's go!'. I too was a male chauvinistic pig. If that Attagirl could do it . . .? This foolish pig rang ATC . . . we would leave on schedule. We filed our flight plan. Lyneham in Wiltshire — Falmouth in Cornwall — Cape Finisterre in north western Spain — Cape St Vincent in south-eastern Portugal — Rabat-Sale in eastern French-Morocco — Ras el Ma: nine hours. We were on our way.

We taxied out with the rain sheeting against the windscreen but the double row of white runway-lights, starry in the sparkling raindrops, stood out splendidly. The take-off was wholly uneventful and, in spite of the full fuel load, the wind lifted her off like a sparrow. I wriggled my bottom comfortably on the seat-pack of my parachute and settled down for the climb. At 8,000 feet we still had not broken out of the clouds but I didn't want to risk picking up ice on the wings by going higher. We levelled out and switched on George. He took over splendidly. The dozens of dials, taps, knobs and switches around me were all set correctly and reading normal. Sitting back, it was a great feeling, being on our way to warmth and sunshine. Life was good. It should not be long before someone produced a cup of coffee.

The navigator told me the time we should cross the coast of

Cornwall, outbound, near Falmouth. He had noted it on a slip of paper which he clipped in front of me, in case I wished to refer to it later. I did not pay a great deal of attention at that moment. It was bumpy, the windscreen leaked round its edges and there was nothing to be seen, inside this black rain cloud, for double checking his calculations. He had nothing else to do except keep me well informed; the course he had given was certainly in the right general direction and we had all night ahead of us, so I would study it later. I relaxed my muscles deliberately in preparation for the long hours ahead while I watched the many instruments as George did the flying. Life in the warm cockpit, seeing the rain sheeting across the glass, would have been really quite pleasant except for water squirting on to me through the cracks, and it was devilishly bumpy. She wallowed. She was a far cry from the smooth, crisp Lancaster on the way home some days earlier.

Suddenly, about 30 minutes into the flight, all the electrics failed; *all* of them. No cockpit lights. No speech on the intercom. Nothing. A lot of the instruments, worked by electricity, flipped back to zero. All dead as dodos. It was horribly frightening, totally cut off in the dark, water pissing on my lap and no idea what on earth was happening. Praises be, the engines still turned sweetly. The Squadron Leader engineer was standing beside me and I leaned across, shouting into the edge of his helmet, 'Get the navigator up here!'

When he came, we bellowed into each other's ears as I tried to find out what the hell was going on. He said: 'The W/Op is searching for a fuse or a circuit-breaker which must have blown. He seems to be having some difficulty from not having brought a torch.'

'Lend him yours!' I yelled.

'I haven't got one either,' was his reply.

'Are there any emergency lights?'

'We don't know.'

'Tell him to come and speak to me in ten minutes if he can't repair the trouble.'

'Yes Sir.'

I fought back a rising temper, fuelled by a significant amount of fear. Navigators *always* have a torch; or should have. About the only thing that stopped me blowing a fuse myself was that much of the blame was mine. With such an unimpressive pair to fly with, a good pilot would himself have thought to bring a torch, just in case. Pilots didn't normally carry torches, but from that moment onwards there was at least one practising pilot in the RAF who never failed to take a torch on his night trips!

To make matters even worse, a few minutes later George also failed. I tried everything I could think of, but nothing would make him work for more than a few moments before he pulled the machine into a steep climbing turn, like the previous day. In broad daylight, that had not been too alarming. But, at night, in a bumpy black cloud, with no cockpit lights, and no electrical instruments, it was positively nerve-racking. Assuming George's demise must be due to lack of electric power, very shortly I gave up the unequal contest and resigned myself to flying it by hand, without respite.

The W/Op came forward and yelled into my ear that he confessed himself beaten. He could not get the electrics back at work. I then made the navigator understand that we would fly the courses and times on the flight plan he had made out; he said he couldn't remember them. Then he had hysterics, gibbered and said we were all going to die. Uncharitably I wished he would, right beside me, at that instant.

I sat there, on course, flying by the luminous needles of the magnetic compass and a few air-driven instruments while I took stock. Nothing was encouraging. The operator had gone back to his desk. The Squadron Leader told me he could just faintly see him, sitting there in the dark, doing nothing and with nothing to do. The navigator seemingly had crossed his forearms on his desk, buried his face and, so far as Macnama could judge, was weeping uncontrollably. He offered to help me in any way he could but, to be honest, I could think of nothing useful. The three of them, for all practical purposes, were a dead loss. Four lives — theirs and mine — were in my hands alone. After a lot of desperate thinking, I could find only three things I might do, and I disliked them all intensely.

The first was to bale out here and now, over England. This would bring us down on land, but the idea of being swept along by a 50 mph wind in the dark conjured up some hair-raising and probably lethal possibilities. At the best of times, coming down with a Service parachute is like hitting the ground after a jump from ten feet up. In the dark with the wind, this choice would be like jumping blindfold off the top of a bus doing 50, through the rain and black of night. We might well land on a house, in a wood, or a river, or be swept against high tension wires. Landing on the roof of a house at 50 mph sounded very messy.

The second option was to go back and forth till dawn. Then we could try for a hole to come down through and, if none appeared, bale out anyway. There were some pretty strong cons to this one, and very few pros. Everything depended on six hours of navigational calculations, all done in my head, to keep us over land in spite of the wind. A fifty mph wind, for six hours, carries you three hundred miles, to where? I knew its speed fairly accurately on the ground, but how about direction and strength up here? And would it strengthen or weaken later? And would I make a mistake in my mental arithmetic during a long and exhausting night? If I got it wrong we could be anywhere by dawn — over sea, land, or mountains . . . An equally messy prospect; but of course, in daylight, we would at least have the dubious pleasure of seeing *how* we were going to kill ourselves.

The third possibility was to carry on going as best we could. We had no working navigator and no help from outside — and couldn't see the maps inside. The navigation from England to Africa would have to come straight out of the top of my head. We had six hours till dawn. I would be flying by the primary instruments alone, with the luminous paint getting fainter and fainter as the hours went by. No gunners for our machine-guns, and the coast of France was bristling with radar-equipped German night-fighters. All the problems of forced bale-outs remained, but in this case we would with absolute certainty come down in the sea, and drown. Almost as messy as the other two.

Another imponderable was me. Would my brain cope for six hours under all that strain without breaking down? It was an interesting speculation.

Behind everything were two fundamental unpleasantnesses. First, we had no radio so, if something catastrophic occurred, it was curtains; no one in the world could know or give us any help whatsoever. Worse, they would assume that all was well because we had kept radio silence, as one did in wartime. Nobody would have the slightest idea what I had tried to do, where we had headed, where we were or, later, what had happened to us. Second, could the engines suck all their petrol up from the tanks, or were the electric pumps essential? No fuel, no fly.

The entire situation was so horrible and scary that I bet our lives on the third option. After all, conditions at the other end would be better. It couldn't be worse — *provided* the pilot and the engines kept going. All or nothing. Ho for Ras el Ma! Here we come!

As we ploughed through the bumpy cloud I thought out a flight plan. It was a very bow-and-arrow affair but, with no lights and no maps, I could only hope it would succeed. If the original course for Falmouth was reasonably accurate, I reckoned it would take about one and a half hours to get there. Then, straight on to a total of three hours, over the inhospitable Atlantic. That ought to put us beyond the attention of the much more inhospitable night-fighters based around Brest and Lorient, *provided* that bit of France didn't stick out too far west of Land's End. I couldn't visualise the map properly and had to hope we were going far enough. Then I would swing round left and aim due south by compass, plodding on till dawn.

We should be through the bad weather by first light and, looking down, I would see one of two things — land or sea. Land would have to be Spain, so we could edge westwards to reach and follow the coast. Water would be the grey-green Atlantic and we would edge east, to find land. From there on I could coast-crawl and any forced landing, at worst, would be in a neutral country. Carrying on south, a moment would come when the coast swept off to our left — away to the south-east. That would have to be Cape St Vincent. A gentle turn left would point us at Africa, which was far too big to miss. Then, if no early-morning fog interfered, I would identify one of the coastal towns and fiddle my way along the roads to Meknes and Fez. This was assuming, of course, that the engines kept turning all the time. I went over it all carefully once more. It was brutally rough, but God willing, it might come out all right. I muttered,

'God, please, please be willing.'

I wriggled my bum again to settle it as comfortably as possible on my parachute seat-pack for the long, long slog of flying by the fading luminous paint. I hoped to high Heaven that it would not get too faint to see. That would be a certain killer. I had never before flown as long as six hours without cockpit lights to perk up the luminosity.

So it was. The engines, blissfully, ran like sewing machines (but noisier) without missing a beat. At 2 am we turned on to our southerly leg as planned. At 3 am we ran out of cloud. It was a massive relief from seeming to fly inside a black velvet bag. There was no moon but the black vault of the sky was dotted with a zillion stars which, I was sure, could be used to give my eyes a rest from peering at those damned and barely visible needles on the panel before me.

Why should I not look up through the roof panel at a bright patch of the starry heavens, and hold it in place up there, just like pointing the windscreen towards a horizon in daylight? Simple, and restful. I chose my patch by glancing up and memorising its brightest stars. Then, feeling relaxed and comfortable, I switched my concentration away from the needles and leaned my head backwards. Before you could say 'knife' that movement had tumbled the balancing mechanisms in my head and they went crazy. The most appalling vertigo smote me like a hammer and the whole world spun round. My eyes went muzzy and I felt the aircraft going out of control. Trying not to be sick, I fought mentally to get my eyes focussed on the faintly luminous instruments, and then battled physically with the stick and rudder-bar in a mighty effort to chase those pestilential needles back to their correct readings. After a time the aircraft settled down again, but the experience left me trembling, badly shaken and 4,000 feet of height had got lost on the way.

By 3.30 am we were still droning southwards and a fresh problem struck me; somewhere ahead were the Pyrenees, sticking up into the blackness. How high were they? I had no idea. I thought a bit and recollected that the highest mountain in Europe was Mont Blanc in the French Alps. Its top, I knew, was at a bit over 15,000 feet, so I drifted the machine gently up to 16,000 feet. Now, for certain, we would clear any Pyrenean peak, even if pointing straight at it.

At 4 am, below and ahead, lights appeared. Of course! Joy of joys and wonderful to behold! I had totally forgotten that neutral countries had no wartime blackout. An irregular line of them stretched from east to west, so it had to be the northern coastline of Spain. Knowing that land was within gliding distance, and in good weather, did wonders for my peace of mind. We let down to 5,000 feet and turned right to follow the coast. When the line of lights turned sharply left towards the south, it had to be Cape Finisterre. Suddenly, the world had become a far, far better place. We followed round to the left, continuing our coastal crawl.

Finally, at long, long last, there was a greying in the east, followed by a blueing, and then pink streaks. Then, joy oh joy, oh frabjous joy, a horizon ahead — a real honest-to-God fixed horizontal line across my bows, and not an almost extinguished luminous mark dancing on a dial. Over to our left was the dark outline of land — Spain or Portugal, I cared not which.

Squadron Leader Macnama, who had been dozing most of the time, came forward. I asked him: 'Have you ever held the controls?'

He admitted that he had, once or twice. Stiffly, I got out of my seat and beckoned him to take my place. Holding the stick to keep her level, I explained to him, 'You're going to fly this while I take a breather. All you've got to do is to keep that horizon, out there in front of you, looking like it does right now. It's level and it's parallel to the bottom of the windscreen-frame; if it leans over either way, a gentle touch sideways on the stick will level it up again at once. Also, it cuts across the upright edges of the windscreen-frame, *there,* just where it does now; if it moves up or down, a light pressure on the stick, forwards or backwards, will promptly bring it back again. As far as you can, let the machine fly itself. Take care to keep all the movements smooth and gentle; just sit, doing nothing in particular but watching that horizon and keeping it just as it is. At all costs, don't try and follow the instruments on the panel, or the compass; that's a totally different technique and they'll screw you into heaps. Now, fly it. Fly the beast while I watch how you get on.'

To my intense pleasure he got the hang of it extremely fast and in a few minutes was flying straight and level like an old hand. I continued, 'Next lesson; keep an eye on your wristwatch. *Not* more often than about every three or four minutes — it will seem to be much longer — glance at the altimeter. Pay no attention to a change of less than 500 feet. If you have gained or lost *more* than 500 feet, move the horizon down or up just a whisker and sit back. She'll drift herself back to the right height. Above all, don't try any big movements. Make little changes and let the old girl take plenty of time to arrive at the correction you wanted. Lastly: over to your left you can see land. If it gets noticeably closer, edge out to your right a bit.

'Now; I'm going to lie down, here, on the floor beside you and have a rest. She's all yours. If you lose sight of the coast, kick me. Also, kick me if anything at all happens which is not happening here and now. In any case, kick me in 45 minutes' time. Are those instructions absolutely clear, and do you think you can cope?'

He nodded and grinned.

I lay down on the floor and passed out like switching off a bedside light.

Sure enough, he kicked me on time and I stood up. The Portuguese coast was turning sharply away to the east — Cape St

Vincent. I took over the controls and turned to a south easterly-heading, over the ocean. That would hit Africa, for sure. When land appeared, I turned right to coast-crawl once more along the line of golden beaches and palm trees. Soon we were over Rabat-Sale and all my problems were over. It was just a matter of following the main road to Meknes and then on to Ras el Ma.

On landing, it came home to me that a remarkable amount of luck had been on our side; the 'coastal' Wellington had had plenty of fuel for all the turning, going far out to sea, climbing and diving which had occurred. And the engines had never missed a beat.

A very tired and very chastened Wing Commander passed the still-dazed and silent navigator over to the station doctor before tottering off to breakfast and then bed . . . he also, glancing up, muttered under his breath gratefully,

"Thank you, God!"

Chapter 17
Eighteen Hours

Where the Bristol Beaufighter came from originally, I never knew, but it was now in Casablanca and was due for delivery to Cairo. It appeared on the boards as a perfectly normal task, passed on to my ferry control. There were plenty of competent ferry crews, including several qualified to fly Beaufighters. However, on investigation this task proved to be somewhat different from normal.

The Beau was said to be needed urgently for Coastal Attack work in the eastern Mediterranean. So far, so good. But it had no radio, no navigation devices and no guns fitted; it was just a flying shell. It had wiring fitted to take some particular kind of radio, but that radio didn't exist anywhere in the region of Casablanca. It also had a lot of extra fuel capacity to give it super-long range and, for a fighter, that was a very long way indeed. All in all, it was an odd beast.

Ordinarily the task would have presented no significant problems. A ferry pilot could have had a delightful drive-cum-holiday, picking fine weather and following the coastline, more or less at his leisure and pleasure, all the way to Egypt, the Nile Delta and the fleshpots of Cairo. However, it was an urgent delivery and, unfortunately, a significant part of the coastline was still populated by highly efficient and distinctly unsociable German forces. Their fighters would dearly love to have met an unarmed, unaccompanied lone British aircraft. To circumvent that particular difficulty gave rise to other unattractive possibilities. One was to wriggle along the Mediterranean, well out of sight of land. This, with no navigation checks and no radio would spell certain death for the pilot if anything went wrong with the engines. Who would know of the emergency? Another was to go south, behind the fighting zones, over the trackless and featureless desert. This would produce the same answer if the

Beau came down out there. A third was to fly by night, but blackness with no radio (for positioning, or for homing in at the other end) was not run-of-the-mill ferrying.

My planners had come to me saying, 'Please, Sir, concerning this special Beau with no radio or other equipment but which they say they want urgently; we suggest that HQ Middle East airfreight its particular radio here, in one of the Dakotas. We can then fit it and deliver the aircraft in the normal way. Do you agree, or what do you want us to say to HQME?'

If I followed their suggestion, the delays in getting the radio, and then fitting it, would be substantial. On the other hand, if it went without radio it might not be fair on my crews. They were modern pilots who had little experience of barnstorming their way about. They were ill-equipped to go long distances with no outside facilities whatever to call on. I said I would think it over.

That evening, in the early dark after supper, I was sitting outside my little hut in the balmy evening air with a glass of Moroccan plonk in my hand. So? It was wanted very urgently although it was unequipped, without even a radio — odd! One solitary Beaufighter, with greatly extended range, and no guns, yet said to be for 'Coastal Attack duties' — odder still! Things didn't quite jell, somehow . . .

The full moon came out from behind some clouds and shone on the Atlas mountains away to the south, giving that fascinating look that a mountain range gets in clear air — cardboard, shaped and stuck against a backdrop; in this case dark-charcoal cardboard, slightly shaded, against dark-blue velvet studded with the diamonds of the night sky. I took another sip, letting my thoughts wander. Mountains, and moonlight. 'Moon's men'; thieves and highwaymen. Were there Arab highwaymen up there in the Atlas hills? I sat up abruptly; suddenly, the Beau could make sense. Or, at least, there might be a sensible answer. How about it being destined for the Middle East clandestine operations unit, working with and dropping people and arms to the beleaguered partisans in the Yugoslav and Moravian mountains? Great range, special radio and no armament . . . I could not be sure and no one would say so, but it fitted the facts I had. This changed the problem from 'how do we minimise the risks?' to 'what risks must we accept in getting the job done promptly?'

Then, two little horns sprouted from my temples and a forked tail jabbed wickedly, zip-zip-zip, from my trousers. Thoughts came tumbling out, one after the other. Why should I not fly it to Cairo, myself? 'Let's face it,' I thought, 'I am an old pilot (27) with plenty of experience It is years since I first navigated at night without radio. Also, (most helpful) I am the boss; no one here can gainsay me. And (craftily), if Headquarters aren't told about it, they can't cancel it. It will be a savoury challenge, with a salad of several problems to be met and overcome.'

Because of wartime security, forecasts and plans were never sent out unless for operational necessity — and my trip was not in that category. This meant that there was no way of letting Phyl know I was coming. Never mind; my actual decision to go (I persuaded myself) had been based entirely upon pure logic — hadn't it? Surely it had never entered my head that Phyl was in Cairo and I had not seen her for some months because I was 2,000 miles away in Fez — had it? Oh hell, who cared anyway; seeing her was what mattered, nothing else. I went happily to bed, thinking through the salient details. This trip was not going to be like the Wellington debacle when I flew solo a similar distance from Lyneham. The lack of radio in that case was from my mistake. This time it would all be meticulously planned. Nor would there be a repetition of the events on my very recent Beaufighter reverse-ferry from Algiers back to Casablanca for repairs. That memory was still extremely vivid.

Reverse ferries were always fraught tasks, to a greater or lesser degree. With the best will in the world, the people at the business end just wanted to get rid of a machine for which they had no more use. Often, the preparations they gave for its flight were skimpy. This was hotly denied, of course, but . . . just a ferry pilot, flying it away . . . the engine turns and the compass points . . . what more does he need . . .? Usually, it was enough. Sometimes, less so.

All my time at Ras el Ma we had been building up towards the big push which, obviously, was not far off — to drive the Germans, still clinging to Tunisia, clean out of Africa and follow up by invading Sicily. Casablanca was turning out aircraft at a magnificent rate and we were moving them as far foward as possible. After the invasion, we would be poised to move a total fighting force into Italy quickly for the drive towards France. Every available airfield eastwards towards Sicily was becoming stacked out with parked aircraft. On Algiers airfield there must have been something in the order of 200 to 300 Spitfires, not to mention the other types of aircraft. They were lined up, wingtips overlapping, all along both sides of the one solitary runway. It was like landing and taking off along a school corridor.

I got to Algiers by the simple process of ferrying yet another Spitfire there. Having got rid of that, I signed for the Beau coming inwards to Casablanca and did all my pre-flight checks. Then I took her out to the end of the runway. Knowing that Beaus had a slight tendency to swing to one side, caused by the twist of the two great engines, I lined her up accurately on the centre line . . . then opened up the throttles slowly, and very carefully indeed. We were picking up speed steadily, nice and straight when, suddenly, at about 60 mph, it was as if a giant hand had given the tail of my aircraft a massive shove to the left. One instant I was bowling happily and accurately along the centre line of the tarmac and the next moment I was turning irresistibly towards a double line of aeroplanes to my right — at 60 mph, which is below take off speed in a Beau.

It is simply unbelievable how fast one's brain works, quite by itself, in moments of grave emergency. It is far quicker than the time taken later to say what happened. With no conscious analysis on my part, my mind grasped that the chances of getting back to the centre line, and retaining control, were minimal — even with engine power; the necessary immediate action was produced automatically. My left foot promptly thrust out to force the rudder the way it ought to go; it checked the swing, but nothing more. While my left foot still gave all the rudder pressure it could, my left hand pushed both throttles through the 'emergency' gate and hard up against the stops. Now my brain permitted me to think and apply judgement. Would we attain flying speed before we reached the machines along the edge, or not?

There was nothing I could do but wait till the last possible moment; that is, wait for about five seconds and then act. I seemed to have all the time in the world to watch things happening. Everything unreeled in slow motion. As the nearest parked aircraft came to within 40 yards I eased the stick well back and hoped. Quite deliberately and ladylike, the tail went down and it felt as if she was never going to come off the ground. Running into a jam-packed mass of aircraft at speed, all filled to the brim with high-octane petrol, would be an exciting moment. Then there would be a big 'whoosh!' and the billowing black mushroom-cloud of exploding fuel would draw matters to a close, so far as my personal interests were concerned.

Fortunately, she just lifted off in time. The wheels didn't hit a Spitfire, although I believed they were going to do so. As a Scottish fitter once said to me: 'Ye cudn'a slippit a ceegaret-paper in b'tween.'

I eased the stick forwards again, in case it induced a stall and we fell back. But she hung in the air, barely and precariously held there by the emergency thrust from the two engines, and all was well.

The entire performance left me shaky but, which intrigued me — totally baffled. How on earth could it have happened? It was not till we got back to Ras el Ma that the mystery was solved. At the back of the fuselage there is a trap-door, covering an emergency exit. The door, opening downwards, forms a wind-break to stop the gunner or radar-operator catching in the opening as he drops through into the 200 mph-plus slipstream. That is a breeze that otherwise would pin him to the edge of the hole beyond hope of getting free. The catch was faulty and the door had opened, flipped itself down and become like an extra rudder, set sideways. Its effect was like a penny which, dropped into a bucket of water, swings wildly from side to side till it reaches the bottom. The open door had swung me sideways, before I had been able to catch it. It had been a very close shave, and it just showed how, in aeroplanes, you can't be too careful. The fault in the catch had been noted some time back on the servicing documents, but it was also recorded as having been mended. If I had read them more attentively, I probably would have given the rear door an extra thump to be sure it was not going to try and kill me.

My forthcoming delivery for the long-range Beau had to cover two inescapable essentials. The first was that the machine had to go to the vicinity of Cairo and, without radio, that had to be achieved by map-reading. Ideally, that postulated good weather and daylight. The second was that between me and Cairo were some unfriendly Germans; they must not see me as I sailed overhead. That cried for thick clouds or the dark. Somewhere between those two opposites an answer had to be found. As we could not fix a big, black, solitary cloud over the Germans on an otherwise nice fine day, how else were we to go about it?

My first thought had been to go by starlight. However, map-reading by starlight borders on the impossible except for certain contrasting features — a river, or a snowfield, or a sandy beach — and even then a mistake could be both easy and fatal. When the penny dropped, the answer was simple. Four days later the moon was due to rise at about 10 pm and be three quarters full, so we could tailor the flight around the moon: start in daylight, pass over the Germans in the pitch dark, and map-read by moonlight for the rest of the way. The job would be done in one full day. The morning leg would be Casablanca to Algiers. That was 800 miles which would permit excellent checks on compass accuracy and the fuel consumption of each engine. Then would come lunch and last minute titivating at Algiers. With everything topped up, we could take off again after a late tea. The couple of hours of light left, before dark, would be long enough to show me the effects of any strong winds. Then, darkness: happily for me, the Germans did not have radar-controlled night-fighters in that area, so two hours in the dark would suffice. Then we would have moonlight, all the way to Cairo.

With luck I would see, and so have, three pin-points at night for my navigation during the 1,760 miles between Algiers and Cairo. The first, by starlight over the Germans, was chancy. The other two, coastlines by moonlight, were very probable. Fortunately, at that time of year, one ought to have very light winds and stable weather. If it started good, it should stay good, almost for sure.

To a purist or specialist air-navigator my methods would probably have been thought heretical. Over the distance of 1,760 miles it was of no concern if we drifted to one side or the other of the line pencilled on my map, provided only that I learned how *much* we had gone adrift. We could be anything up to 80 miles off course and the increase to the total distance flown would only be a few miles — say another minute or two on my flight. What did I care, and what magic was there, about a pencilled line I had drawn as an ideal? I would rub it out, draw another and make the correction to drift her back again; give or take a bit, one correction every three hours. Even *two* corrections ought to be enough if the flight-plan was good, and accurate. In between? Just bowl along contentedly, waiting, not knowing where I was, but capable of making an educated guess.

A particular worry was that of falling asleep during the seven and a half hours of night flying, with no one to talk to, dead earphones and practically no activity except for the three (and maybe only two) short bursts during the navigation checks. I went off to discuss it with the station doctor. He looked at me with a knowledgeable nod and disappeared into the other half of his medical tent. Soon he came back with a little bottle of white tablets, rattling them happily. He beamed with the satisfaction of a man who really knows, beyond doubt, the answer to someone else's problem. Twisting his fingers together like a tailor who is about to measure you for a very expensive hand-sewn suit, and with his head slightly on one side, he said, 'At your service, Sir. I am sure we can fix you up perfectly. With no trouble. Here are some tablets. They're caffein citrate. Each is roughly equivalent to two cups of strong black coffee, without sugar. Put 'em in your pocket. On the way, when you first feel slightly sleepy, take two tablets. Then take one more every hour thereafter — till you arrive. A word of warning — one slight difficulty — although they keep you properly awake with no significant effect on your mental faculties, they make you want to pee. Be sure you have a pee-bag with you. Next gentleman, please.'

I smiled at the doc's little play acting, thanked him sincerely and left, clutching my little bottle. This promised to be a new experience. My lower half always went on total strike when I was in the pilot's seat, even for several hours. Why, I did not know, but nevertheless it had been very convenient sometimes. For instance, a compulsory six and a half hours in the seat of a limping Wellington at night had not, luckily, been interrupted by nature.

The Beau handled beautifully. I had taken off from Casablanca, after an excellent breakfast, at roughly 9.30 am. It would be four hours to Algiers, nicely long enough to be sure that everything was working correctly. We were cruising at the most economical power, bumbling along comfortably at 185 mph and 8,000 feet, so as to measure its maximum range for the long second part of the trip, by night. The engines, sleeve-valve radials built by Messrs Bristol, were incredibly quiet and smooth — but they gave a feeling of lurking power . . . no wonder the enemy had nicknamed the brute 'Whispering Death'. But, with no guns, this was not for me to prove.

It was a lovely day, auguring well for the second stage. We had passed Rabat-Sale with its harbour, sailed gently over Meknes with its white houses, and noted Ras el Ma with its gravel runway and green tents. Eight thousand feet had been too high for me to identify the 24-holer, but the bathing pool stood out clearly. From my height, and on such a clear day, the Atlas mountains made a wonderful brown, snow-white and blue jagged-topped wall, all the way round from the south to the north-east, cupping the towns, villages and greenery in their lush countryside. I remembered the 'black cardboard' effect of the same mountains, four nights earlier, when I had dreamed up the reasons for this trip. After Fez, it was over the Taza Pass with its memories of a fixed-undercarriage Wimpey being coaxed out of the mountainside field. Beyond the Pass, I was flying over or near towns with fascinating names like Oujda, Mascara, Sidi bel Abbes, Tagdempt and Oran; each, if only I could get inside, with its own stories, atmosphere and smells. Finally, I sank down towards Algiers, making a safe landing between the serried rows of aircraft waiting for their call-up. According to the gauges, the forthcoming ten-hour trip was going to be a doddle, but to be quite certain I would have to wait till the tanker-drivers told me the exact quantities they had actually put in each tank when they were refuelling, and therefore precisely how much had been burned.

The young American in front of me in the lunch-tent, with his slow Texan drawl and the ubiquitous crew-cut, had just come back from somewhere up at the front. He looked battle-tired. The sergeant cook leaned over me and said, 'Whaddya want for afters, Limey?'

I was too inured to our hosts at Ras el Ma to indicate that 'Limey' might be improved on, from a Sergeant to a Colonel. I answered, copying his accent as closely as I could, 'Whaddya got?'

'Apple-pie-and-ice-cream.'

'Oh no! Not that. We get apple pie and ice cream seven days a week, in your Mess back at base. Don't you have anything *else* on offer?'

At this the battle-weary young American chipped in, *Jee-zus!* I come back from up there,' he nodded towards Tunis, 'not having seen apple-pie-and-ice-cream for weeks, and here's this guy bitching about it! Shit!'

The measured fuel consumption told me that there was the possibility of eleven and a half hours in the air for that night, if needed. I wanted, according to my flight plan, a little over nine and a half, so I had nearly a couple of hours, or 370 miles, in hand; it ought to be ample.

I took off at 6 pm with the sun behind me and headed, climbing, to the south east. The Atlas mountains ranged ahead of me were truly beautiful. They stood parallel to the coast, rising to 6,000 feet, and the rays of the vivid pink and yellow sunset coloured the hillsides in a myriad soft mauves, purples, browns and greens. For the thousandth time I longed to be a painter, to record them as they were in my eyes, original and individual. Soon we had got to our cruising height and I settled down on my first course. Beyond the Atlas, we were over desert. There were no significant signs of wind so I made no alterations. The night gently folded me in.

I sat very still. The temptation to wriggle my bum on the parachute seat-pack was strong but I knew the penalty; later, the restricted circulation seeping through my muscles would cause agony. If I did not move, the muscles would gradually pass from mild discomfort directly to numbness and, after a couple of hours, all feeling would vanish from that area. My backside would feel physically comfortable and not distracting: total 'numb-bum' would have set in.

The desert below disappeared. First one or two, and then in a rush the diamond sparks of the stars all appeared above me. Below, here and there, could be seen the yellow light-spot of some Bedouin camp fire. The coastal strip, ahead, was a German hornets' nest and I was already in wonderfully dark darkness. With luck, if the starlight was strong enough, my first checkpoint would come from little islands in the Gulf of Bomba where the contrast of sand and sea might just be identifiable. They should come in to view, if I was reasonably in position, nearly three hours after take-off. They would not necessitate a change of course yet — that was plannned for an hour later, about 20 miles off Tripoli, which would be fully blacked out. If I did not see the islands, I would have to turn on to my new course on calculations alone. That would leave me without navigational check till after seven hours from take- off. It would feel a long time to fly with no reassuring checkpoint on the way.

I was lucky. The air was clear enough to let me pick out the Tunisian coastline, because the faint starlight got a boost from sharp-white salt lying in the drying-pools behind the beaches. Beyond, shaped grey patches in an even darker sea showed me the islands I had hoped for. As nearly as I could estimate, we were only 15 miles off to one side of my 'ideal' line, and four minutes ahead of schedule. Four minutes and less than two degrees of error let me calculate a wind of barely 5 mph. As is so often the case in the desert, the night winds were mere zephyrs.

This check on my navigation made me feel really good. I now knew that things were apparently panning out as hoped for.

Secondly, I would be able to turn on to my second course, including a very small correction for the wind, in the sure knowledge that the aircraft was safely 20 miles out to sea from Tripoli. Tripoli was in our hands, but only a madman would guide a 'silent' (and therefore potentially hostile) aircraft towards it from a seaward direction. Anti-aircraft fire might not at that time have been especially lethal, but it was always alarming and a hit would surely kill, even if it was luck and not skill that made the strike. Moral: keep away, if possible.

It was getting on for 10 pm, and well over an hour before my next checkpoint could be expected. I yawned. Ha! I pulled out the little bottle and took two pills.

The doc was as good as his word. In a quarter of an hour I was as bright as a button and started to sing to myself at the top of my voice. Belting it out and hearing nothing is a peculiar sensation, but it is fun and, in a sense, one of a pilot's privileges. You bellow a wrong note and nobody knows nor cares; not even you. At 10.15, as promised, up came the moon in front of me; dull orange as it peeped over the horizon, but becoming more and more silvery as the bright near-full disc slid imperceptibly upwards. A wonderful shimmering metallic pathway, reflected off the wavetops, spread itself out ahead and into the distance. It began as gold and changed to silver with the moon.

It must have been at 11.15 that I saw the black Cyrenaican coastline slicing across the sparkling pathway. I bowed in homage to the beneficent deity that follows careful pilots. My watch told me that we had more than 40 miles to go before overflying the beaches. 'Beaches', because I aimed to cross the coast about 30 miles south of Benghazi. Benghazi also was in our hands, but its port was of tremendous importance for our supplies. The defences were therefore powerful and definitely to be avoided by lone intruders. Being able to pick out landmarks up to 40 miles ahead gave me ample notice of our landfall. It meant that, even if I had unknowingly drifted northwards 30 miles towards the danger, I could easily have identified the port itself and turned aside to safety long before disaster hit. One more pill.

Our landfall, south of Benghazi, proved to be right on target. It was plainly picked out because of little indentations to the coastline. I bowed again. This time it was to the man who had adjusted the compass. He had done a superb job; spot-on after hours and hours of unchecked flying. As the coast passed below I made my second, and this time tiny, change of course in order to head for a point ten miles south of the coast at the Egyptian border. There was all the time in the world to think, reflect and enjoy the night as that marvellously smooth Beaufighter droned along. Above, the moon hung steadily while a myriad stars twinkled brilliantly. Below, all was velvety blue-blackness with faint blotches, useless for navigation, coming from the different coloured sands and dried up watercourses. It was restful, and a million miles from any unfriendliness . . . or so it felt.

All was going so well on the flight that I was becoming positively nervous. An hour (another pill) and 40 minutes after we had crossed the Benghazi beaches I went past the unmistakable sudden northwards turn of the coast at the Egyptian/Libyan border. I knew just where the port of Bardia must be on that short stretch — it had often been my bombing-target — but I couldn't pick it out. I made no detour to take a look 'for old times sake'; it too had Allied defences and should be left severely alone.

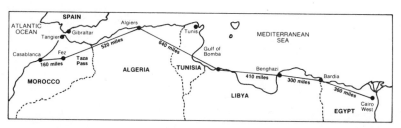

I made the third — and last — alteration of course to take me straight to Cairo-West airfield. I worked out my estimated time of arrival; after all that flying it would be accurate to within half a minute — at worst. Cairo, beyond it and not blacked out, would shine into the night sky like a beacon. Surely, if the propellers just kept turning, it was in the bag . . .? I shook my head violently, muttering 'Bloody idiot! For God's sake don't stop concentrating now!' I took another pill.

However, it *was* in the bag and I touched down a minute or two after 3.30 am. Having parked, I climbed out stiffly. I had been sitting still for almost ten hours since I climbed aboard at Algiers. The blood was coursing through my buttocks. The doc's pills were wonderful but, what price for his second prognostication? I smiled. The waterworks had not let me down. With pleasure I had a satisfying pee on the hard desert sand under the tailplane.

Flying solo for roughly 13½ hours out of 18, I had had a long, but very satisfying day — so far: nearly 2,500 miles and 30 still to go. Now, for the remaining 30 miles into Cairo itself; how at this misbegotten hour was I to find wheels?

At about 5 am I thanked the Cairo-West driver sincerely for his lift, before he pulled away from outside a block of flats on Gezira Island in the Nile. I knew that Phyl had taken in a couple of war-working girls to live in our flat while I was away, so the problem was how to avoid waking everybody up at such an unreasonable time? I decided to shin up an old creeper round the back of the flats and get in over the balcony. When I looked through the french-windows of Phyl's room, I was perfectly silhouetted against the greyness of the dawn sky. She was sound asleep. Very softly, I pushed the window open. Sleepily, she raised her head and looked at me. Two powerful and conflicting emotions struck her, crowding one on top of the other. First, she recognised me instantly; second, she knew beyond all shadow of doubt that I was 2,000 miles away. Words sprang to her lips as she flung out her arms, saying,

'Darling! . . . . who are you?'

Chapter 18
Diplomacy

We did not have to wait too long before the 'Big Push' came off and the Germans were finally ousted from Africa. The Americans, using hundreds of C47s — Dakotas to us — launched the invasion of Sicily with masses of gliders and paratroops. Most of the Mediterranean became safe from enemy attack and was used again, relatively freely, by our surface forces. Gibraltar, with its Coastal aircraft capacity turned itself round, facing the other way, to do less over the Atlantic and more towards the Mediterranean, supporting the drive on Italy. From Ras el Ma our ferry outfit worked like mad to keep the forward airfields in Algeria and Tunisia stocked up with all the operational aircraft back-up that came on stream. Life was very exciting.

One of the spin-offs was that Gib passed over to Ras el Ma most of what they considered to be their aviation ullage. This was perfectly right as they were an important operational station, supporting the war directly. We were a non-operational backwater, even if our indirect support was vital to the war effort further east. They gave us a much greater proportion of the fly-in reinforcements from the United Kingdom, to be sent onwards, we got the diplomatic mail to be forwarded, and we had a number of passenger aircraft — which did not appeal to me, much.

A major inconvenience was that we were not equipped nor staffed to handle passengers. Although we could get plenty of tents and camp-beds from our American hosts, we had neither sheets nor blankets for outsiders. Nor did we have the cooks and house-servants to feed them and tidy up after them. Passengers, even in the most makeshift transit camp, never clear up after themselves; they just walk away, as in a hotel, and leave it all to 'someone else'. We didn't have odd bods to nanny them, and no permission or money to hire locally. Passengers became an unending source of petty complaints and irritations for me.

Anyway, they seemed to get in the way of my first-priority job —
getting fighting aircraft up to the battle area. This was wishful
thinking on my part, persuading myself towards the task which,
to be honest, was the most fun for me. I chose to overlook the fact
that many of the passengers were extremely important to the war
effort.

Irritating though some passengers might be, it was intriguing
how they could be graded in nuisance value. There was no
question that those who were the least trouble were the high-level
civilians and serving officers — Ministers, Admirals, Generals
and Air Marshals. They were so used to being jollied along,
having their hands held by aides and lackeys, that they always
expected to be told their next move. One could put them
somewhere, and they would stay put, until somebody moved
them somewhere else; delectably simple. If they weren't there
when you returned, it was extremely easy to find them. The only
thing that would shift them, by themselves, was a need to go to
the loo.

Others who were comparatively easy to cope with were those of
the more junior ranks — that is, everybody who was junior to me.
One of my team, freely using my name and rank, would collect
them together in a block or body and give them instructions. On
the whole they did what they were told. The teller knew that his
expectations were met by results, usually. His only problem was
to make his instructions *complete.*

One day, the captain of a slightly delayed Dakota kicked up a
tremendous to-do. He was due to leave and make a connection
with another machine somewhere or other and, if he did not get
airborne fairly soon, the flight would be abortive. His passengers,
en masse, had completely vanished. My minion, it turned out (he
very sensibly did not identify himself to me), had told them to go
off for a while, having assumed (wrongly) that the aircraft would
surely not be leaving shortly — might even be an hour or more.
He had failed to complete his instructions by saying '. . . but
come back every 30 minutes to check up.' The passengers had all
cheerfully evaporated and, when the captain eventually asked for
them, we had to find them one by one. The Flying Officer skipper
gave me hell, keeping it just off the edge of insubordination by a
liberal sprinkling of 'Sir's in every sentence, to soften the
vituperation a little.

By far and away the worst problem children were the Group
Captains, the Colonels and the Captains Royal Navy, in that

order. Normally, things happened when they wanted them to. They were junior enough to do the actual fighting, in the air, on the ground and at sea; they were senior enough to be used to getting their own way and, moreover, they were senior to me. If they found something which they thought wrong (their breakfast eggs weren't cooked to their liking, the mirror in their tent was cracked, the American shower they used did not squirt its water properly), they would demand to voice their complaint to the CO in person — me. After all, they claimed, it was my job to see that things were done. If the organ didn't play, you spoke to the organ-grinder, not the monkey. It was I who was supposed to require efficiency, wasn't I? And so on. As their junior it was hard to argue with them forcefully. They gave me a pain where I hate having a pain.

Worse, individually all Group Captains believed that they knew more about my job than I did. Perhaps so, but I had to run the place without their daily help and I swore a deathly oath that, when and if I became as senior as they, I would let the chap doing the task get on with it, and I'd reserve my comments till later on, or when asked. That vow was kept. Well, nearly always.

Nineteen years later I was travelling in a Hastings aircraft, as a passenger wearing civilian clothes, from Singapore to England. The Hastings was slow, and it wallowed along. The trip seemed endless and the discomfort made the several days feel like forever. Luckily, I had a job to do in Aden and so I was 'slipped' to a following aircraft, 48 hours later. All its passengers except me, loaded aboard during the morning, were airmen. After some hours had gone by, with no contact from the crew and nothing to eat or drink, I poked my nose round the door of the crew compartment and spoke to the nearest crew member. He was a Sergeant, munching a sandwich. I asked him if there was any prospect of lunch? He brushed me aside with a shrug of his shoulders and told me that the passengers weren't getting any lunch. I opened my mouth to make some very tart comments, for the ear of the Flight-Lieutenant captain whom I could see flying the aircraft, when I remembered my vow from Ras el Ma all those years ago. I shut it again and went back to my seat, muttering the old adage from the Wild West gold rush of 1849: 'Please do not shoot the pianist — he is doing his best'.

Around half an hour later, the Captain came out with a piece of paper in his hand. Somewhat hesitantly, he said, 'Er . . . was it you who spoke to the Loadmaster, a little while back?'

I nodded.

'Er . . . this is the passenger-manifest. . . er . . . is this you (he pointed to the sheet) AC Dudgeon?'

I nodded again. He said: 'Er . . . is that Aircraftsman Dudgeon?'

I shook my head.

His eyes bulged. 'Are you — er — *Air Commodore* Dudgeon?' Again I nodded.

His voice became vibrant with anguish. 'Dear God! They never told me I had an *Air Officer* on board!'

I licked my lips as I foresaw what was coming. He was going to try and smooth me over. In fact I was not cross with him in the slightest; the luckless fellow merely needed to have it brought home to him firmly that an RAF skipper's duties do not start and finish in the cockpit. The basic fault lay with the Movements staff at Aden who had let him down by not producing food. However, he should have beaten the drum and used his status as aircraft captain to give them hell, and *insisted* on food for his passengers — or an apology directly to the passengers with an explanation for them, if food was unobtainable. He hadn't tried hard enough, and his future would be improved by a swift metaphorical kick up the backside for not doing so.

Mentally he cast around for something to say which would pacify an enraged senior officer. At last he blurted out: 'Er . . . would you like the navigator's lunch, Sir?'

Here it came. . . 'No,' I said, 'not the navigator's; as you don't check that your passengers are looked after as effectively as you look after yourself and your crew, I'll eat *yours*!'

'Oh God, Sir! I would willingly give you mine — but I've eaten it!'

'In that case, I'll go without lunch.'

Miserably, he tottered back into his crew-compartment and shut the door behind him. Poor fellow! But assuredly it must have made him a better skipper afterwards.

Colonels, on the whole, tried to use their rank to make life go the way they wanted. That is, to have *us* go *their* way. One such, who came to Ras el Ma on his way eastwards, tried very hard. His story went round the Middle East grapevine like lightning.

He was waiting for his Dakota to take off for Algiers. The delay irritated him and he wished to know the reason, so he demanded to see the captain. The skipper was a Flying Officer, a mere subaltern so far as the Colonel was concerned. When the 'subaltern' told him why they were waiting — for the weather to improve in Algiers and it was not expected to clear for a couple of hours — the Colonel burst out: 'Bloody nonsense young man! I've been to Algiers frequently and know it well. The weather at this time of year is always excellent. You should take off at once.'

The Flying Officer was not tactful. He gave the Colonel a very dusty answer indeed.

The matter then came to me. The Colonel now wanted two things instead of one. First, that I have the Flying Officer's head brought to me on a charger for outrageous insubordination to a senior officer. Second that the aircraft should leave at once with another, more competent, captain at the controls. Persuading him to go to the waiting room tent, and stay there, took a lot of effort. He was only half satisfied with my assurance that I would enquire personally into the matter, and that his aircraft would leave as soon as I deemed it correct, proper and safe to do so.

The Dakota captain got a flea in his ear from me, not on account of waiting for an improvement in weather (that the Colonel *knew* was good), but for failing to recognise a Colonel with a very short-delay fuse.

Naval officers, almost without exception, caused me no direct trouble. However, they always engendered in me a certain unease. I felt a *je ne sais quoi* of looking down their noses as they thought 'they don't jump to it like our lads' or 'a bit of grey paint would do a world of good around here' or even 'it seems odd not to be piped aboard', and all this with an aura of impeccably and inflexibly good manners. On my side, deep-down I knew it was totally unjustified and recognised my own inferiority complex as a member of the junior Service confronted with the Senior Service. Luckily for me there weren't too many of them. I certainly grew out of it very quickly, as soon as I had Naval personnel under my direct command. We both had a lot of fun.

I hoped that I might turn these complaining passengers to my own profit. I encouraged anyone who found our results to be unsatisfactory in spite of our strenuous efforts, to report so at the other end. I thought that this might get somebody to listen to my squeaks, and I would then be given a hand with supply or local hire of necessary hardware and warm bodies, so that I could improve matters for everybody. That was very naïve of me. All that happened was that these whinges stacked themselves up in somebody's 'pending tray' as indicators of my general incapacity and inadequacy to run things properly in the field of air-transport. Unknown to me, I was getting 'black marks'. In retrospect, I think they were justified: I was concentrating too much on the things which interested me most, which were, of course, the fighting aircraft. However, these black marks were each like an angel's shining, golden halo compared to a special one I earned.

Everyone knows today what a diplomatic bag is like. It is anything from a sealed envelope to a massive steel-bound case containing guns, drugs, and people who are being moved reluctantly from country to country without going through Customs. The 'diplomatic bag' as it went through Ras el Ma was one or several canvas sacks of various sizes, padlocked, sealed, numbered and accounted for, arriving from Gibraltar. We loaded them into óne of my twice-weekly Dakotas and sent them on to Cairo.

In late summer, when the invasion of Sicily was requiring every ounce of effort from us and we were stretched to the limit, the movements officer came to me for advice. The 'bag' would not go into one Dakota, and should he call out a second one? A Dakota carries two-and-a-half *tons*, so I asked to see the 'bag'. The sacks proved to be fascinating: some clinked with the sound of bottles, some of which could be identified clearly by shape as Gordon's gin, Johnnie Walker whisky, and sundry other brands of liquor. Another contained, patently and obviously, golf clubs. These were but some of the contents and we had an enjoyable hour, guessing which held what. A most perplexing one took a long time; it was finally identified by weight and shape as having a sewing machine inside it.

For the obvious reason of operational pressure at that time, we had only minimal resources for non-operational tasks. We could not, therefore, send two Dakotas to Cairo and still have one left for the mid-week run. Therefore, believing that there was a war on, which took priority over golf and sewing (a misapprehension), I decided that we would send all the unidentified and therefore probably urgent sacks in one Dakota; then, hold the bags containing non-essentials (another error; there is never a non-essential in the 'bag') till the second Dakota three days later. I was trying to keep the second aircraft up my sleeve (another mistake) for high-priority passengers and freight which otherwise would have no wings at mid-week. I sent a signal to HQME, saying one aircraft load was on its way, and the remainder was to follow in three days, in my second Dakota.

The first reaction, in code, was received in a few hours. It said that the Americans in Algiers were being asked to provide a Dakota, with a special security-cleared crew, to replace my second Dakota which I had indicated would be unserviceable for the next three days. I must provide an armed guard to go with the high-priority British mail which, completely exceptionally, would travel in a foreign aircraft. I promptly sent a long and explicit coded cable. It said that in no way was high-priority mail of any nationality being delayed. That mail was, quite properly, speeding on its way already. It was only the booze and golf clubs which would not arrive till mid-week. The remaining ton of sacks would arrive, properly guarded, in ample time for Christmas. Thus, any priority passengers and freight at mid-week would have wings available, thanks to my foresight . . . or words to that effect.

The expressions from HQME would have paralleled the reactions of the Archbishop of Canterbury if he had come upon me holding a Black Mass in Saint Paul's Cathedral on a Sunday mid-morning; a mixture of shock, distress and general dismay. I was left in no doubt that the Big Book of Diplomacy ruled that diplomatic mail was, and is, diplomatic mail, and that was the way it was always going to be. It was no duty of mine to infer that a deck chair or a chinking bottle of liquor could be identified by my tactile or aural skills. Golf clubs were important documents, bottles equally were important documents, and so were sewing-machines — as far as I was concerned — now and for evermore. Further, what would they be able to tell the Americans who had so generously offered to lend us an aircraft and crew? I had placed them in a ridiculous and highly embarrassing situation . . . There was more, much more, in the same strain.

I did not say, but felt like saying, that they should give the Americans the facts. They would have their biggest belly-laugh for years and, moreover, mutual co-operation would be enhanced. I regret that I am not, and never was, a natural diplomat.

The nearest I ever got to anything 'diplomatic' in Morocco was through a British Consul, his wife and his only child, Caroline. She was 13 and, as may be imagined, a lonely girl. She had no other English children to have fun with and she had become desperately 'grown-up' from her exclusively adult contacts. Her parents were most hospitable during my time there, and so I tried to repay some of their kindness through the girl.

She came several times, with her parents permission, to visit the station. I did my best to make it 'fun and exciting' for her and not 'educational'. I showed her over whatever large aeroplanes we had in at the time, such as a Wellington, and a Stirling, where she could trot up and down the fuselage from the rear-gunner's turret to the bomb-aimer's station in the nose, asking innumerable questions. She sat in the pilots' seats and played with the controls; she could climb on the wing of my Hurricane, 'Oakley', so as to peer at and then climb into the cramped single-seater cockpit; she talked to ATC on the radio.

But, for the youngster, the American PX was best of all. There she could take her pick of sweets galore, chewing-gum, 'candy and pop' of every description. It was a veritable mine of goodies and, as the wartime subsidised supplies were sold to American servicemen at practically nothing per packet, I gave her *carte blanche* to take as much loot as she could carry. She even collected two cartons of cigarettes for her father; 400 cigarettes for which I paid two dollars — and we were given five dollars for one pound!

She was an enchanting child who met her thrills and discoveries with wide-eyed enthusiasm. I think I enjoyed it more than she did, if possible. Her father most generously and kindly took many opportunities to return, in more than full measure, my favours to her — even after I had left Fez. I remain greatly indebted to him.

Chapter 19
VIP

In early 1943, fairly soon after Headquarters Transport Command was formed, they went deep into the serious business of moving warm bodies around, as well as freight and aeroplanes. Some of these bodies were important — or thought they were. Generals didn't like being lumped together with Lieutenants and felt they were not getting the treatment that their rank and status deserved. Therefore, to help the staff at the receiving end, despatchers were including in their messages little snippets of information like '2 IP' or '4 IP', warning receivers at the other end how many of these 'Important People' were aboard. Minor perks followed, like a car instead of a jeep, or a china cup instead of a tin mug. Unsurprisingly, it soon became a matter of pride for almost everyone to get themselves tagged as an IP, so the currency got debased. A new coinage was required.

HQTC came up with the splendid answer — Very Important Person — VIP. Oddly enough, this sounded the death knell of the IP and he soon faded away. Who wants to be tagged as a second-class citizen when first-class ones are around? At the same time, it is one thing to say you are important, but it takes a peculiar character to claim exceptional importance, *for oneself.* Anyway, china cups and plates were becoming commoner. There was a brief spell when VVIP was tried out, but it never seemed to catch on firmly during the war, and VIP proved adequate.

The next thing needed was a proper passenger aircraft for VIPs. It was one thing to have Colonels, and even Generals seated on a cushion with their backs against the ice-cold metal skin of a long-range Liberator going overnight to the Middle East — but how about Field Marshals and their counterparts? It was no good looking to Churchill for a precedent as he used to spend most of his time smoking (forbidden) cigars on the flight deck.

Luckily Roy Chadwick, the chief designer of Messrs Avro, had sketched out (and the company was already building) what was, in effect, a Lancaster bomber fitted with an obese fuselage for carrying freight: it was called a York. One of these (it was the third one built) was converted inside to a most luxurious passenger aircraft, primarily to become the Prime Minister's personal transport. He would be able to smoke in comfort, in his armchair and (for a change) in safety.

This palatially equipped York flew several thousand miles to prove its reliability, and the time came for its pilot, Wing Commander H. B. Collins, to lift its first real live VIP. The destination was Algiers.

HQTC, having this wonderful new machine at their disposal, developed a bad case of paranoia. Everything else had to be equally wonderful — right down to the tiniest detail of organisation. Their state of mind was aggravated by the fear that, because the aircraft was obviously a very rare bird, German intelligence (if they heard of it) could be reasonably sure that it would contain a juicy target. Shooting it down would be a prime enemy objective. And what a propaganda coup it would be for them! Every possible aspect of its security therefore was kept unbelievably tight.

The chosen route, for safety, would be by night far out into the Atlantic and right round Spain. This was too far to let it reach Algiers in one hop. Refuelling would be at Gibraltar whose facilities allowed VIP handling. Timing and distance to be flown meant that the York would leave England at dusk, and reach Gib in the dawn. This highlighted two more security aspects, linked together. The first was that the aircraft would be seen at Gibraltar from Spain. The second was that a mole in that area might read signals which had to be sent — and get a message to the enemy early enough for trouble. Both problems, they reckoned, could be met by one solution.

The risks at Gib itself were judged to be slight and acceptable, *provided* the machine and its load were given individual and swift treatment. Admittedly, a bright German agent on the mainland, equipped with a good pair of binoculars, might see the aircraft after it had landed and, from its new shape and the obvious attention paid to it, might suspect something interesting. Perhaps even, a mole on the Rock might get a message to him. Nevertheless, whatever he saw, heard or suspected, there was absolutely nothing unpleasant he could do for his masters in Germany or France before the aircraft was well and safely on its way again to Algiers.

Next, that preferential treatment for the York at Gib could also solve the linked problem of leaky messages. They knew our facilities were very limited, particularly for signals and ciphers. We had no decoding machines, so everything had to be done by adding and subtracting figures from books, which was a lengthy process. How to gum up all the signals facilities? It was too simple, really. Send to Ras el Ma all the aircraft which had been booked for Gib, thus doubling our normal load which already was the maximum we were able to handle safely. And, to compound the chaos, give us no warning, tell us nothing at all so we would have no reasons to raise our eyebrows, kick up a fuss, make waves — or ask pertinent questions as to what the hell was going on. The first thing we should know was a fleet of aircraft streaming in, something like bees returning to their hive from a field of flowering clover — and the whole place would become an absolute shambles.

They knew that, amongst professionals, new aircraft are always a matter of curiosity, comment and gossip; no one in our neck of the woods had even *heard* the name York applied to an aircraft. Suppose an early aircraft arrived bearing all sorts of interesting rumours about a new aeroplane called a York? So what? The mass of additional coded messages, and the extra aircraft, would have gummed us up completely. No word, good or bad, could possibly be got out — even if we had a highly efficient mole actually on the airfield. For that matter, the whole of Ras el Ma could go up in flames, and the news would be totally unknown to the world at large.

The fact that their solution would virtually crucify my organisation gave HQTC no apparent concern. Security at Gib would be assured, come what may.

Next, they considered the weather. This should present no special difficulty. The only risk was of early morning fog at Gib; this was long before the days of automatic landings or talk-down radar. Fog sometimes occurred there as the airfield was literally sticking out into the Atlantic. But, fortunately, fog was forecastable. This first VIP departure could be kept flexible; the aircraft would merely leave on an evening when there would be no fog there next morning. The project could be kept on ice till the Met men said it was OK to go. Then — Bingo! They're off! Clear Gibraltar of all traffic, ensuring that Ras el Ma was a crowded ant-heap because nothing but aeroplanes could get in or out — and there would be masses of those — and the York would sail serenely through its stop-off on the way to Algiers. Everyone could then pat themselves on the back: so easy, really, and diabolical for Ras el Ma.

On a Saturday morning a few days later, two things happened at just about the same time. One was that the Air Commodore Meteorology (in wartime all the Met men were in uniform) flung his scrambled-eggs hat to the ground and pronounced, in clarion tones, something like 'I and my colleagues say, beyond any shadow of doubt, there will be *NO FOG* at Gib tomorrow morning!' The other was that Mademoiselle Pravosoudovicz, daughter of the French Foreign Legion CO in Fez, got married.

In England, the plan swung into action. Reinforcement crews for Gib were switched to a new route; tracks were redrawn; chaos at Ras el Ma was assured. The VIP was escorted to Lyneham in Wiltshire for the take-off.

In Morocco, life was placid. I am bilingual in English and French so I had come to know the Pravos fairly well; they even went so far as to amuse themselves by teaching me vulgar phrases in Russian. It had been not only an honour but also a great pleasure to be invited to the wedding and the celebrations afterwards. Mademoiselle Pravo was given away in the French Foreign Legion chapel and, after the ceremony, the new Madame Whatevershethenwas gave me a duty kiss and a ravishing smile in the reception line. Thereafter Colonel and Madame Pravo took over and plied me with unlimited wine (and none of it was Algerian or Moroccan plonk, thank you!) at the wedding lunch, at the afternoon reception, at the wedding tea, at the wedding cocktail party and at the wedding dance that night. I did not get away until the small hours. Luckily, I had foreseen something of the kind and was driven home to my little hut, in no fit state to drive myself. Blissfully unaware of the disarray ahead of my team, I sank on to my camp-bed and passed into unconsciousness.

When I had been having my first dance with Madame Pravo in Morocco, Collins had been lifting the York into the air over England. At the same time our wireless operator in his tent was beginning to become slugged as he sat in a virtual trance, listening and writing down automatically block after block of incomprehensible priority figures for all the aircraft due in — a separate set for each one. These, decoded, would give the type and its anonymous four-letter callsign allotted for the journey.

By midnight the cipher officer, laboriously turning the pages of his code books and looking at the little pile of decoded signals on his left and the mountain of untouched ones on his right, said 'My God! What are they doing to us? Obviously they are all aircraft movements, from their priority, but it'll be lunch-time before I can get through this lot.' He sent a word of warning to the Air Traffic Controller on duty next morning.

In actual fact, the wireless operators and the cipher officer were slaving away at a useless task. The delay caused by that volume of work meant that any aircraft was going to be on the ground at Ras el Ma — or at the bottom of the Atlantic — long before its signal could be unscrambled to tell us that it had left England.

By 5 am, when the first shafts of dawn were greying the night sky, the controllers and the operations officers were reeling under the blow. In the air, dozens of W/Ops were trying to elbow themselves on to the frequencies to give us the announcement of their arrival times. On the ground, from the heap of signals already decoded, it was obvious that one hell of a morning was in prospect. More warnings were passed to the sleepy eyed mechanics and the cooks. The controller had already worked out that any mishap blocking the one solitary runway, even temporarily, could escalate rapidly into a major catastrophe. It would be necessary to land an aircraft every 90 seconds for the first four hours after daylight — or maybe even faster than that . . . and to do it with inexperienced crews, tired, short of fuel, and with no talk-down system. If we got away without a minor disaster, we would be damned lucky.

By the kindness of Allah, the weather as seen in the dawn was good. The men did not call me because they judged, correctly, that there was nothing whatever I could do to make things less than bloody awful . . . It would probably be better if I was kept in ignorance, as I might waste vital time by asking questions. The one crucial task was to get the flow down on the gound safely, somehow — for there was no other airfield they could go to.

It was about 4.30 am, pre-dawn, when an exchange of morse signals began; they were between Gibraltar, other airfields in the area and the York which was then near Cape St Vincent. Each message had to be written down in code and passed to the W/Op who tapped it into the ether. His opposite number in his turn wrote it down and passed it to the recipient for decoding. This made an inescapable delay of several minutes for each message.

First, from Gibraltar to the York: 'Early morning fog. Not expected to clear soon. Divert to Casablanca.'

Dutifully, Wing Commander Collins swung the aircraft to his right, aiming for his new destination on the north African coastline.

The morse-code signals followed one after another:

'York to Casablanca. Arriving with you at 06:15 hrs.'

'Casablanca fog. Divert to Port Lyautey.'

Collins contacted Port Lyautey which answered, 'Fog. Divert to Rabat-Sale.'

And then, 'Rabat-Sale fog. Divert to Gibraltar.'

'Hell!' said Collins. 'This is where I came in.' He decided to abandon the coast with its sea-fog everywhere. He would look for an airfield inland. A new exchange of signals began to be tapped out in simple code, received, and turned over to the controller or the captain, in turn.

'To Ras el Ma. Arriving with you at 06:45 hrs.'

'Roger. You are number 54 to land.'

'Request priority landing.'

'What is your emergency?'

'No emergency. Require priority landing.'

'State your fuel endurance. You are now number 49 to land.'

'Two hours 30 minutes after overhead Ras el Ma.'

'Understand two and a half hours endurance. You are now number forty-one to land.'

The next signal, to the controller's amazement, came through uncoded in plain English: 'Y O R K insists (repeat) insists on priority landing.'

The controller studied this last signal. Y O R K meant nothing to him. All aircraft had four-letter callsigns; he supposed it was merely one which happened to make a word. *Priority* with over *two hours'* fuel? Hells bells! Who in blazes did he think he was? With remaining endurance measured in *hours,* he was demanding priority over machines with spare time to be measured in *minutes*! Pure bollocks! He tossed the paper on to the growing heap and got on with his prime task of getting those aircraft down safely whose emergencies were genuine.

In due course this unrecognised aircraft appeared with its Lancaster wing, four engines, deep square-sided fuselage and three rudders. The controller looked at it with some surprise and not a little curiosity. He had never seen such an animal before. Still, it had plenty of fuel so he told the skipper politely to stand

In the Western Desert during 1940/41 the Blenheims were mostly used for daylight bombing in formation. They were very fragile and ideally they would fly just above a layer of cloud, being largely invisible to the enemy on the ground, but with occasional breaks through which they could see to navigate and to pop down for aiming the bombs. Over the desert this ideal was not found very often.

(via The Aeroplane)

After we had captured the airfield at Benina, burned out hangars, pitted roads and damaged Italian aircraft showed the efficacy of our bombing. However, we soon repaired the runways, put up some tents and brought it back into use again.

(Imperial War Museum)

When the leader dropped his bombs, all aircraft in the formation would drop theirs also, so that the bombs hit the ground in a pattern, causing damage over a considerable area. (via The Aeroplane)

Benghazi harbour, after we captured it, was a sorry sight. In this picture can be seen many sunken ships, some with oil dribbling out. In the background is the harbour mole, which was covered with anti-aircraft guns to protect any ships and tankers unloading. (Imperial War Museum)

During our time in the Western Desert, the Air Force was madly trying to get its hands on a complete Italian CR.42 biplane fighter, so that we could fly it and determine any weaknesses to be exploited. Mostly, the retreating Italians put them out of action before leaving or surrendering. One of our fighters, however, managed to force an Italian to land his CR.42, undamaged, 'behind our own lines!' Before we could get there to assess it, our British soldiers had looted it, happily machine-gunned it, and effectively prevented it ever flying again. Two disconsolate RAF officers scan the wanton damage. (Imperial War Museum)

Dust-storms or 'khamseens' in the desert, which make life seem like living in the bag of a working vacuum-cleaner, are often heralded by the arrival of a 'haboob'. This is a great big rolling wall of sand, blown along by a 30mph gale. It is very unpleasant. One minute you are in clean air, and the next your eyes and mouth are full of grit and your teeth grind when you bite. Horrid.

On the last lap. A BOAC Dakota parked at Gibraltar and silhouetted against The Rock, waits to take Phyl and me to England in 1943 – with another 22 properly authorised passengers, of course. (Imperial War Museum)

During 1943 I put my career in jeopardy for the safety and health of Phyl and our unborn baby. This was what we got for it; Mike, at 4 hours old. Luckily we had enough friends who could, and would, suppress rumours of all my 'heinous' crimes!

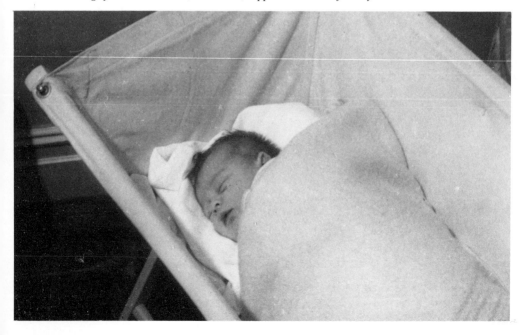

off for half an hour as he was already down to number 23 to land. There were many aircraft, far shorter of fuel than he was, ahead of him. He would be called into the circuit when he had progressed to about number 5 or 6.

To the controller's horror and fury the York ploughed into the landing pattern and made his approach, scattering lesser fry right, left and centre. The controller fired a red Verey flare — an absolute and unequivocal order, saying 'KEEP AWAY! — to try and land will be dangerous!' The York apparently paid no attention and came straight in with the other aircraft pulling away all over the sky.

The controller was angry beyond belief and not a little scared. It was a miracle that there had not been a fatal accident. Saying to his assistant, 'You hold the fort while I go and give that idiot skipper hell for being so bloody dangerous', he ran across to the parking area and stood waiting beside the closed door.

First, when the door was pushed open a pair of steps was lowered, down which came, stepping delicately, an obvious steward in black trousers and a white bum-freezer jacket. The next person to descend was not the aircraft captain upon whom the controller was waiting to vent his bubbling and barely concealed wrath — it was King George VI.

The controller's jaw dropped. He only just remembered to spring to attention and produce a cracking salute. His Majesty, who stuttered slightly and had a very soft voice said 'I w-was told we were going to l-land at Gibraltar. I have to g-get on to Algiers. I understand you c-can refuel my aircraft quickly. I am s-sorry if we are causing you t-trouble.'

The controller assured him that all would be put in hand instantly, with no trouble, and asked to be excused to make the necessary arrangements. Turning, he grabbed the nearest airman and, with all the urgency he could get into his voice, said, 'Go at once to the CO's hut. Wake him and tell him the King is on the airfield.'

'Yes, Sir!' said the airman and turned to go.

All organisations have one or two inoffensive idiots. Normally they get sinecure jobs requiring no brain — like making tea, or taking letters to the nearest pillarbox. The airman that the controller grabbed was such a one. He went towards my hut, repeating the message to himself, over and over so that he would not forget it. He had done about 30 yards when the sense of the last six words sank in — 'the King is on the airfield'. He stopped and thought about it.

Yes. Even on careful reflection, he distinctly remembered that the controller had said 'the King' . . .? This was most remarkable. He had never been near a King, alive and in the flesh. Also, near Fez, in Morocco, it was positively unlikely. He must go at once to see what he could see. He turned and came back to join the growing number of spectators, nearly all of whom were polite enough to try and look as if they were engaged in something obviously useful — but actually finding cover for a look without staring.

It was half an hour before the controller, in desperation, gave up waiting for me to appear and came himself to fetch me. I was asleep. Slowly, I became aware of a human being standing beside the bed and saying something. I felt simply terrible. I concentrated on his words. He said, 'Sir, the King is on the airfield and wishes to shake you by the hand.'

My response, in my slugged state, was short and vulgar. Though two words only, its total meaning was clear. He should go away, for I was not interested in far-fetched practical jokes; and especially not at 7.30; and particularly not on a Sunday morning; and anyway it was impossible, for we were in deepest Morocco.

He said slowly, beseechingly and carefully, as to an idiot child, 'Sir, our Monarch, His Majesty King George the Sixth is standing on the airfield. Due to an error he has already been standing there half an hour, waiting to shake you by the hand.'

To say that I was startled by this virtually impossible piece of intelligence would be a masterpiece of understatement. I must have broken the world record for the lying-high-jump and not come down for some seconds. Thoughts came racing to, but barely through, my addled brain. I felt my chin — could I get away without a shave? The stubble grated against my fingers; no escape. I turned to the looking glass. It was terrible, seeing my ghastly hungover visage with a couple of eyes looking like eggs poached in blood. Behind it, I saw the agonised controller, and remember croaking at him to go and tell the King I would be there in five minutes. A few moments could be saved by not soaping my face. I grabbed my razor. Thank God I had a reasonably clean uniform to put on.

The result was entirely predictable to any normally sane person. My quivering fingers so misguided my razor that, before I realised what was happening, I had some deep slashes across my face, spouting blood like the fountains at the Chateau of

Versailles. I eventually reached the aircraft parking area, dressed and clean except for blood spots on my khaki tunic. In my left hand was clutched a handkerchief, trying to staunch the flow of blood from three vicious razor slashes. Firmly gripping the handkerchief to my chin, my right hand was left free to salute my Monarch and then, after bowing, to shake him by the hand — as he had proposed to do much earlier. He looked a trifle taken aback which, from what he was seeing above and below the handkerchief, was hardly surprising.

'Your Majesty, would you like breakfast? We can give you as many scrambled eggs as you can eat.'

This, I judged, was a good opening gambit. In England, food rationing during the war permitted one shell-egg per week and the Royal Family took no more than their loyal subjects were allowed. I still swear that he was on the threshold of accepting my offer with pleasure, but black-trousers-and-white-bum-freezer sprang between us, saying petulantly, 'His Majesty has *had* breakfast, already, in the aircraft!'

The King, politely, took a pace backwards. I begged leave to oversee the arrangements for his onward journey; also to guide his high-level helps and the aircrew towards the scrambled eggs which they most obviously craved. I had already noted their eyes shining like undipped headlamps at the mention of *real* eggs, scrambled, in quantity.

Refuelling and servicing were simple. Our grave problem, thanks to HQTC's foresight, was to send out any kind of signal, to anybody, anywhere. On the way in, Collins had told Gib that he was about to land safely but, prudently, omitting to mention his destination. Gib, naturally and wrongly, presumed it was Casablanca . . . which it wasn't and *they* didn't know where he had gone. So, from that moment, the King had vanished off the face of the earth so far as anyone outside Ras el Ma was concerned.

Two people in particular, in Algiers, were especially interested in getting some indication of where he was, and whether he needed assistance? These were his hosts, the Land and Air commanders, General Eisenhower and Air Marshal Tedder.

I got hold of the cipher officer, who was bleary-eyed and dropping with fatigue. Together we concocted and wrote out the shortest safe and yet perfectly lucid signal that we could devise. It went under 'Most Immediate' priority; this was specially reserved for imminent air attack. For me, a mere Wing Commander, harbouring the Monarch of the British Empire (whom his hosts had mislaid) sounded as perilous as any air attack. The peril was not imminent either; it was already in my lap. The signal just said: 'Personal to Tedder from Dudgeon. He arrives ten-thirty.' Tedder was plenty sharp enough; he knew me well; he knew where I was; 'He' could only mean one person. Two and two would be put together with no difficulty.

In due course we recovered the lackeys and aircrew from their mountains of scrambled eggs, stowed them in the aircraft with the VIP, and sent them all on their way.

HQTC had done a sterling job. No one, but no one, could beat the security blackout. The airwaves were well and truly clogged and the signal took two hours to arrive — imminent air attack or no. The result was a sight treasured for their lifetimes by all witnesses. To be seen were two cars with flags flying, flanked by outriders with screaming sirens, driving like lunatics from the town headquarters to the airfield. In the rear seats were Eisenhower and Tedder, teeth gritted, clinging on to the sides for dear life, trying to reach the airfield tarmac before the King Emperor did so.

They didn't. He was already standing in the shade under the York's wing. For the second time in one morning the King was waiting to greet somebody and shake them by the hand, instead of the other way round. I doubt he was very impressed with 'military efficiency'.

Chapter 20
Baron

Some days after the King George VI affair, a signal arrived saying that a Group Captain Worrall would be arriving from 216 Group Headquarters in Cairo. I was delighted. 'Baron' Worrall and I had known each other, in the Desert, for a long time. He was tall, slim, and with a widow's peak and pointed chin. His face was shaped rather like a brown Ace of Hearts and his skin took on a leatherlike tan from the sun, emphasising the blueness of his eyes. He had always struck me as an efficient officer and showing him round would be a pleasure: I was proud of my outfit. Also, with luck, there could be some additional profit; he might be persuaded to go back and do something really positive to solve our endless problems in handling passengers comfortably and well. Certainly, the many transient passengers whom I had asked to emphasise our difficulties hadn't produced any practical results so far.

In good Service tradition I was standing on the tarmac to meet my senior when he got out of the Dakota on its scheduled arrival. We greeted each other as old friends and, after a cup of coffee in my office-tent, he asked to be shown all round. This was just what I wanted, and we went round everything — including showing off the marvellous American equipment 'acquired' in exchange for semi-illicit scotch whisky.

That evening we were sitting drinking my best grade of plonk on the little verandah of my hut. Baron had laughed immoderately when he saw it taken from the coffin, and voted it a splendid idea to combine seat and store in one space-saving item, at a very low price.

He told me he had heard and was curious about the conflicting stories which reached the Cairo end of the line. Several people had made outright complaints that the facilities were far below those which should be accorded to their rank and status. On the other hand, some had been more than complimentary about our efforts and successes, considering the obvious difficulties. Indeed, the loudest praise of all had come from the Secretary of State for Air and his entourage, who had been accompanying the King in the York. He had eulogised loud and long at the way the unexpected aircraft had been efficiently handled, and how well the passengers had been fed before sending them on their way to the next stop — Algiers. I made a mental note always to give VIPs massive helpings of scrambled eggs for breakfast, whenever they arrived from England. It seemed that a propitious moment had arrived to make my plea for help from above. I began: 'As you have doubtless noted, all this tented accommodation and the primitive messing facilities don't really give an opportunity to handle passengers properly. I hope that when you get back to Group HQ you will be able to . . .'

Baron interrupted me. 'Don't you know why I'm here?'

'No, Sir. Just the signal to say you were arriving from Group . . . on a normal staff visit, I assumed.'

'Frankly Tony, this is very embarrassing! I'm not going back . . . I've been sent to take over this place from you.'

To say that I was surprised would have only told the half of it. He went on, 'Some weeks back, Whitney said he was dissatisfied because of complaints that were coming through. He had decided that the place was a shambles which needed cleaning up and it had to be run properly. He told me to come here and do it. Admittedly, he was a bit startled when everybody on the royal York took endless pains to tell him how simply marvellous everything was here and what a splendid outfit you had — but he had already given me my marching orders, HQME had authorised the switch, and so that was that.'

'He gave you no letter for me? No details of the complaints?'

'No; nothing. I came here, assuming he must already have written to you.'

'No, he hasn't. And what happens to me?'

'I've no idea . . . I suppose you go back to Cairo.'

'And do you find the place the shambles that Whitney told you you would find?

'Frankly, no,' said Baron. 'I think what has been achieved, in the circumstances, is first class — and, so far as I have seen, "cleaning up" doesn't come into it.'

Dissatisfied passengers had been asked to voice their complaints where they could produce some action. They had, and there certainly was action. The action was to fire me!

Nevertheless, the Baron was incredibly generous and kind in his awkward situation. I am glad to record that it did not stop us remaining good friends for many years to come.

Two days later, metaphorically shrugging my shoulders, I set off for Cairo.

Chapter 21
His Return

Baron Worrall had been warming his chair for only a few days, trying to get a grip of all the multifarious duties that faced him, when he was told the interesting but somewhat startling plans for the King's return to England after his Middle East tour. It would be far too dangerous for him to be seen at Gib. The German agents in Algeciras and La Linea would have ample time to warn the German night-fighters in France long before the York could get past the danger zone. On the other hand, the 'powers that be' judged that no agent or mole in the Fez area could get information out of French-Morocco, past Spanish-Morocco, to the Germans in Europe, quickly enough for it to pose a danger during the night flight. So, on some unspecified day in the future, after the final decison on weather suitability for the whole trip had been made, the King would leave Algiers late in the afternoon to stop off at Ras el Ma. That evening he would take off for England, going over the Atlantic by night as he had done on the way out. In between his arrival at Ras el Ma, and before take-off, Baron could give him dinner at a local hotel.

At first glance that sounded grossly insecure for any royalty but, on second thoughts, why not? And it might be fun for the King — if a little nerve-racking for Baron, his host. There was, and is, a magnificent hotel on the outskirts of Fez, called the Palais Jamai, which had been built in Moorish style as a palace during the 17th century by the Sultan's vizier. An ex-palace would be eminently suitable for feeding a monarch, even if the food had to come from what could be grown locally — although the preparation and cooking were reputed to be excellent. Baron hadn't yet had a chance to go there but it was said to be both top class and quiet. Baron intended to nip up there in the next day or so, to give it a once-over.

'Some unspecified day in the future' be damned! It was the very next morning that they pressed the button in Algiers. His Majesty would arrive that very afternoon at 6 pm and take off again at 9.30 in the evening.

Baron vowed to himself that, this time, no one was going to be able to point any finger of criticism or ridicule at Ras el Ma. Everything was going to go like clockwork, or else! Although he did not yet know each and every one of his officers personally, I had introduced him to all the heads of sections and he scuttled round his domain making sure that everybody, from controllers to cooks, knew just what was expected of them.

There was no question of him finding time to check out the Palais Jamai as well, so Hoggy, in his official capacity as the Squadron Leader in charge of administration, was despatched to do the job. He was to make sure of a secluded table for two; that would take care of the King. Then, they would need another table nearby, but not oppressively so, for as many hangers-on — number unknown — as turned up in the York. Of course, to maintain security as long as possible, Hoggy must in no circumstances let slip in the morning that the King was coming; he could imply that the elegant dinner for two was directed at a very refined and retiring piece of goods with the station commander. Nothing need be said. Just place one finger beside the nose, lower the chin a fraction and look up quizzically from under raised eyebrows. If the management promptly offered a private room with thick velvet curtains and a luxurious *chaise longue,* and were surprised when it was declined, they could think what they wished of the mad English. Being Middle Eastern, they would perhaps think the reticence less odd when both the diners turned out to be men. And perfectly normal if they recognised the King — they would promptly switch to the idea that the Emperor had some form of *droit de seigneur* over Baron.

Hoggy would use his judgement on whether to order a set menu, or let the Monarch give himself a treat — probably unenjoyed since he was a youth — by ordering his meal *a la carte.* It would depend on what the Jamai had on offer. The hangers-on could take pot luck.

No matter that lunch passed Baron by while he was checking everything out . . . he was booked for a first class dinner. He made sure that he had plenty of time; he was not going to get caught (as I had been) without his trousers up and correctly fastened. Satisfied at last with all his arrangements, he went off to the hut in mid-afternoon to get ready.

Disconsolately he looked over his wardrobe. As with nearly all men out in the field, laundry facilities within striking range did not exist, so proper washing and ironing frequently had to go by the boards. A boiled, creased, sun-dried shirt might be clean, but it doesn't inspire many glances of admiration and approval. His shirts were clean but unpressed; one pair of slacks was in reasonable shape. The only upper garment that looked as though it had not recently been taken from a waste paper basket was his bush-jacket. He weighed it up dispassionately.

The trouble was that bush-jackets were not authorised RAF uniform. On the other hand, it was a serviceable garment. Undoubtedly the game-warden in East Africa who designed it originally had done a fine job. It was an obvious mixture: its lapels, open neck and short sleeves pointed to its shirt parentage, while patch pockets, with rank badges slipped over the epaulettes, were plainly derived from a tunic. But it was passably smart and, above all, it was clean and tolerably pressed. In addition it was cool, having no shirt under it and with his medal ribbons it looked pretty good. Admittedly, everybody out in the field wore them, but what would the minus score be for greeting and entertaining the most prestigious officer in your Service when you were improperly dressed? How many brownie-points might that cost if someone saw, and mentioned it? Oh, well . . . he laid out his slacks and bush-jacket on the bed and brushed them off as best he could.

Early afternoon, two hours before the arrival, he prepared to clean himself personally so that even a most delicate nostril would not pick up any desert smell. And, being dark-complexioned, he would have a shave at the same time to avoid showing a blue chin later in the evening. He undressed, wrapped a towel round his waist and, carrying his wash-bag, sauntered across to the line of shower roses. Hot water in the showers and plenty of it! It was delicious to feel the warm flow trickling between his shoulder-blades. He metaphorically doffed his hat to the Americans who, when they put their minds to it, even in the field did things well. He began to sing as he soaped himself. Hearing the sound of an aircraft he instinctively looked up, as does every pilot, always. It was the York, wheels extended and turning into the landing pattern: say, about three minutes from touchdown?

In 200 BC Archimedes, a Greek mathematician, had a sudden and unexpected revelation while he was washing himself. He was so excited that he sprang from his ablutions and ran, stark naked, to his dwelling, flapping his bath towel and crying 'Eureka!' as an expression of delight. This act has brought him undying fame down the centuries. In 1943 AD the Baron had an equally sudden and unexpected revelation while he was washing himself. He too ran stark naked to his dwelling, bath towel waving in his hand. However, he earned no fame — possibly because he was not shouting 'Eureka!' as an expression of pleasure. His cries expressed no delight at all; he mouthed some very uncouth words and phrases indeed, directed at people who failed to keep to their published schedules. In the end, just before the King came down the steps he ran, panting, up to the aircraft. Fortunately, he had had no time to start shaving, so his chin did not need to be hidden.

King George shook him warmly by the hand, peering intently as Baron tried to still his heaving chest. Baron waited, correctly, for Royalty to speak first. The King shook his head as if to clear his brain and had another puzzled peering look. At last he spoke — and when Baron told me the tale, he did not mimic any stuttering.

'Good afternoon.' Pause. 'Tell me, you aren't the Station Commander whom I met here last week . . . are you?'

'Good day, Your Majesty. No, Sir. I took over from him only a few days ago.'

'I am so glad I was right. It was a little difficult to be sure as your predecessor's face was half hidden by a handkerchief. I gather that the announcement of my arrival came as something of a shock when he was in the middle of shaving, and he cut himself rather drastically. I trust you were expecting us, and that we have arrived at the correct time?'

'Oh dear,' thought Baron, 'what do I say now? I can lie, and what if he finds out later? Here goes . . . the truth . . . and I hope it makes him laugh.'

'Yes, Sir, indeed we are expecting you and I shall have the honour of giving you dinner tonight. Your aircraft is, I must admit, two hours ahead of schedule. Fortunately, I was not shaving when you appeared overhead so you can see all my face. I was only taking a shower.'

The King did not laugh. He was bloody angry and muttered half-audible phrases, the gist of which was that he would have someone's guts for garters if they couldn't come closer than two hours adrift on a tiddly little flight from Algiers. Baron quaked at the thought of the coming five hours, if his mood did not get any better.

He thought that the best thing to do was to get the King off the camp and away to the Palais Jamai. There was a long night ahead of him and it could be bumpy. To relax in a deep armchair with tea, followed by drinks and then dinner, might have a calming effect. Baron took a deep breath and began, 'I think it would be a good idea, Sir, if we went to the Palais Jamai hotel. It is extremely comfortable and we dine there tonight. We have no staff-cars here, nor drivers, so I am driving you myself, in my Jeep.'

The King nodded his assent, saying 'Where is this hotel?' Baron offered up a short prayer as he began to repeat what Hoggy had told him, hoping that the briefing was accurate and well judged. 'It is on the edge of Fez, Sir. We drive a short distance towards the town until we see an old arched gateway in the walls. We then turn left, along the road which runs round the city. The hotel is not too far along that road, on the right, overlooking the ancient town. The panorama is magnificent.'

The King was still scowling and being grumpy as they started off. Conversation was, at best, stilted. To Baron's dismay the 'short distance' to the gateway in the ancient walls turned out to be over five miles. However, thank God, the turnoff before the gate in the walls was there, as briefed.

'How far along here is the hotel?'

'Oh, not very far now, Sir. It's just along here, on the right.' Another mile went by.

'How far now?'

'A little way, Sir. Along here,' spluttered Baron, '. . . on the right . . . soon . . .'

'Tell me, Group Captain, do you know where this place really is?'

Baron's heart sank into his boots. How on earth was he going to explain away that he had no proper idea where he was, or even that the road he was on was the right one? And all this to an irritated King of England sitting beside him in a Jeep!

'Sir, I have not yet been to this hotel. I haven't had a chance to do so in the few days I have been here, taking over. I accept the responsibility for having had the detailed arrangements for the hotel made on my behalf. My informant said that the hotel was 'along the road round the city, not too far after you turn off before the gate.' That is all I can say. It is Sir, of course, entirely my fault and I most humbly apologise.'

The King burst into roars of laughter. From that moment on he was in a marvellously good mood and improving every minute as the road twisted round hairpin bends, climbed up through the trees, passed scattered fields, apparently going miles from the city of Fez — or from any reasonable habitation for that matter — as it headed for the outer edges of French-Morocco; or so Baron felt. He, meanwhile, was getting more and more alarmed and jittery; a breakdown or puncture would be an appalling disaster. The King was clearly delighted. He obviously had never been lost by any official escort before and he thought it was a huge joke. He prodded Baron on the arm and said, 'What's that garment you're wearing?'

'Oh Lord!' thought Baron. 'Here we go again. He's spotted it. More trouble ahead.' He answered, 'I am sincerely sorry, Sir, for being improperly dressed. I put it on because it is the only reasonably clean and tidy uniform I have here. I thought it better to be clean than to be . . .'

The King cut him short: 'I'm not talking about that. I want to know what it is and where you got it from. It looks splendid. They dress me up in all these thick clothes, in several layers, because they tell me I have to be in 'correct uniform'. I want a tunic like yours. How can I get one?'

Baron picked his words cautiously. 'Well, Sir, it's like this. As the result of some thinking not understood fully by me, our top-level masters have decided that these garments, called bush-jackets, are not smart enough to be Air Force uniform. We, on the factory floor so to speak, find that in the hot weather you soon become extremely un-smart with sweat marks and creases when you wear shirts, ties, lined tunics and all that stuff. Also, later, they begin to smell because you cannot wash a tailored padded tunic and, where we work, dry-cleaning doesn't exist — it is only in big modern cities. So we wear bush-jackets whenever no one in officialdom is looking. If you want one, you might get it from the Army, who, I believe, are allowed to wear them. And were you, Sir, firmly to put your Air Force rank badges on its epaulettes, as we do, I am far from convinced that anyone would have the nerve to say you mustn't do it.'

Baron and his monarch had a delightful evening together. The dinner was excellent. The King showed himself to be extremely observant and told many amusing anecdotes about what his hosts had said and done, all around his Middle East tour. A lesser mortal would have been said to have 'sung for his supper'.

One tale about him, which went round the Middle East like a bolt of lightning, showed that his query on Baron's bush-jacket was not the first question he had asked about RAF uniform. Group Captain Ronnie Lees (now Air Marshal Sir Ronald) had worn desert-boots. The King had appeared wearing (correctly) highly polished black shoes with his khaki Air Force uniform. At his request, Ronnie explained that his ankle boots in light-brown suede were comfortable and practical in the desert — if irregular: they kept out most of the sand and didn't show the dust. The King looked wistfully down at his dusty, scruffy, black feet and said: 'How sensible; they never let *me* wear things like that. It's not really worth being a King these days!'

Baron drove him back to the York after dinner — this time followed by an escort which he had sent for — and the take-off went as planned, at 9.30.

About six weeks later, and for no apparent reason which anyone could fathom — except that Baron could make a shrewd guess — London suddenly issued an official instruction. It said that RAF personnel could wear bush-jackets in hot countries.

Chapter 22
My Return

Back in Cairo from Ras el Ma, I trotted off to HQ Middle East to see the postings staff and learn what my next job was to be. 'Posters' have almost unlimited power over your body, but to be on the postings staff is thankless, for those posted are seldom really satisfied. I was no exception. Being a Wing Commander myself, it was another Wing Commander who saw me; this was normal procedure — to relieve a more junior officer from having to argue from lower status. I knew the man slightly and he had held an office job in Cairo all through the war. He had red hair, blotchy skin, small eyes and he was far from one of my favourite people. The conversation was positive, but did not tell me anything I wanted to hear.

'You want to know your next job? Something in England. Transport Command seem to think they want you. You're senior enough to be flown back, via Gibraltar, and they will decide exactly what to do with you when you get there.'

'And does my wife come with me?' I asked.

'No. She'll travel by sea; embark at Suez, when we have a troopship. Then, southwards all the way round South Africa, and back via the Atlantic to the UK. Although the recent airborne landings have got the Yanks and ourselves into Sicily, the Med's not open yet for shipping. Allah alone knows when it will be, and He won't tell me.'

Hah! I thought, I can spike this one if I'm crafty! I said, 'There won't be time to do that. She's going to have a baby, our first, in two months. She'll *have* to be flown home.'

'She won't you know! She's not allowed to travel within three months of a baby — before or after — by air or by sea. So she'll have to wait here till she has it, and then another three months, and then home round The Cape as I said before. Or she might get through the Mediterranean by then, if it's open for non-operational shipping.'

I tried pleading. 'But you can't do that! It'll be six months before she's allowed to leave, and could be up to eight before she gets home. Where is she going to live on her own, for six months, after I go, as a lone civilian, in Cairo? And how is she going to cope with having the baby, by herself, in a foreign country?'

'My dear chap,' he sighed, 'that's *your* problem. Stop belly-aching and remember you've been bloody lucky so far, having your wife out here in a war theatre, living with her and having a proper family life. Most of us out here haven't seen our wives, stuck there in England, since Mussolini declared war three years ago. Some have children who are missing brothers and sisters. Some have kids, over two years old, that they've never seen.'

Hypocrite! Forked tongues! I knew perfectly well that he himself had been in Cairo for yonks years, with his wife and family. I switched to indignation. 'But, look here, what about money? My allowances for being in Egypt will stop when I leave; what happens about enough cash for her to live on, if you keep her here and send me there?'

He raised his eyes to the ceiling, saying unctuously, 'The question of money is nothing to do with *me,* old boy. That's something you'll have take up with the akker-bashers*. There may be some special allowances . . . or not. I don't know.'

I looked at the Wing Commander's wispy red hair, balding in patches, and his pinched face, his large freckles and his pig-eyes. They confirmed in my mind that I didn't like him. I fired one last shot — amiability. 'Well, I know you have a difficult job to do, and no one wants to be the harbinger of bad news, but how about letting me have some kind of posting around here? Anything, even something menial; such as being your assistant, ha-ha! Just for the six months? Then, I fly home when she goes by sea, if we couldn't travel together by then . . .? How about that? I am sure you must have *some* slots needing back-up for a short spell?'

He gave me a stony look for a few moments. Then, 'Be reasonable. You know full well you can talk the hind leg off a donkey — convincingly at that — and you are an ace at getting your own way. However, you have been out of England for over seven years — India, Singapore, Egypt and elsewhere — so your return to UK is long overdue. You've just come to the end of a posting, and this is a good moment to make the break. And you've been asked for in England. It's bad luck that your wife's in the very worst situation so far as timing goes for having her baby — but lots of girls have had to have babies without their

*Akker: troops' slang for an Egyptian piastre – about 1p

husbands around them. There's a damned good Anglo-American Hospital on Gezira. You were born in this country; you must have dozens of local friends — and relatives. You are probably better placed than any other person in the entire Middle East Command, if they were to be faced with the same problem and timing. Go back to your wife. Tell her the awkward news. Make the necessary arrangements, and I'll be in touch sometime to tell you how and when you leave. OK?'

I gave him a look which I hoped was a suitable mixture of sorrow, despair, anguish and stoic resignation, with a spicing of indignation and anger thrown in; in reality, I probably looked like a leering mental defective. The irritation was that he had done his homework splendidly; I was beaten because he was absolutely right, on every count. Greek met Greek. Nevertheless, I still didn't warm to him.

When I got home I talked it over with Phyl. It was absolutely true that I could make perfectly satisfactory arrangements for her to have the baby in due course; my mother naturally would ensure she neither starved nor went in rags before she sailed. It was the prospect of a trooper, six months later, that neither of us liked one tiny bit. That voyage home through the Atlantic was downright frightening: the German U-boat packs were having a lot of successes. The thought of my beloved and her unweaned infant in a lifeboat hundreds of miles from land or, worse, struggling in the grey-green waves . . . it made my flesh creep. Many troopers arrived safely; but some didn't . . .

We also discussed what we believed, wrongly, was yet another risk. We imagined that having a first baby in England would be safer for her, and easier, than in Egypt. We did not know that hospitals, the good ones, were booked up months in advance. To be certain of having a bed for a wartime delivery the girl had to say 'May I book in for the arrival of my baby nine and a half months hence — my husband comes on leave next week?'

Be that as it may, having got acceptance but not wholehearted backing from Phyl, I decided to bet my livelihood against her security — my career for the safety of her and the unborn child. If I was ever to succeed, I would need an incredible amount of goodwill, and good luck, from top to bottom. Failure would, almost without question, result in me being booted out of the Air Force. Next morning I went to see my late AOC, Air Commodore Whitney Straight. The stakes were being laid.

Coming to the point without preamble, I said, 'I wish to ask you a question, Sir. I want an absolutely truthful answer, with no frills or evasions. If you heard a rumour that some woman had been flown away in a Service aircraft, would you make it your business to find out if there was any truth behind the rumour'?

Whitney sat bolt upright in his chair as though somebody had thrust a hat-pin through the seat and into his bum. His eyes bugged out like glass marbles. 'I can't give you permission to fly Phyl home!'

'That is not my question, Sir. I am asking no direct favour. If you are told something officially, you will have no choice but to take official action on it. Of course. That will be that. However, if anybody puts his mind to unearthing the truth behind a chance rumour, it can always be dug up eventually. What I am saying is, if over a dinner party maybe, you hear a wild rumour that some girl got airborne in a Service aircraft, would you then make it your business to establish whether the remark is true?'

'Of course I wouldn't chase up rumours. But you . . .'

I cut him short, impolitely. 'Thank you, Sir; that is all I wanted to know.'

The next hurdle was at Cairo-West airfield. It was the base for the Dakotas which did all the passenger and freight work, up and down the length of North Africa. Group Captain John Rankin was the CO and therefore an absolutely key individual. There was no point in even lifting a finger unless Rankin too was prepared to forgo rumour-tracing. I knew so well how people low down in the military hierarchy cherish their childlike beliefs that COs don't know much of what goes on beyond the ends of their noses. Nothing is further from the truth. I had already experienced, as a boss, how necessary it is positively to turn one's head aside not to see all the things that happen.

John Rankin did not answer my question directly. He gazed at the ceiling for a while as he pondered the outrageous undertaking. As I waited I thought 'this is being nonsensical; how can I be so selfish as to suggest he risks his job by pretending not to know!' Then John started to chuckle, his shoulders shook and finally he burst into a great big belly-laugh. At last, regaining his composure but not taking his eyes from the ceiling he spoke, musingly as though to himself, 'I haven't been keeping up my flying hours properly, recently, and I haven't visited Morocco yet. I think I'll do a trip there in a few days' time. We always have passengers on our regular runs and, if there happens to be a woman's name on the passenger list, who on earth between here and Morocco — including me — could know whether that name ought or ought not to be there? And, of course, all passengers on the list must be on board before take-off. When I get back, who knows but I might perhaps find, on doing a routine inspection, that the Air Movements Section had made an error, which needed to be corrected. For example, they might inadvertently have filed two passenger manifests for one flight, with discrepancies. We should naturally have to dispose of the one that was wrong.'

Whitney indeed had been a generous subscriber of goodwill towards me, but John outdid him by a mile!

Phyl, carrying all before her (she went from 8 to 12 stone) was too uncomfortable to sit, hour after hour, on the hard-arse aluminium inward facing seats of a wartime Dakota. John Rankin had agreed that she could sit in a 'Rookie chair' at the rear of the cabin, facing towards the front. Rookie chairs were a product of the British Raj, in India. Ingeniously, the wooden frame could be dismantled and wrapped in the canvas part which formed the back and the seat. Assembled, it became a tolerably large and very comfortable armchair in which you could sip the *chota-peg* brought by your bearer. However, Phyl was not sipping a small whisky; she was knitting a shawl for the coming baby. She looked very regal upon her throne with the double row of passengers facing her on either side. They could have been courtiers and, if she had held a sceptre instead of the knitting-needles, she would have been queen of the entire outfit.

I was happily flying as co-pilot to John. It was no hard task in a Dak; 'George', the automatic and third pilot, was flying it most of the time. We exchanged an occasional comment, but my mind was far away. Two and a half years earlier I commanded No 55 Squadron, equipped with the ubiquitous Blenheims. We were about to fly across all of my hunting ground. Our operations had spread from our base at Fuka, a couple of hundred miles from Cairo, westwards over yellow desert past the Egyptian/Libyan frontier to Bardia, Tobruk, and Derna. Derna was the area where the Jebel el Akhdar — the Green Desert — began, extending to Benina and the Italian port of Benghazi. Colonisation of the 300-mile coastal strip of Cyrenaica had been one part of Mussolini's efforts to recreate a Roman Empire. I knew the area as I knew the back of my hand and it would be like a movie re-run as we flew over the towns, roads, airfields and tiny regularly spaced farmsteads. Any cultivation, with the general shortage of water, was parched and miserable. Each colonist had been given a tiny house and a plot of land but, in those marginal agricultural conditions, the living extracted must have been a pittance.

My time there, fortunately, was before the Germans arrived with their Messerschmitt 109s and 110s which shot the Blenheims clear out of the sky. On the ground, we dreamed up any and every light-hearted scheme or jest to counter the excruciating boredom between tasks; in the air, every operational flight had been a planning challenge on how to complete a given job while avoiding the calamity which could engulf you and your crews at any time. Airborne, one was endlessly alert for Italian fighters coming from any part of the sky. Now, in astonishing contrast, I was placidly droning along in an unarmed aircraft, keeping a half-hearted lookout and sitting contentedly under a roof because it kept off the sun's rays.

I was seeing the area probably for the last time, and memories came flooding back, clearly and vividly. I encouraged each vignette to return to my mind, even searching back to re-savour the little details.

Chapter 23
Contestants

An hour and a half out from Cairo, a long line of white surf over to my right drew the boundary between sandy beaches of the blue Mediterranean and beige desert beneath us. We were approaching at a slight angle and I watched the white strip getting closer and closer. Then, far away in the distance I could just distinguish a well remembered promontory, sticking out five miles into the sea — Ras el Kenayis. I never knew who Kenayis was but his Ras, or head, had made a superb landmark for us returning in our Blenheims at night or in a dust storm. It was the only significant projection in a more-or-less straight coastline for 50 miles in either direction. Just inland would be the hard, sandy patch called Fuka. This was the name of my airfield. Three Blenheim squadrons, day-bombers each with a dozen aircraft, made up the total Desert light-bomber force. Two of them were Nos 113 and 211. The third, based at Fuka, was No 55 Squadron. Fuka and '55' were mine — all mine. I was monarch of all I surveyed: Squadron Commander, Station Commander, the local god. I was 24. Looking back, I must have been far too big for my boots.

As Ras el Kenayis passed by, I saw the patch of sand that had once been Fuka. Nothing was there. We, and all its later tenants, had followed the retreating Germans far into Libya, Tunisia and beyond. While we were there, however, before the Benghazi Harriers raced past Benghazi for the last time, we had settled ourselves in very comfortably.

*   *   *

In our Mess hut, made from packing cases, we ate, drank and played cards. Because of the need for total blackout, it was hot and airless. But we had electric light, provided by courtesy of our signals officer, from the generator which operated our flashing neon beacon nearby. Cleverly, he had arranged that our lights did not flash on and off in time with the scarlet beacon; they held steady. Also, he had most adroitly wired the Mess lights to the door, so that if anyone went out the lights did too, to preserve the blackout.

The unremitting stress of trying to outwit people of equal intelligence who are doing their utmost to kill you, and the aircrew for whom you are responsible, is mentally very exhausting. Bridge in the desert was a wonderful relaxation. You cannot play bridge and at the same time think over, re-think, plan and re-plan tomorrow's raid. The game completely closes your mind off from work. However, desert bridge had some problems and some house-rules that would not be welcomed at Crockford's!

An occasional Italian Savoia 79 bomber would come and sprinkle bombs on the coastal strip we occupied. Someone each night was the air-raid warden and he would blow the siren if he heard the unmistakable beat of an S.79's three engines. The Mess door would be flung open as everybody rushed to the slit-trenches outside. There would be complete silence as we listened to the triple beat except for one plaintive voice saying, always, 'Goddammit — that was the first good hand I've had the whole evening and that bastard Savoia wrecks it.' Always, it would be followed by a gust of unsympathetic laughter as Mess rules dictated that any hand interrupted by the enemy was null and void; no effort to reconstruct it was permitted. Grumbling, we went back with the 'all clear'.

I regret to record that some of my partners and opponents could be a trifle unscrupulous at times. The nearest place to meet a call of nature was a 'desert lily' some 50 yards away (a desert lily is a funnel made from an old petrol tin and dug into the sand). Although we had little beer, people had to go out sometimes. If someone went out, one of the cries to follow him into the darkness would almost surely be 'For the love of Allah close that bloody door quickly! Someone who has a bad hand is going to upset this damned card table "by mistake" as sure as God made little apples.' It was remarkable how often someone, unidentified, 'bumped into' the card table in the dark.

One day, without warning, we were issued with a vacuum cleaner. It was received with hysterical laughter because the staff officer who authorised its purchase and supply was simply not in our league. It was an ordinary domestic cleaner with a suction tube and the usual six feet of flex. The Equipment Officer told me that the papers with it said it was for clearing sand from the aircraft. He must be joking! Aircraft were dispersed around the edge of our sand patch, and no electric power came near any of them. More: the sole power supply was the generator for our beacon to get us home at night, and I was not going to let anyone wear it out in the daytime as well. The problems in keeping it going by night were already big enough. Anyway, sand in our aircraft needed a small shovel to clear it, or a commercial-size extractor, not a household cleaner. When we sent an aircraft to the Delta for major overhaul, the usual amount of sand coming out was in the region of 100 lbs.

Loath to waste a good piece of equipment, we decided that it could become a makeshift air-conditioner for the Mess. 'Conditioner' might be an overstatement, but at least it could be a powered ventilator to suck out the fug — fug almost thick enough to dig bits out of with a spoon and from which we suffered at night because of the blackout. The extracted fug would, we assumed, be replaced by fresh air drawn through the cracks. In the event it was like a young call-girl taking on an old sugar-daddy; the idea was great but the performance was hopeless. It just couldn't do enough work to achieve the objective.

Our engineer officer, a mad but clever Irishman called O'Hanlon, was quite undaunted. He had the brilliant idea of turning the machine round so that it blew instead of sucked. A suitable hole was drilled in the Mess wall and the tube inserted. Connected to the power system, it was turned on that evening. Congratulations were poured on 'O'Haitch'. Night air that felt positively cold poured through the nozzle and everyone got as close as possible . . . after me. I had used my rank and status to get the best place, right beside its cooling spout. This was too much for Nick Nicholson, the senior Flight Lieutenant. Quietly and without a word he left the Mess. If anyone gave it a thought, they probably assumed he was visiting the desert lily.

Suddenly, the Mess erupted into a bedlam of coughs and sneezes, with me leading the chorus. In the background were peals of ribald laughter coupled with shouts of unheeded advice. Nick, outside, had emptied into the whirring vacuum cleaner a full carton of ground pepper!

Almost without fail, we would have to fly one bombing raid by each squadron each day and a second on some nights: sometimes with a flight of three; sometimes a squadron of nine; and, very occasionally, we put up everything we could get airborne. Our targets seemed nearly always to be airfields and ports, in particular the ports of Bardia and Tobruk — bombing from high level. 'High level' for us meant 12-15,000 ft because, as we did not have the luxury of oxygen, that was our practical physical limit. It is certainly *possible* to go much higher without losing consciousness, but lack of oxygen makes you progressively more stupid. It is exactly like drunkenness — you feel brighter, but you are dimmer. That type of unrecognised stupidity in a car-driver's seat often results in death; in an aeroplane-driver's seat, and with some fighters around who are trying to find you and kill you as well, it is even more risky to become mentally sluggish!

Another of our practical limitations had been from the aircraft itself. A Blenheim, though a marvellous aeroplane when first designed as a civilian airliner, was proved in early wartime days to be not much more resistant to battle damage than an electric light-bulb. We, luckily, only had the Italian Fiat-made CR42 biplane fighters to contend with. They, too, were wonderful machines for their time and very manoeuvrable, but they suffered from a couple of problems which saved a lot of our lives. First, the mountings of their machine-guns were not tough enough, and the barrels wavered about; therefore most of the streams of bullets went harmlessly past, even if the aim had been good. They used a lot of tracer and we called them flaming ping-pong balls. When these glowing red fireworks flipped past your ear, as they did most of the time, it was extremely alarming but fortunately, taken all round, not madly dangerous. The second saving grace, for us, was that the Italian fighter-pilots lacked a lot in determination when it came to closing right in, steadfastly pointing their guns at us for a close kill.

Our main problem with the CR42s was the extreme manoeuvrability of those single-engined biplanes, compared with our twin-engined monoplanes. They knew we had no effective guns firing downwards, nor did we have self-sealing petrol tanks. This meant that a CR42 pilot, who was braver and craftier than most of his colleagues, could sneak up in comparative safety from behind and below, taking his time over aiming careful and leisurely squirts of incendiary bullets at our unguarded and unarmoured bellies. One incendiary, even a lucky one, passing through an unprotected fuel tank was a very upsetting event. As the CR42 was able to wriggle about in the air infinitely better than we could, it was impossible to shake him loose or get his aircraft into a position where the rear-gunner could take the necessary pot shots. The normal safety action, if you were a lone aircraft, was to stand the Blenheim on its nose, go hell for leather to ground level, and then fly so low that there wasn't any 'underneath' he could get into. This forced him up, if he was going to shoot at you, and your own gunner could shoot back. As CR42s didn't like being shot at, any more than we did, they often pushed off, which was splendid so far we were concerned.

*　　*　　*

I sat comfortably in my Dakota seat, remembering the time that Ricky Rixson had been out by himself, minding the King's business, when he was intercepted.

*　　*　　*

As usual, Ricky Rixson was going as quickly as he could — vertically — towards the ground so as to shut off any space beneath him, and hurry home with minimum delay. Low down, he was going flat-out with both engines bellowing at maximum power and emergency boost. The propellers were pulling at every scrap of air they could encompass to drag him along with all the speed he begged of them. Certainly, the CR42 never got underneath him. Ricky made sure of that. He flew down so low that the tips of the metal propeller-blades (six of them, three to each propeller) dug eight inches into the sand. Compared to air, sand is solid. By pulling at the solid sand, the tips of all the blades dragged themselves forwards so that they were sticking straight out in front and doing no useful work at all. Ricky, after the sudden terrifying bang and his immediate alarm, became far from upset. To his surprise and delight he found he had, in just a flash of time, converted the long-bladed high-altitude propellers into short-bladed low-altitude ones. The noise of the engines rose to a scream as, relieved of the work needed to drive those tips, they spun the smaller propellers much faster — which pulled the Blenheim along much faster too — and it outdistanced the fighter easily.

Our immediate request to Headquarters, to take a hack-saw to all the Blenheim propeller-blades at about nine inches from the tips, fell on deaf ears.

My squadron had tackled the same problem from a different angle. We wanted to find a better answer than the dive-down-vertically prank. Firstly, if you were on the way out to an attack, it spelled the end of the job you were being paid to do. Even if it saved your life, you could only come home. Secondly, if you were in formation with other aircraft it was totally impractical to take the whole outfit down in a screaming vertical dive — and anything less than straight down would not keep the fighter away from your bare belly. Thirdly, we had an AOC who took a very gloomy view if we had, as he put it, 'run away from danger'. He felt very strongly that it was our RAF duty, and therefore essential, to hang on up there exchanging bullets and to fight it out to the bitter end — for them, or for us. Inside our fragile Blenheims we, frankly, were less than convinced that this was a good idea. We leaned towards the philosophy of a monk called Erasmus who said, as long ago as the 15th century: 'That same man that renneth awaie may fight again on other daie.' So, we looked for another answer to the problem.

We reckoned we might cash in on the enemy pilots' nervousness. A Blenheim pilot in a great hurry could extract from his desert-equipped machine, flat-out and with all levers set at 'Emergency!', a shade over 200 mph. That is 100 yards per second. A CR42, to get its sheltered shot, sat 400 yards behind and slightly below. In other words, the attacker was flying four seconds behind his prey. Why not leave some unpleasantness behind us, for him to catch up with?

Given that idea, my somewhat ingeniously minded senior armourer, Warrant Officer 'Fatty' Barker, began work with a device which had originally been designed for use at night. It was a parachute flare. This was a sort of black metal canister, to put on the small bomb racks fitted under one of the wings; when released it would hang in the air on its parachute for the number of seconds you chose to set on its fuse. Then, a small explosion would light the million-candle-power magnesium. These he modified so that they became our charmingly simple and special anti-fighter weapons.

He took off the magnesium flare and put a 20-lb bomb in its place. (A 20-lb bomb is equal in explosive power to a 6-in shell.) Fuses were set for four seconds. So, on our bombing raids we carried four of these infernal devices on the small racks. It was absolutely miraculous. If a fighter pilot elected to reach his 'safe' place, behind and slightly below so as to fire from his preferred range of 400 yards, we left a bomb hanging behind us on its parachute. Its appearance doubtless stimulated his curiosity as to what it might be. Then, in four seconds, by which time he had caught up with it and was close enough to satisfy any curiosity in one easy lesson, the equivalent of a 6-in shell went BOOM! in his ear. Fatty Barker never managed to get a 'confirmed' CR42 entered in our game-book from the use of his parachute bomb, but none of them ever hung around our tails to work out what must have happened. And that was our prime objective up there anyway — to be left in peace to get on with our war.

As we were day-bombers, our stock of parachute flares declined and then ran out fairly quickly. We asked for more parachutes and fuses, with or without flares attached. Headquarters wanted to know why, so we told them, waxing lyrical about our device. This, they said in shocked tones, was an unauthorised modification, and they would have to ask London.

London said that there was just a chance, minuscule but it existed, that the parachute might open, catch on the bomb-rack and stop the bomb falling away; then, four seconds later — BOOM! — end of one Blenheim. We must not use it, because it was dangerous. 'Murderers!' we screamed back; the risk from the bomb was a thousand-to-one, and incendiary-firing CR42s were a bloody sight more dangerous than that. We wanted it because it had proved to be a completely effective deterrent to CR42s and, for us, it was a safety device. 'NO!' said London; our makeshift parabomb was not entirely safe, and no more parachute flares would be forthcoming.

We stressed our despair yet again as it was a question of the lesser danger. We were happy to accept a thousand-to-one chance of a quick and certain death, against the far greater chance of a messy and perhaps maiming machine-gun bullet. It was all a question of odds, and the stakes for the wagers being laid were *our* lives, but to that there was not even an acknowledgement.

We were, all three Blenheim squadrons, 'mobile'. This meant that we lived in tents, ready to fold them, put them on our lorries, hitch on the office trailers, up sticks and move at any time. It was a maddening existence: just as one got dug in and comfortable with a nice illicit supply of booze and goodies coming up on the train from Alexandria — by courtesy of the guard or the engine driver, suitably bribed — dammit if a signal didn't come in saying: 'Move forwards, towards Benghazi, for so-many miles to your new landing ground number so and so'. Then, when our Army had become weakened by badly stretched supply lines and our enemy had become stronger by his lines becoming correspondingly shortened, the tide of war would turn against us. The signals then said, 'Move back, in the direction of Cairo, to yet another airfield'. No wonder we became known as the 'Benghazi Harriers'.

*   *   *

Over to the left of our Dakota, some distance beyond the Egyptian frontier, lay a little area of packed sand. I knew almost exactly where it must be, but I couldn't identify it. However, I remembered its details vividly.

*   *   *

From Fuka we had leap-frogged forwards twice and this was to be our next new 'airfield': a patch of sand. The only way we recognised it as an airfield was by a windsock on a pole, and a number of wooden boxes containing tins of aviation petrol. No radio, no wires to attach a telephone to — nothing else whatever. Well, we could erect a radio mast and be in touch with headquarters within the hour, but there were no bombs and 12 bombless bombers made no sense at all. So, while we were putting up the tents, fixing an ops room, laying out the sick quarters, getting the cookhouse under way and doing the 1,001 other things needed, I sent all the aircraft off independently to pick up a load of bombs from our previous base, Fuka, and bring them back. Then, as soon as we made contact with the world once more, the boss would discover that a little matter like 'no bombs' would not stop the splendid 55 Squadron from functioning! We might even earn some satisfactory brownie-points.

What I did not know, and no one could warn me about it, was that a howling *khamseen,* or severe dust storm was brewing. Half an hour later all that the airborne crews could see through their windscreens was a great *haboob* of dust, looking like a gigantic mile-high brown bolster, rolling sideways towards them. They couldn't turn back to reach my unmarked patch of sand as there was no direction finder and, in any case, their job was to get bombs. They went on, into the dust. It was far, far worse inside than they had judged, so, with radios totally wiped out by the dust-static, in ten minutes every pilot was fighting for his life, trying to do something that would end up as a safe landing, somewhere, anywhere. A few climbed up and some sneaked down. Most of them aimed to reach the Nile delta, hoping the sand would be less over the cultivation. It was every man for himself.

One fellow, coming down gingerly, by incredible good fortune managed to distinguish the brown sandy desert underneath him from the brown sandy air he was flying through, just before he hit the surface. Now, concentrating all he knew, he was clinging to it as he raced along at almost zero feet. It was vital to hang on till he or his navigator could see and recognise something helpful and safe. On the one hand he was scared stiff of going up and losing sight of the surface, so that he would have to face finding it a second time. Yet, on the other hand he was terrified of staying down, and flying smack into any sandy-coloured hillock or escarpment which would stick up invisibly ahead of him. Having no radio, he was far from happy about his plight.

Suddenly, underneath him, a dark-brown narrow strip came in sight: tarmac — must be. There was only one piece of tarmac in the entire desert — that long, long road near the coast, straight for nearly all its length, which stretched over 300 miles from Alexandria to Tobruk. He could see the blowing sand, whipped by the gale, streaming towards him and almost obliterating the dark macadam below. He was flying almost directly into the wind, so he snapped the throttles back and, when his speed had dropped far enough, extended the flaps and the wheels. Gently, he put her down on the road and, keeping dead straight, came thankfully to a standstill. Even with both engines ticking over, he could hear the blown grains of sand crackling against the glass and perspex of the cockpit, but, he was safe and in one piece. He breathed a deep sigh of relief.

Out of the murk as he sat there, a khaki Ford station-wagon came straight at him, travelling down the road remarkably fast. At the last moment the driver saw before his nose the astonishing vision of a glass and perspex coc:.pit, flanked by two spinning propellers and a couple of wings sticking out beyond the edges of the road. He braked violently and, at the last second, swung off to the desert under the wingtip. An infuriated Army Major stepped out of the car and came up to the Blenheim. With the help of the rear-gunner, he climbed up on the wing and then yelled at the pilot, 'What the bloody hell do you think you are doing with that thing in the middle of a road? You damned nearly caused a bad accident!'

The pilot was in no mood to bandy words about the shockingly worse accident he had avoided by the skin of his teeth in getting there, and answered remarkably gently, 'I didn't come here by choice — I was originally trying to get to Fuka when this appalling dust-storm blew up and I was completely weathered out. I simply landed . . .'

The Major cut in, brightening visibly, 'Did you say getting to Fuka? I passed there only about five miles back. If you want to follow me in my car, I'll lead you there. *And* I can clear aside, out of your way, any traffic we may meet! Just let me get back into my station wagon . . .

Before you could say 'knife' he had scuttled back down the wing, into his car, and a remarkable procession began. The Major didn't drive too fast and the occasional lorry or staff car was peremptorily waved off the road into the desert. After about 20 minutes they both turned right by the NAAFI, past the barrier of the main gate (dutifully lifted by a somewhat startled guard), through the camp and thus on to the airfield.

It was the only aircraft of my entire squadron which reached its destination that day.

Meanwhile, on my sand-patch, the *haboob* hit us just as we got our wireless mast up, and the gale promptly blew it down again. I fully knew what must have happened to my aircraft and was in agonies of apprehension that some pilot might have tried to run back before the storm, and there was no earthly way we could help him in to land. By nightfall, none had reappeared with me, and they must all be down by then, somewhere, whole, or in bits. For the second time in my life I had lost my complete squadron. It was just as bad — no, worse! — the second time round. Had my lack of foresight killed a crew? I ought to have known better. I prepared a 'request news' signal, specifying each of the 12 aircraft, and asked the wireless-operator to try and get it away in spite of the sand-crackle. At least, the mast had been re-erected and there was a chance.

The W/Op got my signal away in the small hours of the morning, when the wind and sand dropped a fraction, but he could get out nothing else, and we got no signals in. Having no telephone line, we were totally cut off. The *khamseen* blew for three whole days and nights in all, and then the fourth day dawned bright, clear and still. Eleven of my 12 machines came back during the day, with bombs, from wherever they had managed to get down, all over Egypt and Sinai. The 12th crew had hit a palm tree, but managed to bale out and were safe.

A signal also arrived during the day. It came from Cairo, from the RAF supremo himself, an Air Marshal, Commander-in-Chief of all Air Forces in the entire Middle East war theatre and it came straight to me, a mere Squadron Leader. It had left on the highest priority and the sand had kept it from me, till the radios worked again, for more than two whole days. It was brief and to the point. It said: 'PERSONAL FOR DUDGEON FROM TEDDER STOP WHAT THE HELL ARE YOU PLAYING AT'

We got no favourable brownie-points for that effort!

*　　*　　*

Oh well . . . that was all in the past now. I asked the Dak W/Op if there was any coffee left in the thermos.

Chapter 24
Visitors

The Dakota wireless operator had done me proud. In my pilot's seat, clutching a great steaming mug of coffee, keeping a wary eye on the instruments, I recalled some of the visitors we used to get from time to time.

*   *   *

Not many visitors came to our little sand-patches: there wasn't much to see. Certainly, when we had enough booze, we would throw a party but, with just a few notable exceptions, we were graced only by an occasional snooping staff officer trying to unearth our latest bit of skulduggery before it became serious. However, the rarity of visitors usually ensured that their presence was something out of the ordinary and therefore to be enjoyed.

One whom I remembered very clearly was Group Captain Judge. He was an Operations Officer from Group HQ and he came mainly to be sure that our briefing room was effective and that its material was fully up to date. However, it was pleasing that he accepted our invitation to lunch, with a courtesy drink beforehand. He sat beside me at the bar and nonchalantly produced a pack of cards from his pocket. 'Take one,' he said, 'any one you like . . .' This was the beginning of a series of card tricks. Gradually the officers began gathering round and soon he was the centre of a craning, fascinated group. I had often seen stage shows, and amateur conjurers, but never before or since have I been so mystified and infuriated by card tricks — and by those done within a foot of my nose. He was quite brilliant. When I tried to catch him out — perhaps by refusing to take the card he was obviouly *forcing* on me — he would switch smoothly to a different trick, using instead whatever card I *had* picked. He drove me nearly crazy, partly because I couldn't see how he did his tricks and partly because he wouldn't show me the secret of a single one. I felt sure that he must have started a misspent but profitable life, a long time before the war, probably as one of the card-sharpers who made fortunes milking cash from rich passengers on the Atlantic liners. He was always welcome with his one-man conjuring show; it brought a pleasant and welcome break to the monotonous part of our life — waiting for orders to fly.

Another staff visit turned itself into a red-letter day for my navigator, 'Clockwork' Hornby, mainly because things did *not* work out the way the hapless visitor had expected. This business concerned the Officers' Mess accounts. Money and the way it is handled is a never ending magnet for accountant officers from HQ, and rightly so, for money can vanish or be misused only too easily. Clockwork was Mess Treasurer at that time. A little man with blond hair, blue eyes and fair skin, he looked much younger than his 30 years. He was a Pilot Officer. The visiting accountant from Group was a Flight Lieutenant. He was probably about the same age but had been recently promoted and was unquestionably feeling his oats. He complained about almost everything and he trampled all over Clockwork who was two ranks junior to him.

Our visitor complained that the accounts were poorly kept; that they were not in accordance with RAF accounting; that entries did not correspond; that the double-entry should be triple . . . and so on. Finally, he said pompously that he would have to make adverse comments in his report to me, and that it would be copied to Group HQ. Finally the young man, bearing down with the full weight of his wartime-shortened accounting course said haughtily to this 'youngster' before him — and an 'aircrew' member to boot — 'For Heaven's sake, where on earth did you learn to keep accounts like these?'

Clockwork led him on, shuffling his feet and looking embarrassed. He produced a number of 'ers' and 'oh well, you sees' while his inquisitor got more and more cocky. At last, quietly, Clockwork pushed him off his self-erected pedestal: 'I learned to keep accounts that way at Price, Waterhouse and Company. I am a fully qualified pre-war Chartered Accountant.'

The Flight Lieutenant's jaw dropped as he realised that he had advertised his ignorance of procedures used by one of the most prestigious accounting firms in the world. He was so mortified that he never came back to see us again.

Towards the end of November 1940 the AOC had rung me up

to say that two American 'observers' were coming to stay with us for a few days. Although posing as civilians (this was long before the United States joined our war) they were completely security-cleared. They could see and do anything they wished, including flying with me, but not on any account were they to be flown across enemy-held territory. Being 'Neutrals', as America was politically, that potato would be too hot to hold.

These two duly appeared, in gents' natty suitings, and I showed them everything. They looked a lot, asked a lot, and said nothing. One indicated that he was a pilot, and I asked if they would like to fly.

'Yes, please,' was the instant reply.

They were so taciturn and unlike the forthcoming Americans I had met, that I double-checked their credentials with Group HQ. Yes, they were confirmed to be OK, so we went to my aircraft. The pilot sat on the jump-seat beside me, and the other fellow was on the bomb-aiming seat. We took off. We flew around for about half an hour, and got no reactions, so I asked the pilot whether he would like to do some aerobatics.

'Yes, please.'

Neither of them could be properly harnessed in, so my performance was limited to manoeuvres which would hold them on their seats — a loop, a wing-over and a barrel-roll. Still no reaction. Would the pilot like to fly it?

'Yes, please.'

We changed places and he showed himself to be a genuine pilot by driving competently and decorously around the sky for a quarter of an hour with no word nor change of expression. Then he announced, mystifying me completely, 'The elevators go out before the rudder. That's good.'

Unreasonably, his taciturnity irritated me. I decided to try to make this fellow put some more feeling into his remarks: I would show him what could really be done with a Blenheim on landing. By then I had flown about 600 hours on the type and I must have been just about at my peak in flying competence, even if undoubtedly low on wisdom and maturity. We changed places again.

I came back to base in the opposite direction to that for landing, and obviously rather too close to the airfield. When overhead, I closed the throttles and swung into a very steep descending turn, round and back for the landing. I kept the near-vertical bank steady, then the wheels went out sideways, followed by the flaps. I felt behind my left hip and pulled the pair of knobs which changed the propellers into fine pitch. Every ounce of skill I had ever acquired was summoned up to perform this biplane-type manoeuvre perfectly. Beads of sweat were probably starting out on my forehead; they might even have been drops of blood. Out of the corner of my eye I could see the blanched knuckles of my silent friend as he gripped the sides of his seat grimly, staring ahead with frog-like eyes. Good! I held my turn right down, down and down, till the bottom wingtip had almost reached the ground. Then, holding the wingtip where it was, I smoothly rolled the fuselage down so that the wheels came gently to ground level. I never touched the throttle levers once, not an iota all the way. Finally, he could just hear the wheels and tail-wheel brushing the sand together as she greased down, smooth as a baby's bottom. I braked to a standstill and waited for the applause.

This time I got reaction. He turned in his seat, looking at me with shining eyes as, spluttering with excitement he said, 'Gee!! What a ship!! You can just fling it on the ground, *any* old how!!!'

Feeling somewhat piqued at this apparently libellous appraisal of my effort I said, tartly, 'Well — you couldn't do that in one of your Lockheed Hudsons.'

Like a flash he retorted, 'Yes indeed you could — but only *once!*'

I never did discover who he was or what he did, but he knew a lot about aeroplanes and it was clear that he certainly knew damned well how close to disaster I had taken him with my bout of unwarranted showmanship.

*   *   *

Two hundred miles westwards, ahead and slightly to our right, was Derna. There were marshes on the seaward side of the town where I had once seen large numbers of geese. That reminded me of another visitor in January 1941, an Army officer.

*   *   *

Our forces had just made one of their great leaps forward, capturing scads of Italian equipment of every kind. The time was shortly before the 'Benghazi Harriers' had to make their next leap backwards. My brother-in-law, Colonel Dick Hobson, was CO of an Army unit and he rang me with a request that I should give house-room to his emissary, Major Peter Dollar. Peter and his driver would come by car and they needed nothing but food, and their beer-ration if possible. Daily they would go out and about, trying to pick up, and spirit away, captured Italian transport-vehicles of every shape and size before somebody else got them first. Some would be for use directly, and some would be cannibalised for spares. This 'liberation' of enemy equipment on an individual basis was heavily frowned upon by HQME, who had grandiose ideas of doing it centrally and then parcelling the booty out piecemeal. None of us at the sharp end believed any of it would ever get back to where it was needed and paid no attention, so naturally I agreed with Dick.

Peter Dollar arrived the next day. Typically of Peter, who was generous and unorthodox, he arrived with a house-present (tent-present?) for me, consisting of half a bottle of whisky and a Fortnum and Mason tinned grouse — both unheard of in the desert. He was a tremendous character and an ideal looting officer. Later on he was taken prisoner-of-war, and finished up in Colditz; he said that Colditz, the escape-proof mediaeval fortress was far and away the best place to be, for it was where all the nicest, most exciting and enterprising prisoners-of-war were to be found . . . and some escaped.

Within only a few days of his arrival quite a sizeable motor transport park could be seen growing at the edge of my airfield.

One evening we were having a lukewarm beer in the Mess. Very diffidently, Peter opened up a conversation. 'There is one thing I'm very interested in. I see you and your chaps going out and coming back. I listen to them talking. I would dearly love to know what actually happens. Do you think there is any chance of my being squirrelled away somewhere, in one of the aircraft, on a raid?'

I put my beer down and gave him a disapproving look. 'Peter! You're mad. Why on earth do you want to stick your neck out, looking for more trouble than you have to? What if you get shot down, and probably killed. Apart from that inconvenience to yourself, I should have some pretty unpleasant questions to answer. I don't mind about Dick — he'd be pretty angry with me for losing his looting officer, but he's my brother-in-law and I can handle him. But my Air Force bosses . . . they'd sack me on the spot, as like as not!'

'Please,' he cajoled, 'can't you think of any way at all that would let me come? I've got a crazy urge to see your work as it really is . . . and not the guff you read in the papers.'

I considered his lunatic request for a little while, then said, 'Why not? Let's suppose that next time I go out, you come with me. If nothing occurs, no one need ever know. If we get shot down, neither of us will be around to answer questions and everybody else can say, truthfully, that it was nothing to do with them. What about that?'

Peter was delighted and for 48 hours he could hardly contain himself while waiting for the 'off'. He even stopped stealing enemy transport in case he missed the show. The chance came at last: it was to be a squadron raid. Target: the airfield and hangars at Benina. (Benina was a minor town some short distance from Benghazi.) I would lead the formation of nine aircraft.

Clockwork, navigating, sat at his table beside the bomb-aimer's seat, up in the nose. This left his jump-seat, beside me, free for Peter, and he would have room to stand up, look around, put his head into the perspex blisters at the side to look behind, and generally get a grandstand view of whatever went on. Unfortunately for him, we had no provision for a crew of four, so there was no way we could plug him into our conversations in the air. He could shout into the edge of my helmet, and I into his, but that was all. It was just his bad luck and he would have to lump it; after all, as I said to him, if he objected he didn't *have* to come! After that remark, I thought for a moment that he was going to strike me. We took off, picked up squadron formation and set course.

It was a perfect bomber's day. We went far south over the desert to avoid detection, and the weather was ideally clear, so navigation was easy and accurate. There was nothing of special interest for Peter to get excited about, but he learned something about airborne map-reading. As we neared the coast and after our final course had been set with great accuracy, we ran over a heaven-sent sheet of cloud at about 12,000 ft, completely hiding us from eyes on the ground. Five minutes before overhead-target I nosed the formation gently down through the cloud and popped out below, just in time to see Benina airfield. The air was so smooth that it was like flying on silk. Clockwork took perfect aim and pressed the bomb release. I nudged Peter and he watched the pattern of bombs fall from the other aircraft. Immediately we had got our bomb-strike photographs I promptly nosed back up into the cloud again and stayed there for 50 miles on the way home. It couldn't have been better: accurate flying and navigation, total surprise achieved and best of all, according to Clockwork, smack on the target.

After de-briefing back at base and reporting our success to the AOC, I explained to Peter what a marvellous raid he had been on. 500 miles over enemy territory; nine aircraft out; nine back; no ack-ack; no fighters; no interference. Far from having been damaged, none of us was even alarmed.

Peter shifted his feet and said 'er' several times. At last he found his tongue. 'It wasn't at all what I expected, or hoped for.'

'Why not? It was wonderfully quiet.'

'That's it!' exclaimed Peter. 'I wanted to see action! Guns! Fighters! Ack-ack! Battle!!'

'You're off your head. My prime objective on a raid is, admittedly, to drop the bombs in the right place but, having said that, also to try to keep away from all trouble . . . if it's humanly possible.'

'May I come with you on another raid, if you judge it's going to meet up with trouble of some sort?' asked Peter.

'You're stark, staring, raving insane!' I cried. 'Who in hell wants to poke his nose into trouble by choice? I don't like trouble one little bit. But, O madman, if one comes up for me to fly during the next few days — before you leave with your trucks — and which looks likely to be dicey, I'll take you. But, believe me, don't think I'm going to stick my neck out just to satisfy your curiosity. I think you're as nutty as a bag of almonds and, if you have as much brains as would fill an egg-cup, I think you should say you don't want to come.'

A nasty one came up two days later. The Italian soldiers were fleeing in their thousands by any and every means of transport that they could lay their hands on, all along the road from Tobruk to Benghazi. Many were on a particularly tricky twisting section, like being in a narrow ravine with no escape, between Marua and Barce. The AOC directed us to send out nine aircraft, not as a formation giving mutual protection, but bombing individually so as to cut the road and bottle them up in as many places at once as we could.

I decided that this could best be done by having the aircraft fly well to the south over uninhabited desert, one behind the other, about 15 miles apart. We would all turn north together, descending to about 2,000 ft to get the greatest bombing accuracy. As the enemy had no radar, he would get no warning of our approach till the last moment. Then, each of us would bomb his allotted stretch of the coastal road as he came to it. Finally, after bombs-away, we would escape promptly by carrying on flying northwards out to sea, and would come home from far out over the Mediterranean. Peter could come with me.

The risks were obviously going to be high. Flying low enough to be reasonably sure of our bombs striking the road took us down to within range of rifles, let alone the deadly low-level pom-poms. Yet, it was not low enough to stop a lucky enemy fighter getting underneath. The first news of that could be the slam of a successful flaming ping-pong ball. Lone bombers, particularly Blenheims, are sitting ducks . . . no, it wasn't pretty. I offered fervent prayers that my ewe lambs, my vulnerable Blenheims, flying singly at low level, would not be picked up and become sacrifices to be slaughtered. Being shot down from the ground — although possible — looked unlikely if the enemy was scared and busy enough with running away. Peter, the fool, was delighted.

The selected crews agreed that my plan probably gave the best compromise between success and escape.

Some hours later, as we approached our bit of road, Sergeant Bennett my gunner said, 'There's a Savoia, flying fairly high, westwards, a few miles behind us. He has an escort of seven CR42s. At the moment they may not have seen us as they are not paying any attention. I'll tell you if anything happens.'

I said, 'Clockwork, get a move on. I'll turn and give you one good run, putting your stick of bombs diagonally across the road. That'll give you the best chance of getting a strike on the tarmac. Then we go home, pronto.'

I swung into my turn and levelled out again. Clockwork said, 'Stand-by!'

Bennett kept us up to date: 'They've detached two fighters who are coming after us, fast. I can see black smoke from their exhausts, so they've gonε to full throttle.'

Clockwork said, 'Hold it — straight and level — steady — ten seconds to run . . .'

Bennett interjected: 'They're just coming into range . . . coming in to attack now . . . one from each quarter . . .'

I heard the giant tearing-calico noise of the Browning machine-guns in his turret. I hunched my shoulders to make myself as narrow as possible behind my steel seat-protection of quarter-inch thick armour plate — and concentrated wholly on my flying.

Clockwork reported, 'Bombs gone!'

I banked towards the coast, nosed down, pushed the throttles through the gate and pulled the emergency boost-lever.

Peter, whom I'd totally forgotten and who, of course, could

not hear our conversation on the intercom, had sprung up at the first crackle of firing and thrust his head into the blister to see behind. I crouched motionless behind my armour plate and listened to the battle-talk, going flat out for the ground and the coast. Bennett was giving us a running commentary; the flaming ping-pong balls flipped by.

Peter looked at me sitting rigidly and expressionless. Then he looked out of the blister again. He looked along the inside of the fuselage, seeing Bennett swinging his turret from side to side. Then he looked at me again. Finally, seeing me sitting there motionless, staring straight ahead, he could bear it no longer. He put his mouth to the side of my helmet and shouted above the roar: 'I don't want to upset you, but we're being followed!'

I nodded; by this time we were crossing the marshes, low over the water at the coast's edge. I beckoned to him and pointed downwards at a startled skein of geese and, pulling his head down so that I could shout into the edge of his helmet, yelled, 'Plenty of good shooting down there, isn't there?'

We had been lucky that there were two fighters, as they couldn't both sit below and behind in safety. In their attack from the side and above, they made excellent targets. Bennett shot down one and hit the other, which turned away streaming white vapour — probably fuel. After that, the journey home was uneventful.

When we got back to the Mess, Clockwork was slightly depressed, saying, 'As we were running up the road to bomb, there was a truck crammed with soldiers belting away from the battle zone. It was full to overflowing and one chap was sitting on the bonnet in front of the windscreen. Seeing us coming towards him, he was so frightened that he jumped off . . . and the truck wheels ran right over him. Poor sod! How bloody unfair to lose your life in a war by getting run over, miles away from the front. It seemed such a waste, somehow. I know that he was an enemy, but it gives no satisfaction or feeling of success, does it?'

At first, Peter pretended to be cross with me for having pulled his leg about the geese when he was genuinely trying to be helpful. Really, he was happy as Larry with the whole performance, chattering away and behaving like a dog with two tails. He had been 'in action' in the air.

I was miserable as sin and said nothing. Eight crews came back but Peter Blignaut, my charming South African pilot and his crew did not return. I assumed — correctly, as I heard later — that they had been shot down and killed.

In the Dakota co-pilot's seat, safe and comfortable, I remembered vividly all the agonising and the mental pain of wondering, hour after hour, 'Could I not have saved Peter Blignaut? If I had thought more adroitly . . .? If I had planned better . . .? If I had briefed better . . .? If . . . If . . . If . . .' So many 'If's! Any loss tore my heart out — because ultimately it always came round to being *my* fault for not having been good enough in planning that raid. I was never able to ride over the loss of a crew and shrug people off as expendable. The fact that in my time we lost fewer crews than either of the other two Blenheim squadrons could never compensate for the death of a colleague. The odds of war are brutal: eight 'successes' to one 'failure'. Perhaps the loss of only one had been a fortunate outcome in the circumstances; who could say? But it could never seem fortunate to Peter Blignaut's parents.

*   *   *

I said to the wireless operator, 'Any more coffee?'

Chapter 25
Spenny

Over to our right I could see the notch in the coastline which identified the port of Bardia, one of our most favoured targets in the early Western Desert days. It was then a small Italian port, just north of the place where the Egyptian-Libyan border meets the Mediterranean coast, and it was as colourful as a rainbow. Seen from above, the water inside the harbour entrance widened into two bulges, making its shape resemble the end of an enormous thigh-bone. The colour was purest sapphire, nestling below ochre-coloured sandstone cliffs which sheltered a pier with several storehouses and some quayside equipment on it. It never looked like a military and naval depot; it was more like a picturesque little fishing harbour, which, pre-Mussolini, is presumably what it was.

Once, when we bombed it with a formation of three Blenheims in January 1941, Clockwork said in a puzzled voice as he peered down to note and photograph the strike of our bombs, 'How big a blast can a 250-lb bomb make?'

Before I could ask him 'Why?' there was a thump which threw me hard up against my shoulder-straps. Clockwork, not strapped in because of his bomb-aiming, struck the cabin roof and came down again painfully on all-fours. His maps and navigation instruments were chucked around the flight-deck like useless scrap. Everything not anchored down — such as the emergency dinghy-pack — was thrown all over the aircraft. Something *much* bigger than a 250-lb bomb had gone off two and a half miles beneath us!

Later, our intelligence told us that we had hit a store of naval mines. Eighty-six *tons* of them had gone off and that thump was the concussion at 12,000 ft. It was reported as a 'very successful' bombing raid. The damage to the port itself was horrendous; the buildings, their occupants, the cranes and so on, disappeared as if they were stubble shaved off by a gigantic razor. On the other hand the sandstone bluffs on either side of the harbour had made a funnel, or chimney, directing the shock-waves upwards to us. The buildings of the hamlet above the cliff-tops escaped the full force and, apart from losing all the windows, were comparatively unharmed. Secretly, I was rather pleased because, though seen only from high up, it looked as though it ought always to have been a pretty little fishermen's village.

Even though we were ostensibly classed as day-bombers, we got quite a number of night raids to do. These were of doubtful damage-value as we had no electronic gadgets to help us identify our targets, and all navigation had to be achieved by map-reading. Fortunately, we could enlist the help of the enemy in getting some of the pin-points necessary, by cashing in on the Italians' nervousness. Normally, you flew happily all around their area in peace and quiet as long as you kept clear of towns and ports. However, if you needed a navigational fix, you aimed at where you reckoned a town must be: any sizeable town would do. All would be as silent as the grave while they waited to see if you proposed to disturb them. Then fairly early, when their nerve cracked, minor or major hell broke loose. Streams of multi-coloured tracer came groping up, and the point from which they came gave the navigator the precise fix that he wanted. Naturally, you immediately turned to one side or other and went round the source. The ack-ack promptly stopped because they (presumably) assumed you had been 'driven away'.

Italian ack-ack in the Desert was spectacular and that over Tobruk was unquestionably the most breath-taking of all the pyrotechnics in the area. Hundreds and hundreds of flaming, coloured projectiles would erupt into the air, looking like the Grand Fountain of a firework display. Most were reds, greens and yellows, but there were some whites thrown in. You could see from the great glorious fan-like shapes of coloured tracer snaking upwards that the guns weren't being aimed; they were waving from side to side, spraying the sky with shells as the enemy was hoping to scare us off, and (one supposed) trusting to get 'a bird or two by browning the covey'. It looked beautiful, as fireworks always do. It was hard to believe that each and every yellow, pink, green and red light of the thousands coming up was borne by a shell, fully capable of killing you if it hit.

We had a gunner on the squadron who had been in Bomber Command. He swore that the visible anti-aircraft fire over

Tobruk was heavier than any he had ever seen in all his raids on Germany. In many ways it was scary but, although it looked awful, it proved not to be particularly dangerous; I never reasoned precisely why. Perhaps it was because we flew a little above the optimum range for low-level pom-pom guns, and their high-level ones were without radar for aiming.

On a typical steady bombing run at medium height in the dark, all the coloured blobs of fire left the ground slowly, oh so slowly. You felt you would be gone far into the distance long before they could possibly reach you, and they looked so pretty. However, although many blobs were being sprayed all around the sky for discouragement, there were always a few which insisted on coming straight for you. These were vilely unpleasant for there could be no escape; there was nothing on earth that you could do except sit there, on your run, waiting for 'Bombs Gone!' Surely, your brain told you, by the law of averages not *all* of them were going to pass you by? As they approached they came faster, faster and ever faster (even though reason assured you that, coming up against gravity, they must be slowing down) and you watched, thinking 'this is it, boys; this is the one, coming up now!' Then, in the last fraction of a second, it appeared to swerve away, in a sharp curve, flashing past at an incredible speed and disappearing into the darkness above — another near-miss, luckily.

No one could be indifferent to sitting and being shot at, but you concentrated utterly on the job of flying a perfect bombing run for the aimer. This made you so busy that unpleasantness got pushed into the back of your mind. The near-misses went by all the time, every second or two, all over again, and again, and again . . . worrying, yes, but you were not frightened *then,* during those particular moments, nor in the euphoria of being safely on the way back to base. Fear, or something like it, came later after landing, particularly when you were lying in bed, at night, waiting for sleep.

The port of Bardia also brought back an unsavoury recollection. Our AOC in the desert at that time — 1940 — had been renowned as a World War I flying ace. I remembered and admired him personally as a very brave man. He would never have asked anybody to do something he would not do himself. Nevertheless, I could not subscribe to his somewhat First-World-War approach. The potential cost, in lives, appeared to be only a minor factor among the pros and cons of his planning for the tasks he set us. Sometimes we felt that we were sent off, as soldiers had been sent 'over the top' from the trenches, like cannon fodder. He must have had long-term objectives, but often they were hard to discern. I thought back with crystal clarity to a certain raid, made on his say-so, which for my squadron had been neither satisfactory nor successful.

On December 11 he told us to bomb Bardia with a few aircraft, at 3 pm. Next day on December 12, he sent my whole squadron there, nine aircraft in formation, one hour earlier at 2 pm. Then, on the 13th, he told us to go *again* one hour earlier at 1 pm. We thought it was tempting providence to make three raids on successive days, to the same target, with the same one-hour time change on each. Further, it was Friday the 13th, held deep in Scandinavian mythology to be a particularly unlucky day. I demurred, but he brushed my reluctance aside. However, we came away from Bardia unscathed as the Italians had not reacted.

When the boss rang up that evening telling us to do another strike on the same target, again with the whole squadron, on the *fourth* day running, *again* exactly one hour earlier this time at noon, I nearly had a stroke. This was scary stuff. I remonstrated with him: I tried to say as inoffensively as I could that, having attracted the enemy's attention with our first raid, and then reinforced it with another, then stamped it indelibly on his controllers with a third — each one to an easily recognisable time-pattern — they probably would consider it, at worst, a reasonably sound bet to put up a reception committee of fighters for us at midday. It could become mayhem.

He answered, and I could hear him slapping his thigh as he usually did when he was making a point, 'Nonsense Dudgeon! We'll fox 'em! They would never expect us to do it *four* days running. I'm putting all three Blenheim squadrons in together — all at the same time. I tell you, we're going to fox 'em.'

'But, Sir,' I remonstrated, 'can't we break the routine a bit? The nearest fighters are at El Adem, 50 miles away; if they sit there on the ground till we are seen approaching Bardia, they can't get up to us before we are well on the way home. If they are waiting over the target at 12:00, as one would expect, they will have to go back for fuel before 14:00. Can't we delay the timing by three hours, say? Best of all, can't we skip a day? I feel we're booked for serious trouble if we fly to the plan as you've outlined it.'

Back came the vicious and unanswerable question: 'Dudgeon, are you trying to tell me that you haven't got the guts to do your job?'

There was no sane reply. I answered, 'Very well, Sir. As you wish. We'll do it as you say.'

To preserve secrecy, I didn't ring up either of the other two squadron commanders beforehand — 'Bishop' Gordon-Finlayson commanding 211 Squadron or Bob Bateson commanding 113 Squadron — but I wondered what their reactions had been. They would see, as I did, that very precise timing was needed to get three squadrons arriving together, to give and to get support from every rear-gunner for the fighters that I feared. We, anyway, were lucky; Clockwork was inordinately proud of his navigational accuracy. If the boss said noon, Clockwork would do his utmost to make sure that, within a few seconds either way, the bombs struck at that instant. He took it as a challenge to be met between us, his navigation and my flying, achieving the near-impossible.

The day was brilliantly clear and, flying some miles out to sea parallel to the Egyptian coast, we first picked out the other two squadrons about 20 minutes before bomb-release. They were well behind us and it looked as if they would be late. I slowed up as best I could but a squadron of bombers in formation is a pretty unwieldy affair. When we started our bombing run they were still five miles, or two minutes away.

I glanced up and saw the glint of sunlight on biplane wings. I took a careful look and then said to Bennett: 'We have about 20 CR42s diving down, in front and on both sides.'

Bennett answered, with no trace of emotion in his voice, 'There are 30 coming in behind. That makes 50.'

Apart from Clockwork's bombing corrections, nothing more was said. Bennett's guns were firing in an almost unending chatter. Then, half a minute later the bombs had gone and we nosed down gently to pick up more speed, turning left towards our territory and home. For me, it felt as if it took me forever to get the squadron round, unable to turn quickly in case I lost the wing-men and yet striving to get my team away from that purgatory of blazing fighters shooting at us from all directions. That anyone escaped alive could only have been due to the fighters' lousy gun-mountings and the pilots' reluctance to close right in and make sure of their kills.

Milly Singleton was the first to be hit hard, and flames began to stream from his left wing and engine. When his machine was seen to be on fire we called him on the radio, telling him to bale out before things got beyond control. He refused and, in flames, he held formation with me for as long as he could so that his gunner gave us supporting cross-fire all the time. Then, suddenly, probably when some control or spar burned through, he flipped over and went straight down. Some of the navigators, who had no productive task in the battle itself, watched him all the way. No parachutes had broken clear of that impersonal object, streaming flames and a black trail, till the sea swallowed it with a great big white splash and a black mushroom belch of smoke and flame. Its trace of smoke drifted away in the wind.

Black Metcalfe, Nick Nicholson, Fanny Hunt and two others had engines shot up so that they failed then and there. I slowed up all I could, looking over my shoulders and flying to give them the best chance of holding in formation, each with his remaining engine at full throttle. Not only could we thus give and get some protection from their gunners' cross-fire but, if I drew ahead, a lone, limping Blenheim would be money for jam to the enemy.

Due to the remarkable skill shown by the maimed ones, we managed to hang together somehow till the enemy swarm broke off the combat. One could only assume that it was for some reason such as shortage of fuel, for the battle had lasted barely eight minutes and we had only managed to shoot down three of them. Then, Bennett started counting my squadron off for me as each one fell away. After Milly, the next man went at the very end of the battle, just as the fighters started to break off combat. Mercifully, none followed him down. All the other Blenheims, except one, fell away and went. down on the way home. In a Blenheim, one engine is not powerful enough to let the pilot maintain height if the other propeller is still windmilling or stopped. They could, however, stretch the descent quite a bit. I hoped fervently that most of them could cross our lines and crash-land in friendly territory. My aircraft was the only one to have two engines working. I got home and landed safely.

The one other pilot who got home, some time after me and on one engine to my astonishment, was David Potter. David was 'accident prone'. He was one of the unluckiest men alive because, if things could go wrong for him, they did. He stayed alive only because he was one of the most skilful pilots I had. He too had been extensively shot up, but this time, for a change, he had one piece of luck. One of his propellers, hit by an explosive bullet, had been shot clean off. His good engine, going flat out and relieved of dragging a dead propeller through the air, allowed him to keep the machine just airborne. With consummate skill he managed to nurse it the 125 miles home. He wasn't lucky enough to have any hydraulic oil-pressure to put the wheels or the flaps down so he had to land it on its belly — which he did with minimum further damage. Poor Potter! In spite of sterling efforts with his machine, it proved to be no more than a flying colander and it had to be scrapped.

After landing I rang up the boss to report in as usual. I told him we had attacked as he had directed, and our reception committee had been 50-plus fighters — CR42s. Of the nine Blenheims that went out, I and one other had got back to base — and that machine was so badly shot up as to be of no further use. Seven out of nine were missing. One had been shot down and its crew, for certain, was dead. Of the other six aircraft and crews, I had reason to hope that some had succeeded in making a crash-landing on our side of the lines. After refuelling, I would go off to see how many I could find. Hornby, my navigator, had told me of a couple that were uncomfortably close to enemy troops, but at least neither appeared to have had a bad crash . . .

The AOC merely said: 'Well done. We'll get you some more aircraft as quickly as possible.'

While I was speaking to the AOC, my machine was being refuelled and we went back immediately to search. Clockwork's spotting was magnificent. Each machine was precisely where he had said it would be and no enemy soldiers were beside them, even the two just inside enemy territory. We had seen enough of unfriendly fighters for one day, so we wasted no time hanging around. The sand beside the belly-landed machines looked smooth and, judging from the marks they had made, appeared to be hard. Scared stiff we landed alongside first one crashed Blenheim, and then the other. In both cases the sand proved firm enough, and my relief was almost as great as that of the two crews who scrambled aboard and tucked themselves into the belly of my aircraft for the flight home. Unbelievably, four more pilots had also pancaked down safely and, being well on our side of the front, all the crews had no trouble in hitching lifts in trucks back to the squadron by nightfall. At the final count, 24 out of 27 aircrew members were alive, home — and safe.

When we had settled down at base, and before I knew the good news about my missing crews, I telephoned the Bishop to ask how he had fared. He had met no opposition other than the usual ineffective ack-ack. I complained gently that his lateness had let me get the whole weight of the fighter attack, while he had got away scot-free . . . he had not played fair.

He replied, 'It was patently obvious that the Italians were going to turn out in great strength today, or tomorrow if the AOC was fool enough to do it a fifth time. Everybody knows your lunatic passion for being precisely on time, so I reckoned that the best way to protect my crews was to be just a tiny bit late. You would then catch any fighters for me so that my squadron could bomb in comparative safety. Somebody was going to cop it, hard — and I didn't see why it should be me.'

I didn't ring up Bob Bateson because he, obviously, must have come to the same conclusion. War cannot be a fair business. But, if you can save some men's lives by playing it unevenly, it is presumably fair for somebody.

The drinkers in the Messes that evening were a bit subdued. One officer and two sergeants were beyond my power to land beside, pick up and bring home. Pilot Officer Milward 'Milly' Singleton had been an Old Harrovian and a delightful colleague. We had known him as a very gentle person, quiet and socially shy. Naturally, he got teased on this account and he protested at the effeminate nickname we gave him. But, by any standards, he showed he had guts . . . he was just twenty-one years old.

I tried to recommend Milly for a Distinguished Flying Cross; it was refused because that recommendation may not be made after death. However, he could not be accepted as 'dead' because I did not have his body to prove it. The contradiction was odd and unfortunate. We felt he had earned something by which his family and friends could see his bravery had been recognised by his colleagues and his country.

Bardia was bad news for us on that occasion. However, Benghazi was worse for a friend of mine earlier in the campaign. The Italians were using that port as a major supply base for their forces in Libya and Cyrenaica.

The AOC decided to bomb shipping at the quays by three Blenheims, flying in at low level in daylight. He rang up the CO of a Blenheim squadron, Squadron Leader R. H. Spencer, to tell him so. He was known as 'Little Spenny' as he was only about five feet six tall. Little Spenny was staggered at the news, for we Blenheim crews in the Middle East knew only too well the horror stories from England, resulting from WWI-type attacks made earlier in the Second World War. Squadrons of 12 Blenheims had been ordered to bomb naval targets by daylight, such as Kiel harbour or Wilhelmshaven — and only two, or even one, aircraft had got back from such raids. Benghazi, we knew, was very heavily defended. Surely the boss must be familiar with these reports?

Spenny explained to the AOC as tactfully as he could that this was a highly dangerous mission; the value to us of hitting a few unloading enemy merchant ships would be minimal.

Spenny could hear him, on the telephone, slapping his thigh as he always did when he enthused, 'Nonsense Spencer! We'll fox 'em, if you come in from over the sea at very low level.'

Spenny pointed out that photographs showed the harbour wall looking like a thorn fence from the number of guns along it.

The boss then, as later he did with me, delivered the wicked query: 'Are you telling me, Squadron Leader Spencer, that you are too lily-livered to do the task you have been allotted?'

Spenny went to his office-caravan, made his Will and gave it to the adjutant. Then he wrote a letter to his wife, went to his tent and tidied up his personal kit. Having looked after his own affairs he got down to the official ones. He handed over his squadron to the senior flight commander; then he collected the two most junior (and therefore presumably the least valuable) aircrews, briefed them on the raid and took off in due course.

Four hours later the senior flight commander had become the new commanding officer. All three Blenheims had been shot down before they had even crossed the harbour wall to drop a bomb. Not many men have that kind of cold, determined courage.

A little while after I had left the desert campaign to have a rest in Iraq, the boss tried to task a squadron of slow and ungainly Wellington night-bombers for a raid on Benghazi harbour shortly before dawn. The squadron commander was an old sparring-partner, buddy of mine and a cadet with me at Cranwell. He was Tommy Rivett-Carnac — a tough character from South Africa. He, seasoned in Bomber Command, knew the calibre of German fighter pilots who by then had joined the desert war in support of General Rommel and the Afrika Corps. He telephoned the AOC and demurred, indicating politely that he had no wish for his Wellingtons to try to get home, across 400 miles of enemy-held territory, contending with German Messerschmitts in daylight. Indeed, the chances for *any* of his crews to reach base would be negligible.

When the AOC asked him if he was gutless, Tommy ended the call and put down the telephone. He thought it unreasonable that his determination should be questioned, and he had some justification too, for his chest dripped with gallantry medals. He picked up the telephone again and spoke to the Air Commander, Air Marshal Sir Arthur Tedder, in Cairo: Tedder would always listen to a squadron commander. The Wellington dawn raid on Benghazi was cancelled and, not long after, the AOC was quietly replaced by another, more modern, individual.

*   *   *

Later, after our Dakota had landed at Benina, refuelled and taken off again, I watched Benghazi and Cyrenaica, with all the memories they evoked, disappear astern, under the wing for the last time. It crossed my mind that my desert bombing experience might well result, for the future, in my flying for Bomber Command. German opposition would make an interesting, if not very desirable, comparison.

Now, in our Dakota over the Gulf of Sirte, we had no reason to foresee or to seek out trouble: it was a snug and comfortable feeling.

Chapter 26
Last Lap

In our Dakota, after the stop at Benina, we headed out over the Gulf of Sirte, 400 miles across the sea to Tripoli. We dined and spent the night there. I could show Phyl the parched gardens and broken-down Italian facilities which I had first seen with Whitney, Prince Bernhard and Captain Moll. Next day it was on to Algiers, taking a straight line over the Gulf of Bomba and the high Atlas Plateau because there were no longer any Germans to worry about. Algiers, where the King once waited for his hosts, had lost all of the hundreds of fighters parked beside the runway. After lunch and fuel it was onwards once more, past Oran, over the Taza Pass and the horse-shoe of the High Atlas Mountains before dropping down to Ras el Ma to off-load passengers and freight.

I chatted with Baron Worrall and learned his delightful story of the King's passage through Ras el Ma on the return trip. I was quietly gratified to see that the great 'clean-up', for which he had been sent there, had effected no visible changes to what I had left behind. Finally, it was onwards again to our last landing, Rabat-Sale. The first leg of our trip home had been completed. The second and final leg was still to go.

John Rankin watched Phyl being helped as she awkwardly negotiated the four steep and narrow metal steps down from the Dakota. He gave us an inquiring look before saying, 'Well, that was a great effort. Considering her shape, overweight and the general lack of comforts, I think she took it all wonderfully. Nevertheless, it looks to me as though you are now "out of the frying pan and into the fire." You have a gigantic problem on your hands. Look at the facts. According to the records, Phyl has never left Cairo. The passenger lists say she never flew in my aircraft. Officially she isn't here . . . or, if she is here, it's totally irregular.

'How on earth do you propose to get an illegal or non- existent person any further?'

I gave him a long, slow look. He had done so much, I wanted to answer his question honestly and in full. I decided I didn't dare. At last I said, 'Sir, don't get me wrong. I am in the pit, up to my neck, with no lifebelt; far and away past PNR — the point of no return. I might bring it off, or end my career in a shower of sparks. A new batch of risks is ahead — for me alone — and I have my fingers well and truly crossed. Hardly anyone is going to know what chances, or how many, I shall take; or, how I find a solution — if any.

'Look at it this way, Sir. Anybody who doesn't know can't tell me to stop, or tell someone else to stop me, or get into trouble for knowing something and doing nothing. And, if the world blows up about my ears, there will be fewer people for me to try and protect.

'But, most important, IF I succeed I don't want somebody else to try — and fail, and then, then, under pressure or as an excuse, to say "Why hit me? *He* got away with it!"

'So, Sir, not a single thing will I tell you. One fine day, far into the future, you will know. Meanwhile, as you said yourself, Phyl isn't here, is she? So you couldn't have brought her here, could you? Just remember that, whatever happens to me, you have my undying thanks for having never ever done anything for either of us. And, in any event, that will never change.'

John grinned and said, kindly, 'I get the point!'

The British Consul looked at me across his desk and raised his eyebrows just a little. The news I had given him led him to decide that his staff had slipped up somewhere: most regrettable. How could it happen that, unknown to him earlier, there was an English civilian woman in his French-Moroccan area? It was a war-zone and English civilian female non-combatants were forbidden to be there, unless specially authorised like his own wife, and daughter Caroline. The woman must somehow have slipped through the earlier checks. It could not be tolerated and, even if she protested, she would have to be evacuated at once. Evacuated, naturally, to her country of domicile. He gave the necessary orders.

The lady would be packed off the very next day, bag and baggage. She would leave in a British Overseas Airways feeder-aircraft from Rabat-Sale to Gibraltar; from Gib she would continue on a civilian overnight Dakota service to Lyneham,

Wiltshire. Her husband, being a Service individual did not have to be evacuated but, as he was around and was going home anyway, he might as well travel with her. His office made out two tickets for travel all the way to England — and to enter that country legally, as evacuees.

In Gibraltar, the hotel we found to stay in was clean and attractive. The staff were hard-working and efficient. The two days Phyl spent there, waiting with me while the UK Dakota was arriving, were entirely delightful.

In England, the one nursing-home that we found with a bed to spare was dirty and repulsive, and the staff were idle and inefficient. The two days Phyl spent there, waiting while our son was arriving (51 hours on the way) were entirely horrible.

I have an enormous debt to three prime pairs of blind eyes; Whitney Straight, John Rankin and the Consul. However, the number of others is legion. Consider one antagonist for whom in the end I acquired quite an affection — the red-headed pig-eyed Wing Commander in the postings staff. At some time he must have been told that he was missing a couple of people due to be sent home. He can only have suppressed the questions and dropped his movement instructions into the waste-paper basket. A host of others, of greater and lesser power, saw something and said nothing; they kept the doors open for me to go on developing in the flying career which I so keenly enjoyed. I am sincerely grateful to each and every one.